Criminal and Social Justice

Criminal and Social Justice

Dee Cook

SAGE Publications
London • Thousand Oaks • New Delhi

First published 2006

 SAGE Publications Ltd
1 Oliver's Yard
55 City Road
London EC1Y 1SP

SAGE Publications Inc
2455 Teller Road
Thousand Oaks, California 91320

SAGE Publications India Pvt Ltd
B-42, Panchsheel Enclave
Post Box 4109
New Delhi 110 017

British Library Cataloguing in Publication data

A catalogue record for this book is available
from the British Library

ISBN 17619 4009 X   978 0 7619 4009 8
ISBN 17619 4010 3 (pbk)   978 0 7619 4010 4

Library of Congress Control Number available

Typeset by C&M Digitals (P) Ltd., Chennai, India
Printed on paper from sustainable resources
Printed and bound in Great Britain by Athenaeum Press, Gateshead

For Glyn, with love.

○○ Contents

Acknowledgements   viii

Introduction   1

1 Justice as a Two-Way Street   4

2 Constants and Dissonants in the Study of Criminal and Social Justice   33

3 Signs, Posts and the Third Way   61

4 'What Works' and Criminal and Social Justice   94

5 The 'Upside Down Duck': Participation and Engagement
   for Criminal and Social Justice   120

6 Locating Middle-England: 'Otherness' and Criminal and Social Justice   151

7 Reconciling Criminal and Social Justice   171

References   190

Index   204

○○ **Acknowledgements**

This book has been a very long time coming – three and a half years to be precise. I am very grateful to Caroline Porter and all at Sage for their patience and their support throughout this very unhealthy time for me! More than thanks are due to my colleagues at the Policy Research Institute at the University of Wolverhampton – Martin Roche, Paramjit Singh, Angela Morgan, Kully Thandi, Derek Bunce, Chris Lyle and Christine Vallely who have all stepped in for me whenever needed, and have always been responsive to my need for help, advice, a coffee, a chat and a laugh. (Particular thanks to Martin for his support and good humour throughout, and to Pram, Kully and Ian for helping me edit and prepare the manuscript.) Mentions and thanks too for: Marigold, Jane, Sam, Amanda and Mandy for being such good friends to me; to Adrian Sinfield for his advice and inspiration; and to two wonderful GPs – Peter Coventry and Chris Brown – and to the late Osman Shouli who all helped me to mend. Thanks to my son Haydn and daughter-in-law Katrina for giving me a beautiful granddaughter, Harriet, who has brought so much joy and laughter into my life. Most of all, I want to acknowledge the constant love, care and support of my partner (not a good enough word for him), Glyn, who has seen me through the bad times – and now for the good...

Dee Cook
July 2005

◯◯ Introduction

Justice is a concept which many of us take for granted: its meaning and its existence are assumed to be the foundation of the 'British way of life' and integral to the society in which we live. *Justice* is often assumed to be that which is automatically produced through the workings of the police, courts, judiciary and related criminal justice agencies. When prefixed with the word 'social', *justice* takes on different meanings, conveying ideas about citizenship, public services and social equality. Criminal justice and social justice may therefore seem, at first, to occupy different spheres of policy and social relations. In the past this separation applied to study, research and policy in these areas, but the last decade has witnessed significant changes (described in Chapters 3–4). At the same time, the central argument of this book is that criminal and social justice are not (and never have been) in separate spheres, but they are inseparable – you cannot really talk about one without the other.

To take criminal justice first: the concept is rooted in the exercise of (legitimate) power in particular contexts – spatial, cultural, historical, political, economic and social – and this includes societies that are stratified along lines of class, income and wealth, status, gender, religion, 'race' and ethnicity, and so on. Criminal justice is therefore not a free-floating or abstract concept that is devoid of social context and so, inevitably, this raises the question *How do we ensure criminal justice in a society which is basically unjust?* Many critics argue this is a question we continue to face in contemporary Britain.

Turning the question the other way around, we could ask *How can we work towards social justice in a society in which criminal justice and equal treatment before the law cannot be guaranteed?* Whichever way around we pose this question, it is fundamentally about asking *How do we start to reconcile criminal and social justice?* This book attempts to explore this question, and to offer some positive ways forward.

One key concern of this book is therefore to illustrate the ways in which criminal justice and social justice are interconnected and interdependent concepts, in theory and in the day-to-day realities of our lives. The focus of the analysis throughout will be Britain, although there are two riders here: firstly, as the legal systems of Scotland and of England and Wales differ in key respects, I will at times refer to them separately. Secondly, although European and North American politics and research will be drawn upon here (as will historical themes), the primary scope of this book is contemporary Britain.

Any book with such a broad title as *Criminal and Social Justice* is bound to disappoint and to be seen by some as 'thin' or inadequate in its analyses. This may well be the case, as a high degree of selection is inevitable in the choice of key issues raised, literature surveyed, questions posed and in the comprehensiveness of policy proposals put forward. In all of these respects – *mea culpa*. In addition, this book is somewhat of a *hybrid*: it seeks to cover some important theoretical ground for readers who are new to the fields of criminal justice, or social justice, or indeed both. At the same time, it attempts to critically engage with *some* of the key contemporary issues in both spheres and so must be, in this sense, selective. It draws on published research and 'grey' literature in both fields, in addition to new or unpublished research conducted by the Policy Research Institute at the University of Wolverhampton. In this way the book is three things: partly text book; partly a critical review of policy and practice in criminal and social justice; and partly a discussion of original empirical research.

The book is structured as follows: the first chapter attempts to examine and unpack the different (and competing) understandings of the concepts of criminal and social justice. This chapter then goes on to gather a range of research evidence in order to assess the current state of justice – criminal and social – in contemporary Britain. The second chapter reflects back on the historical themes that underpin this state of affairs and that run through representations of criminal and social justice issues. It will analyse those elements which are constant over time (and place) in these discourses, and also the dissonants – the 'new' issues, representations and themes – that have emerged as the twentieth century drew to a close. The chapter will then apply these themes – old and new – to a case study of criminal and social justice: the differential treatment of tax and welfare benefit fraud.

The next two chapters (Chapters 3 and 4) address issues of theory, research and policy more explicitly. The third chapter (while drawing on the constants and dissonants that emerged from Chapter 2), brings us into the twenty-first century. It aims to equip readers with the 'signs and posts' they may need to navigate their way through, and beyond, the criminal justice and social policy space, which is the 'Third Way'. This will include discussion of issues including globalisation, postmodernism, the vexed issue of trust, social capital and 'criminalising the social'. Chapter 4 takes forward the issues of policy-making and implementation in the criminal and social justice fields by addressing the issues of evidence-based policy (EBP) and the 'what works' paradigm. Having promised to 'back anyone' who could deliver 'what works', the New Labour government's efforts in this direction, since it took office in 1997, are critically assessed. The uses, misuses and implications of this paradigm – for policy, for research and for governance – are also highlighted.

Chapters 5 and 6 critically examine the delivery and the outcomes of criminal justice and social policies, to date, under New Labour governments. Chapter 5 takes the analogy of an upside down duck to visually indicate the panic and flailing at local levels which the plethora of national policy initiatives (and their requirements for consultation) have given rise to. The chapter examines community participation and engagement for criminal and social justice and, in particular, looks at consultation (in theory, and in practice on the ground) and at the diverse impacts of policies geared to reducing crime through social inclusion. Chapter 6 examines the ways in which social justice and criminal justice issues are allegedly perceived by the 'middle Englanders' identified by pollsters and politicians. It focuses on the construction of mythological 'Others' who are cast outwith the bonds of social inclusion, and against which middle Englanders may unite (and vote!). In so doing, this analysis uses the three themes of area, asylum and anti-social behaviour.

Finally, Chapter 7 attempts to bring together the themes that have emerged from the preceding chapters and examines and critiques the ways in which, over the past eight years, policy initiatives within and across the two spheres of criminal and social justice have often led to contradictory and mutually defeating outcomes. The chapter starts with a personal reflection on the May 2005 general election and also sketches out the implications of the terrorists attacks in London in July 2005 for progressive criminal justice and welfare futures. Finally, the book ends with the identification of ten 'good-enough' (Williams, 2000) principles which could usefully inform ways forward to reconciling criminal and social justice.

○ *one* ○ Justice as a Two-Way Street

Introduction

At its most symbolic level justice is portrayed, in a classical sculptured form, as a woman holding the scales of justice in one hand and the sword of truth in the other. She is often blindfolded to signify the impartiality of justice, which is 'balanced' and equally applied to all, irrespective of place, gender, sexual preference, age, (dis)ability, ethnicity, 'race', religious belief, wealth or status. But this abstraction becomes problematic when it is applied in the 'real world' of twenty-first century Britain.[1] This chapter will raise questions about the diverse experiences of criminal justice for a range of groups – the advantaged and the disadvantaged; the successful and the vulnerable; old and young; men and women; and white people and those from minority ethnic groups. In so doing it will also question to what extent struggles for criminal justice collide with manifestations of social inequality which characterise the wider society within which the law is (re)produced and operates. The chapter will start by examining *competing understandings of the concepts of social and criminal justice*: although both terms are laden with 'common-sense' meanings, they present challenges when they are unpackaged and subject to deeper scrutiny. Secondly, this chapter will go on to analyse *evidence on the state of justice* – criminal and social – in contemporary Britain. Finally, it will begin to explore the complex *linkages between these two concepts*, to pave the way for later chapters which explore ways in which criminal and social justice may be more effectively reconciled – in theory and in practice.

---
1. Justice, Citizens and the Two-Way Street

According to the North American writer Jeffrey Reiman (1990), criminal and social justice are inseparable and, in a just society, should be part of the same 'two-way

---

[1] 'Britain' will be used in this volume, except where the differing legal systems of Scotland and of England and Wales are being discussed.

street' along which citizens navigate their way, attending to the rules of the highway, which everyone is obliged to follow. However, in his book, aptly titled *The Rich Get Richer and the Poor Get Prison*, Reiman argues that while justice *should* be a two-way street, criminal justice effectively only goes 'one way':

> Individuals owe obligations to their fellow citizens because fellow citizens owe obligations to them. Criminal justice focuses on the first but looks away from the second. (1990:124)

Criminal justice, he argues, focuses upon the obligations that the state owes *to us* rather than the obligations that we owe *to others*. In this way, the **social contract**, which we enter into with the state and with our fellow citizens, is not one that strikes an equal balance between criminal and social justice – they are not part of the same two-way street. In order to flesh out this proposition and to better understand the relationship between criminal and social justice, we first need to explore the roots of this contract. This entails examining what is meant by citizenship – the rights it confers and the obligations with which it is endowed.

The seminal academic work in the field is that of T.H. Marshall (1950) who, writing in the late 1940s, identified three essential elements of **citizenship**: *the civil, the political* and *the social*. The first is associated with the rule of law and includes freedom of speech and the right to 'justice'. The second concerns the ability to participate in politics, whether by voting or standing for office. The third – social citizenship – includes:

> ... the whole range from the right to a modicum of economic welfare and security to the right to share in the full social heritage and to live the life of a civilised being according to the standards prevailing in the society. (1981:10)

Here citizenship is a relative concept as it uses the 'standards prevailing in... society' as benchmarks for fully social citizenship: this remains a problem to assess in practice. Also problematic are some of the 'clashes' that occur between the rights and autonomy of the individual on the one hand, and the duties of citizenship on the other. Dwyer (2004) suggests that the components of Marshall's theory that refer to 'duty' are less developed than those concerned with 'rights'. And so, for example, the duties to obey the law and pay taxes may seem straightforward yet they can pose dilemmas – as we will see in Chapter 2, the dividing line between illegal tax evasion and (legal) avoidance is a fine one, and may be crossed by seemingly the most 'responsible' of citizens.

Marshall's theory has many critics, some of whom doubt that social rights can be seen as 'rights' at all, as they are far from universally experienced or accessed: Barbalet (1988) sees them as, at best, 'conditional opportunities', which depend on professional and bureaucratic structures and, crucially, are underpinned by politics and the constraints of fiscal policy (Dwyer, 2004:43). As we will see in Chapter 3, the politics of New Labour and the Third Way challenges the concept of a welfare state predicated on universal rights of citizenship, instead stressing the primacy of opportunity (in work and education) in the context of a 'social investment state'

(Giddens, 1998). Leaving these challenges aside for the moment, the framework provided by Marshall offers a useful starting point for a discussion of what might constitute full citizenship, offering an insight into the links between citizenship and social exclusion, and between criminal and social justice.

Figure 1.1 summarises the key elements of citizenship as identified by Marshall, to which the dimensions of environmental and human rights have also been added. In relation to the former, it is not surprising that the late twentieth and early twenty-first century have been characterised by increased concerns over the *environmental risks* of late modernity – global warming, pollution, genetic modification – and the threats they pose for biodiversity, the physical environment and both human and animal health (Beck, 1992; Giddens, 2000). While many of these risks apply to rich and poor alike, others disproportionately affect those poorer individuals and groups who are likely to have fewer life choices and to live in the most blighted environments – locally, nationally and globally (Foley, 2004; Lister, 2004). Ways of forging synergies between environmental sustainability and social justice at the level of policy are at a relatively early stage of discussion and development (see Julie Foley's 2004 edition for a fuller discussion of issues around sustainability and social justice).

The concept of *human rights* emerged from the Holocaust of the Second World War. The Universal Declaration of Human Rights was signed in 1948 by members of what was later to become the United Nations, although no nation came to the table to sign it 'with clean hands' in the aftermath of war (Kennedy, 2004:309). It attempted to lay the foundations for rules that were universal, binding and would ensure the humanity and dignity of all. Subsequently, in 1950, members of the Council of Europe signed the European Convention on Human Rights (ECHR), to be safeguarded by the European Commission of Human Rights (1954) and the Court of Human Rights in Strasbourg (1959) to which any individual could take a grievance or 'petition' as a victim of an alleged breach of the convention. In this way the ECHR goes beyond boundaries of nation states and their legal jurisdictions.

More broadly, the very language of human rights offers a way of discussing relations with one another, and with the wider world: it transcends national boundaries and engages with the personal, community, national and global dimensions of human existence. In this sense there is no issue of conditionality – human rights are universal and indivisible. One of the core elements of the United Nations system for the protection of human rights is the International Covenant on Economic Social and Cultural Rights (ICESCR): the Covenant gives legal force to the civil and political rights enshrined in the Universal Declaration of Human Rights of 1948, namely:

- Equality between men and women
- The right to work
- The right to fair conditions of employment
- The right to join and form trade unions
- The right to social security
- The right to protection of the family

Elements of Citizenship	Undermining Citizenship
Civil and Political Rights Freedom of speech and association. Freedom from discrimination. Protection from the law (for self and property). Political participation.	Limitations/conflicts over public order, political protest and civil liberties. Harassment and discrimination: along lines of 'race', gender, sexual preference, age, religion and (dis)ability. Institutional racism. Differential patterns of criminal (and repeated) victimisation. Erosion of legal rights (to legal advice, the right to silence, the right to jury trial). Increasingly limited political participation. Lack of trust. Disempowerment and disengagement.
Social and Economic Rights Education. Housing. Health care. To own (property). To consume (goods and services). Work and participation in economic life. To an income (welfare rights).	Inequalities in the provision and quality of: education, health and social care, housing, transport and social amenities. Inequalities in health (mental and physical), unemployment, under-employment and low pay. Erosion of levels of welfare benefits. Asset and pension inequalities. Benefit sanctions and restrictions. Welfare policing of, and for, 'the family'.
Environmental Rights To the benefits, in amenity and health, of a safe and clean environment.	Lack of basic amenities – water, housing/shelter. Air, water and soil pollution: urban, rural and global. Poverty, sickness, mortality and disease. Genetically modified crops and food. Threats to biodiversity.
Human Rights[a] Respect for the dignity of all members of the human family.[b] Economic, social, cultural rights which ensure that dignity. Freedom from fear and from want. Interdependence (and indivisibility) of all these aspects of human rights.	Poverty. Lack of voice/powerlessness. Political repression. Denial of a 'fair trial'. Conditionality of citizenship rights, e.g.: • Social security withdrawal and sanctions for those who will not work/train/comply • Anti-social behaviour legislation for those whose behaviour is deemed 'unacceptable' • Criminal justice conditional upon admission of guilt.

[a]See Faulkner (2001:143–4) and Lister (2004:158–65).
[b]OHCHR (2002:42).

Figure 1.1   Undermining Citizenship
(*Source*: adapted from Cook, 1997b:30).

- The right to an adequate standard of living (including the right to food, clothing and housing)
- The right to health
- The right to education
- The right to culture.

(*Source*: House of Lords Paper HL183, 2004:7)

Although compliance with the Covenant forms part of the UK's international human rights obligations, the UK has been slow to pick up the challenge of incorporating human rights into domestic law: it was not until 1998 that the law enshrined the principles of the ECHR in the Human Rights Act (HRA) 1988. Critics argue that the Blair government's approach to human rights is deeply problematic for several reasons, most of which centre on the issue of 'universal rights'. The rights which are endowed to the UK citizen are still regarded as, in many ways, 'conditional' on the citizen's responsibilities: if citizens are seen to fail in discharging their responsibilities to the state, or to behave in ways which are inappropriate, then such rights are not ensured (Faulkner, 2001:143). To expand on this point further, David Faulkner persuasively argues that key government policy themes (most notably evident in the Crime and Disorder Act, passed in 1988, the same year as the HRA) display a clear tension between the concept of rights and the notion of responsibilities – as in many policy areas only the latter can guarantee the former. This clearly runs counter to the universality and indivisibility of the concept of human rights itself. Consequently, he and others identify a 'retreat from human rights' and a profound gap between the *promise* of human rights and the *lived reality* within which legal and social-economic rights are effectively denied (Faulkner, 2001; Kennedy, 2004). These contradictions run through a range of criminal justice and social policy areas. Examples cited by Faulkner include: the imposition of anti-social behaviour orders (ASBOs, to be discussed more fully in Chapter 6) and criminal penalties for their breach, where the behaviour for which the order may have been imposed was not in itself criminal; benefit sanctions for offenders who breach community sentences (thereby making the payment of welfare benefits conditional on 'responsible' behaviour and not on individual rights and entitlement); and the benefits which the criminal justice system offers those who admit their guilt (and in so doing speed up the wheels of the criminal justice system): the possibility of getting a 'discounted' sentence for pleading guilty effectively means that denial of guilt becomes an 'aggravating factor' in sentencing, rather than a way of asserting the right of any suspect to challenge the prosecution. This serves to penalise those who insist they are innocent and so runs counter to the spirit of human rights (Faulkner, 2001:143–4).

Lister (2004) traces the relations between human rights and poverty, arguing that being poor by definition involves a lack of power, voice and citizenship which denies human rights (issues of 'voice' and empowerment will be discussed further in Chapter 5). The Vienna Declaration on Human Rights (1993) was important in formally affirming 'the equation of extreme poverty with denial of human rights'. (Lister, 2004:159). Nevertheless, more than a decade on, there remains a gap between the global/universal promise of human rights and the local/domestic reality of poverty. In this sense, poverty (in the UK as elsewhere), powerlessness, lack of voice and the conditionality of many rights of citizenship all serve to subvert the full realisation of human rights.

2. Unequal Citizens

The framework in Figure 1.1 (see page 7) begins to illustrate some of the ways in which fully social citizenship may be undermined and denied through a multiplicity of inequalities, which can be legal, civil, political, social, economic and environmental in character. Poverty denies human rights and 'corrodes citizenship' (Lister, 1990) because the poor are more likely to suffer from criminal victimisation, illness (mental and physical), unemployment and low pay, and live in the midst of 'geographies of despair'. If we initially select health and housing as examples of how this corrosion is manifested, the extent and multiplicity of inequities becomes apparent (see the selected data presented in Figure 1.2). The indicators brought together here demonstrate the multiple nature of disadvantages suffered by those poorer groups who inhabit the most deprived areas of the UK. These include: poor quality accommodation; rent arrears; enhanced risks of disability and serious illness (including stroke, heart disease and cancer); reduced life expectancy; and mental health problems.

Poverty is not the only condition or social relation which may lead to exclusion from the rights and benefits of citizenship. For instance, many British citizens are excluded from full civil, political and social participation because of their religion, culture, 'race' or ethnicity (Cook, 1993; Collins, 2002; Lea, 2003). The increasing incidence of racial harassment and attacks – particularly in the wake of the events of 11 September 2001[3] in the United States – shows that, for many black and Asian subjects in particular, even the basic right to walk the streets in Britain freely, without fear or harassment, is illusory. Between 2002/3 and 2003/4 *racist incidents*[4] officially recorded by the police rose by 7% from 49,078 to 54,694. But this was clearly 'the tip

---

[3]On the morning of 11 September 2001, terrorist attacks were mounted on the United States by hi-jackers from the militant Islamic group, Al Q'aeda. Two planes ploughed into the World Trade Centre's Twin Towers, another into the Pentagon and a fourth (aimed at a Washington target) was forced down by passengers. A total of almost 3000 people died (9/11 Commission, 2004).

[4]The most often used definition of *racial incident* is that used by the Metropolitan Police and accepted by the Association of Chief Police Officers. It is: 'Any incident in which it appears to the reporting or investigating officer that the complaint involves an element of racial motivation; OR any incident which includes an allegation of racial motivation made by any person.' Most racist incidents involve damage to property or verbal harassment. Racially or religiously aggravated offences most often involve harassment (59%), criminal damage (14%), 'other' wounding (14%) and common assault (11%). 'Statistics on Race and the Criminal Justice System 2004'. (Home Office, 2005a:8–11). See also http://www.racialharrassment.org/about.htm

---

- ❑ One third of all dwellings in England in 2001 were 'non-decent' (in terms of good repair, heating etc.) and over 4% were 'unfit'
- ❑ Lone parents and people from minority ethnic communities are more likely to live in poor quality, non-decent accommodation
- ❑ 33% of tenants of social housing/housing associations were in rent arrears in 2001 compared with 8% of homeowners in mortgage arrears
- ❑ Experience of multiple housing deprivations increases the risk of severe ill-health or disability across the life course by an average of 25%
- ❑ Life expectancy differences between social classes one and five are 7 years in men and 5.5 years in women
- ❑ People on lower incomes are significantly more at risk from diet-related diseases such as heart attacks, cancers and strokes
- ❑ The death rate from coronary heart disease is three times higher in unskilled manual workers than among professional men
- ❑ 35% of lone parents on income support (principally women) suffer from a longstanding illness
- ❑ Fewer GPs are working in deprived areas
- ❑ A survey conducted in 2003 found that one-third of people on low incomes reported suffering from stress, isolation and loneliness. 36% were 'anxious or depressed'
- ❑ Suicide rates among young men in Manchester (with 27 of its 33 wards among the 10% most deprived in England) are twice the national average
- ❑ Between 36,000 and 52,000 young people aged 15–24 were 'found homeless' by local authorities in England in 2003 (this estimate does not include the 'hidden homeless'). Of these, an estimated 13% may have had recent experience of rough sleeping

Figure 1.2   Poverty, Housing and Health

(*Sources*: Flaherty et al., 2004:119–27; Pleace and Fitzpatrick, 2004:4)

of the iceberg' as racial incidents are grossly under-reported to the police: estimates derived from the British Crime Survey suggest that around 204,000 such incidents may have taken place (Home Office, 2005a:8). At the same time, racially aggravated *offences* recorded by the police in 2003–4 (35,022) showed a 13% increase on the previous year.

Citizenship is also undermined by the experience, and the effects, of institutional racism. The McPherson Report (1999) into the death of the black teenager Stephen Lawrence stated that 'institutional racism... exists both in the Metropolitan Police Service and in other Police Services and other institutions countrywide' (McPherson, 1999:6.39). The recommendations of McPherson and the subsequent passing of the Race Relations (Amendment) Act (2000) were both watersheds which opened up the possibilities for positive challenges and for change. The Act placed a 'general duty' on all public authorities to 'eliminate unlawful discrimination' and 'to promote equality of opportunity and good relations between persons of different racial groups'. But disappointingly, so far, there is little evidence of the 'culture change' necessary to make these duties real in enhancing the experiences of minority ethnic communities in Britain (Collins, 2002). In an interview marking the fifth anniversary of the McPherson enquiry, the Head of the Metropolitan police's Black Police Association (Chief Inspector Leroy Logan) acknowledged that:

the well meaning soundbites from the senior management do not get rolled out at a lower level... The force has failed to change the structures that underpin the culture of institutional racism. (Quoted in the *Guardian*, 24 February 2004)

Further, he argued that the force was failing to address racism within its own ranks and, consequently, 'If you cannot treat a diverse workforce right, you can't treat a diverse public right'. Clearly both claims exemplify the gap between the promise and the reality of citizenship for minority ethnic communities in contemporary Britain.

The lived experience of social citizenship – civil, political, economic and social – is also a gendered experience. In terms of civil and political rights, although women constituted just over half of the UK population in the 2001 Census, they comprised only 18% of Members of Parliament (compared with, for instance, 45% in Sweden) and 24% of Members of the European Parliament (compared with an EU average of 30% and 58% in Sweden) (ONS, 2002; EOC, 2005). In 2002/3 women constituted around 45% of the British labour force, yet women working full-time earned only 81 pence an hour for each £1 earned by their male counterparts. Moreover, data for 2004 indicates the 'gender gap' between the pay of women working part-time and men working full-time was wider still at 40% (ONS, 2004). Women from minority ethnic groups suffer a double disadvantage: Pakistani and Bangladeshi women earn on average 84% of the hourly rate of white women (Fawcett Society Briefing, 2004). If, to experience poverty is to experience a denial of fully social citizenship, then women (particularly minority ethnic women and lone mothers) suffer disproportionately. Around 90% of the 1.5 million lone-parent households in the UK are headed by women, who have the highest risk of income poverty of any social group (at 53%), which far exceeds the risk of pensioner poverty (at 22%) (Flaherty et al., 2004; Lister, 2004). Where citizenship is seen in terms of civic rights and criminal justice, gender also plays a significant part. For example, where gendered experiences of criminal victimisation are concerned, it is significant that the British Crime Survey estimated that there were 635,000 incidents of domestic violence in England and Wales in 2001/2 (with 81% of the victims being women), although less than 35% of such incidents were reported to the police (Mghill and Allen, 2002). Rates of repeat victimisation are higher for domestic violence than for any other crime at an estimated 57%. Taken together, all the data above serve to indicate that political, economic rights and civil rights (in terms of safety and protection under the law) are differentially experienced by men and women in contemporary Britain.

In general terms, citizenship is often regarded as a matter of 'give and take': if individuals wish to take advantage of the **rights and benefits** citizenship offers, they must give, by exercising the **duties and responsibilities** that accompany it. The responsibilities include working, saving, paying taxes and being a dutiful and active citizen. Do these same rules apply equally to the poor and to the relatively rich? Giddens thinks not, suggesting that:

The civic concerns of elites are plainly not separate from questions of taxation; avoiding taxes, or pulling out all the stops to pay as little tax as possible, are at the same time evasions of civic duty. However, obligations and commitments go well beyond fiscal responsibilities. Those moralists who make extensive civic demands of welfare recipients would do well to make them also of business leaders and other elite groups. A social contract of mutual obligations... must stretch from bottom to top. (2000:119)

The rich therefore benefit in three ways: they often *pay less* than they ought to into the citizenship deal; *less is demanded* of them than is demanded of poorer groups (who are perceived as 'takers'); and they do not attract the moral *censure* that is reserved for the poor when they fail to meet their citizenship obligations. In terms of fiscal and welfare policy (as we will see in Chapters 2 and 3), I will argue that public and political attention focuses disproportionately on the duties and responsibilities at the 'bottom end' of society while neglecting those at the 'top end' who fail to meet their obligations.

The 'rights', which are so valorised in criminal justice discourses, are therefore not the universal rights of full social citizenship, but the rights of active and law-abiding (and usually older) citizens, as Hudson notes:

When asked about the rights of people not to be filmed by CCTV cameras; the rights of young people not to be excluded from certain public spaces and leisure venues; the rights of young people not to be subject to curfews and similar restrictions in the absence of criminal conviction, the response has been that it is the rights of 'law abiding' and 'fearful' citizens that are important. This zero-sum approach to rights is the antithesis of the positive rights agenda. (2001:110)

Where young people are concerned, rights to counsel – including those under human rights legislation – may not be acknowledged or implemented (Brookman and Pierpoint, 2003). The gap between policy and practice in this respect means that 'a right is an empty right unless people are provided with the means to claim it' (ibid.:466). And so, regardless of formal, universal rights, the fearful citizen and the discourse of *risk* (risky places and risky people) dominates and comes to serve as a mechanism of exclusion. This is antithetical to the concepts of citizenship and justice which centre on the discourse of *rights* and are inclusive in character, as 'no-one is outside the constituency of justice' (Hudson, 2001:112).

3. Justice and the Law

In order to more fully understand the current gap between the promise and the reality of civil and political citizenship, we can usefully examine the historical and legal origins of both our rights and our obligations to others in society. While these are often couched in terms of a 'social contract', ultimately both our 'rights' and our obligations arise from what historian E.P. Thompson termed the 'rule of law'. In essence, the law should guarantee and protect our personal rights and freedoms, while enshrining our obligations to obey the law and not to impinge on the rights and freedoms of others. Thompson considered that:

> ... the rule of law itself, the imposing of effective inhibitions upon power and the defence of the citizen from power's all-intrusive claims, seems to me to be an unqualified human good. (1975:266)

But while the law was seen to protect citizens from the worst excesses of state power, it was nonetheless shaped by the emerging logic of capitalism. Consequently, much of eighteenth- and nineteenth-century English law was effectively law designed to protect private property and to enable profitable trade and commerce to flourish. For example, in relation to agriculture, the Enclosure Acts extinguished many former agrarian and collective 'rights' to land which were:

> simply converted into crimes, some of which were punishable by death. When they protested against these usurpations, the dispossessed were not viewed as rights-holders defending their property but were branded as criminals interfering with the property rights of others. (Cole, 2001:180)

Although the law can be seen as an instrument and a product of elite or class power, it was and is not *merely* this: the law can and does open up the space for struggle and change, as laws perceived to be 'unjust' may – in theory at least – be challenged. The difficulty remains that the law may be both written and used instrumentally to serve certain established, powerful interests over the interests of citizens. Moreover (as subsequent chapters will discuss), there are significant inequities in *access to the law*, which favour the powerful and, at the same time, prevent the powerless from using it as an effective means of challenge and redress.

The growth of the nation state in the nineteenth and twentieth centuries concentrated powers of policing and punishment in the new institutions of criminal justice. The policing, prosecution and punishment of offenders was now administered by increasingly specialised authorities in the name of 'the public' not of the individual. This 'modernisation' of crime control and justice was characterised by 'statization, bureaucratisation and professionalization' (Garland, 2001). Consequently, Garland argues, '"law and order" came to be viewed not as a hostile and threatening power, but as a contractual obligation owed by a democratic government to its law-abiding citizens' (ibid:30).

But, once again, this contract was one that was not equally entered into nor equally honoured. For example, there are important critiques which relate to gender inequalities and the law: it is argued that the law focuses predominantly on what is termed the *public* sphere, which is constituted differently from the *private* sphere. Women are less likely to be represented than men in the former (which includes the spheres of politics, work and public places) and do not inhabit the latter (the home) on an equal basis to men: in terms of financial and physical power, men dominate the private sphere, which laws designed predominantly for the regulation of the public sphere have failed to effectively penetrate (Hudson, B., 2003). As noted already, the scale of domestic violence in England and Wales in 2001/2 and increasing incidences of child abuse, are testimony to the extent of violent crime that takes place within the private sphere and which the law has, historically, been very slow to address. The notion of the rule of law centres on preventing the unjust exercise of power and restricting the powers of the state and the liberty of citizens *only* in order to prevent harm to others. However, it implicitly assumes that such harms are done 'in public' and not by partners, intimates or family members within the private sphere.

Nonetheless, the notion of the 'rule of law' remains both powerful and symbolic: it is largely seen as a necessary (though not a sufficient) condition for a 'just society'. The law alone is insufficient because while its processes and structures may well impose certain constraints on the exercise of arbitrary power, few (or no) constraints are placed upon the *content* of laws themselves. As Chapters 2 and 6 will go on to discuss more fully, the content and the application of new legislation regulating a range of individuals and behaviours deemed 'problems' – such as welfare dependency, asylum seeking and 'anti-social behaviour' – reflect very specific notions of how idleness, threat and deviance are constituted: as such they are all historically and politically (re)produced. Finally, above and beyond debates around the content of laws, there remains the problem that laws themselves are selectively and differentially *applied*, with worrying consequences for criminal justice.

4. What Is Criminal Justice?

At a very simplistic level, criminal justice can be said to be produced by the political, social, organisational and judicial processes through which the criminal law is applied in (post)modern societies. As we have seen, the law itself is not a neutral construct: it is produced within particular historical, political, economic, social and material conditions, all of which are themselves shaped by relations of power. But beyond the letter of the law itself (the *law 'in books'*), there are additional layers of disparity which are then produced by the ways in which the law is applied (the *law 'in action'*) by the differing agencies which constitute 'the criminal justice system'.

Criminal justice is about more than the law and its implementation, at a more sociological level, has been described by Sanders and Young as:

> [a] complex social institution which regulates potential, alleged and actual criminal activity within procedural limits supposed to protect citizens from wrongful treatment and wrongful conviction. (Quoted in Rutherford, 2001:7)

This definition is more useful as it begins to unpack some of the issues and problems that surround the way that the agencies of the criminal justice system operate, in practice, to perform their key functions, here seen in terms of:

- Regulating criminal, and potentially criminal, behaviour
- Applying procedural rules to protect citizens who come into contact with criminal justice agencies
- Ensuring that these rules and safeguards prevent wrongful treatment and wrongful convictions (miscarriages of justice).

What precisely do we mean by 'the criminal justice *system*'? In the context of England and Wales[5], the criminal justice system (CJS) formally consists of:

- The Police Service: comprising 43 police forces
- The Crown Prosecution Service (CPS)
- The Courts Service: Magistrates' Courts, Crown Courts and Appeal Courts
- The Prison Service and National Probation Service which, from June 2004, comprised the new National Offender Management Service
- The Serious Fraud Office
- The Criminal Defence Service
- The Criminal Injuries Compensation Authority
- Victim and witness care services.

A further important question to raise is, of course, *What is the criminal justice system for?* This question is complex as its answer is shaped by our choices, values and politics – the role of criminal justice (like the law) can be seen as essentially ideological. One answer has been offered by Sanders and Young (see above) but the *official* purpose, as stated by the government in its Strategic Plan for Criminal Justice is as follows:

> The purpose of the Criminal Justice System (CJS) is to deliver justice for all, by convicting and punishing the guilty and helping them to stop offending, while protecting the innocent. (Cm. 6288, 2004:12)

The extent to which the CJS is able to deliver 'justice for all' is, however, limited by the broader structural and social inequalities of the society in which the system operates. These inequalities include poverty, poor housing and education, ill-health, unemployment and environmental decay, all of which are associated with the effective denial of fully social citizenship. But, at the same time, it is important to recognise that such inequalities have also been associated with high crime rates and the likelihood of being a victim of crime. This has resulted in crime being seen as both an **indicator** and a **cause** of many of these negative social features: in this way crimes such as burglary, thefts, criminal damage and drug abuse are seen to *indicate* poverty, social exclusion and a limited 'quality of life' in many poorer neighbourhoods while, at the same time, they are also seen as part of the *cause* of those neighbourhoods' decline. Such areas thus become a key target for the interventions of both criminal justice and social policies (as we will see in Chapters 2 and 6).

In such social and spatial contexts, the aim of the CJS in dispensing justice fairly for all is also problematic because of the ways in which a range of decisions are taken about who, and where, is **policed** and the consequences this has in terms of

---

[5]The Scottish CJS differs fundamentally from that of England and Wales, reflecting historical and legal differences, and so what follows will relate to the CJS in England and Wales only.

differential *patterns of criminalisation*[6]. These patterns are to some extent attributed to the working practices of CJS agencies themselves who, both directly and indirectly, tend to employ stereotypes of crime-prone individuals, families, localities and ethnic groups which may lead to their adopting patterns of policing and punishment that are perceived as 'unjust' by local communities. For example, the proportion of black people who felt that the CJS was effective in bringing people to justice fell from 54% in 2001/2 to 46% in 2002/3, and the proportion feeling that the CJS met the needs of victims fell from 45% to just 39% over the same period (Home Office, 2004a:3).

When policing resources are targeted on individuals, groups and localities that are defined by the police as 'a problem', it is not surprising that arrests result, leading to a self-fulfilling prophecy which drives future targeting. But arrests *may* also have resulted from targeting resources on *other* less likely suspects within alternative groups, organisations or localities, as we will explore further in discussing the treatment of some of the crimes of the relatively rich in Chapter 2. Those individuals and communities who *are* targeted may feel alienated and tend to lack confidence in the CJS as a consequence: thus the aim of 'dispensing justice fairly, thereby enhancing confidence in the rule of law' may be subverted by the routine working assumptions of CJS agencies about *who* and *where* is crime-prone, and where the deployment of their resources can yield what are seen to be the best 'results'. If we envisage the CJS as a system of filters located at various stages of the process (from decisions to police, arrest, prosecute, sentencing choice and ultimately to the 'hard end' of imprisonment), then the ways in which it operates can be seen to *filter in* certain individuals and groups, while it *filters out* others.

5. Equal Before the Law?

> Leonard Woodley, the first black Queens Counsel, was sitting as a judge at Wood Green Crown Court when he slid out at lunchtime to go to the bank. He wrapped a scarf around the neck of his overcoat to cover his judicial collar and white bands. When he presented his plastic bank card and chequebook at the bank counter, the teller was immediately suspicious, signalled to some male colleagues and he was detained. The court sitting had to wait because the bank could not believe that a black man bore the initials QC after his name. (Kennedy, 2004:186–7)

This is not an isolated example of insidious racial stereotyping: Kennedy goes on to describe the case of a Birmingham caterer who was stopped by the police 34 times in two years despite having a clean driving licence and no criminal record. Such examples illustrate the ways in which racial discrimination, racial harassment and practices of institutional racism served to undermine the realisation of fully social

---

[6]The term 'criminalisation' is used here to refer to a range of social and criminal justice processes (including policing, prosecution, punishment, penalisation, stigmatisation and blame) through which an individual or group is accorded the 'label' of criminal.

	ETHNICITY (%)					
	White	Black	Asian	Other	Not known/ not recorded	TOTAL
POPULATION (aged 10 + at 2001 Census)	91.3	2.8	4.7	1.2	0	100
STAGE OF THE CJS PROCESS						
Stops and searches	74.3	14.7	7.3	1.5	2.3	
Arrests	84.3	8.8	4.8	1.4	0.7	
Cautions	84.2	6.7	4.7	1.2	3.2	
Youth offences	83.5	6.3	3.1	2.9	4.3	
Prison receptions	80.5	9.7	4.8	2.9	2.1	
Prison population	77.1	15.5	3.1	4.1	0.1	

Figure 1.3   Representation of Ethnic Groups at Different Stages of the Criminal Justice Process 2003/4

(*Source*: Home Office, 2005a:ix)

citizenship for many individuals from black and minority ethnic groups in contemporary Britain.

Taking the analysis a stage further, Figure 1.3 goes on to examine the operation of the CJS and summarises the representation of minority ethnic groups[7] at varying stages of the process (these figures are also fleshed out in the narrative summary in Figure 1.4). Taken together, this evidence shows that the criminal justice processes engaged in by a range of agencies – from stop and search, caution, arrest, charge, prosecution, pleas and sentence – serve to filter black people into the hard end of the CJS and, ultimately, into prison (while white counterparts are filtered out).

Where the relationship between ethnicity and imprisonment is concerned, the data show worrying disparities. In February 2003, ethnic minorities accounted for 24% of the male prison population (with 16% black, 3% Asian and 5% other) and a staggering 31% of the female prison population (with 25% black, 1% Asian and 5% other). But these figures included foreign nationals who are not normally resident in England and Wales, and so this skews comparisons between the prison and the 'general' populations. Consequently, the data presented in Figure 1.3 refers to **'British nationals' in prison** and so may be compared with their representation in the overall population of England and Wales. From these figures it is clear that, in 2004, 'black' Britons were more than five times over-represented in the prison population than in the general population, while 'white' Britons were statistically

---

[7]See Home Office 2005a for details of the ethnic classifications used in the 2001 Census and by criminal justice agencies.

- o Asian (Indian, Pakistani and Bangladeshi) people in 2004 faced a higher level of victimisation (31%) with people of mixed race suffering the highest risks at 39% (compared with 26% for black and for white people)
- o People from minority ethnic communities are significantly more likely to be victims of racist incidents
- o Ethnic minority victims are less likely to be satisfied with police responses
- o People from minority ethnic groups are more likely to be stopped and searched by the police
- o People from minority ethnic groups are more likely to be arrested
- o Black people are less likely to receive a caution than Asian or white people
- o People from minority ethnic communities are more likely to be remanded in custody
- o People from minority ethnic communities are more likely to plead not guilty
- o People from minority ethnic communities are also more likely to be acquitted
- o Black people are less likely to be sentenced to fines or a discharge and more likely to receive a community penalty
- o Partly as a result of the above (proceeding through the possible/available sentences more quickly than their white counterparts), black people represent a disproportionate proportion of the prison population
- o For violent offences, the rate of custody is higher for black and Asian offenders
- o Minority ethnic prisoners are less likely to be released on parole
- o But minority ethnic prisoners have lower re-conviction rates than their white counterparts.

Figure 1.4   'Race' and the Criminal Justice System
(*Source*: Home Office, 2003a:2–10; Home Office, 2005b:7)

under-represented. This disparity cannot merely be explained by different offending patterns of the groups concerned, and the implications of this were acknowledged by the Home Office in its assertion that

> [a] modern, fair effective criminal justice system is not possible whilst significant sections of the population perceive it as discriminatory and lack confidence in it delivering justice... We need to get behind the numbers to understand the process through which discrimination may be occurring in the CJS. (Forword to Race and the Criminal Justice System, Home Office, 2003a).

As already indicated, when we do get 'behind the numbers' we find a notable reduction in the confidence of minority ethnic groups in the criminal justice system (particularly in the police), which is in part due to negative experiences of contact with the police, notably their perceptions of police responses to racial harassment (which are often seen as inadequate), and to stop and searches (which are often seen as too frequent and intrusive). The latter view is borne out by the data presented in Figure 1.3 (see page 17). In 2003/4 there were a total of 738,016 stop and searches recorded by the police in England and Wales under a range of legislation (including PACE – the Police and Criminal Evidence Act, 1984). Of these, 15% were black people, 7% Asian and 1% of people where of 'other' non-white origin (Home Office, 2005a:13–14). In effect, then, black people are 6.4 times more likely than their white counterparts to be stopped and searched in England and Wales. This situation has been even more acute in the capital where the number of recorded stop and searches in the London Metropolitan area rose by 8% for white people between 2000/1 and 2001/2, but increased by 30% for black people and 40% for Asians. Moreover, recent research shows that, once in police custody, individuals from black and minority ethnic communities (particularly those of African Caribbean heritage) are disproportionately likely to be subject to strip searches (Newburn et al., 2004). This research once again raises the 'spectre of police racism' (ibid:693).

Moving beyond the importance of the criminal justice system for citizenship, we also need to address the effect of wider social and political factors on the lived reality of citizenship and sense of 'justice' in the UK. In these respects it is clear that issues of 'race', culture, religious belief and justice have been fore grounded since the events of 11 September 2001 (9/11), and in the wake of the subsequent political and discursive dominance of the 'war on terror' and the military interventions (or invasions) in Afghanistan and Iraq. In Britain, the impact of 9/11 on media, public and political culture and on manifestations of racism has been dramatic. Commenting on the post-9/11 targeting of Britain's 1.6 million Muslim community, the leading civil liberties lawyer, Gareth Pierce, argued that they now faced a 'dark age of injustice' and commented:

> I have never known such venom and such hatred and such constant unchecked fascistic expression of daily, often appalling, often fabricated, always imagined, always exaggerated verbiage as there has been against the Muslim community. (Quoted in the *Guardian*, 1 April 2004)

But expressions of hatred and racism have not been confined to words alone: for instance, following the release of three British Guantanamo Bay detainees and their return to their West Midlands home town of Tipton, an effigy of a detainee, clad in an orange boiler suit, was hung from a lamppost in the town and then set alight (*Birmingham Mail*, 10 March 2004).

The 'war on terror' is being waged in Britain where, according to the Home Office, at 31 December 2004, a total of 702 people in England and Wales had been arrested under the 2000 Terrorism Act. But it is significant that of these 702, only 119 were charged with offences under the Act and only 17 (just 2% of all arrestees) were convicted (Home Office, 2005b). Nevertheless, the political triumph and dramatic publicity surrounding *arrests* is not matched by explanation and equal publicity on the *release* of the vast majority of suspects. At the same time, asylum seekers, refugees and settled migrants are subsumed within the war on terror discourse, all are assumed to be 'suspect' and so increasingly suffer from the corrosive effects of racism: for example, the Scottish housing charity Positive Action in Housing (PAIH) reported in 2004 that 28% of its clients had suffered racial harassment, an increase of 75% on the levels reported in 2003. The organisational cultures and operational logic of criminal justice agencies, together with the racialised British political and cultural context post-9/11[8], provide a poison mix. Under such conditions, it is unlikely that members of minority ethnic communities in contemporary Britain will feel that, for them, 'justice' is being done.

6. What Is Social Justice?

Moving towards defining the concept of 'social justice' we can usefully return to Marshall who provides a useful starting point, as one way of defining social justice is in terms of everyone enjoying the rights and duties of full citizenship. But, as we have seen, citizenship rights may prove illusory for women, for minority ethnic groups and for many of the poor in contemporary Britain, which (in turn) clearly raises concerns for claims of social justice.

Where issues of 'justice' (criminal or social) are concerned, the discourses used – and those eschewed – are crucial. For example, so far I have used the words 'poverty' and 'the poor' in a fairly simple and uncritical way. Competing views and theoretical struggles around the discourses of *poverty*, *social exclusion* and *citizenship* are examined in more depth in Chapter 3. For the time being, suffice it to say that poverty can be considered as, at the same time, a concept, a condition and a measurement (Lister, 2004). As a concept, poverty entails powerlessness, lack of participation and voice as well as the material elements of the condition arising from a 'lack of disposable income'. The often-used 'definition' of poverty (60% of median income) is actually a measurement that seeks to operationalise a particular definition. The term social exclusion is seen as a more dynamic and multi-faceted process which is related to that of citizenship in that it involves a 'breakdown of the major social systems... that should guarantee full citizenship' (Berghman, 1995:20). But, as Chapter 3 will contend, it is highly significant that the 'hard' word (poverty) has over recent years been replaced in the British political and policy lexicon with the rather 'softer' term (social exclusion). This has led to a displacement of concerns about socio-economic rights and at the same time has perhaps blurred what we mean by social justice. For example, when Prime Minister Tony Blair dedicated the second 'New' Labour government to 'delivery, delivery, delivery', most notably in the field of public services, he went on record stating that 'public services are social justice made real'. But this is clearly a limited view of what constitutes social justice; focusing, as it does, on a single element of social citizenship – and on that element solely through the lens of public service provision.

For many, social justice is far more than this – it is also about notions of 'fairness'. Rawls' (1971) perspective on social justice proposed the idea of 'justice as fairness', which could be represented by deciding on how to divide up a cake without knowing how big a slice you would get yourself. But the problem remained of how Rawls'

[8]And, we could now add, post-'7/7' following terrorist attacks on the London transport system on 7 July 2005.

> - 'The foundation of a free society is the equal worth of all citizens
> - All citizens are entitled, as a right of citizenship, to be able to meet their basic needs – for income, food, shelter, education and health
> - Self-respect and personal autonomy are inherent in the idea of equal worth, but their fulfilment depends on the widest possible spread of opportunities and life-chances
> - Inequalities are not necessarily unjust – but those which are should be reduced and where possible eliminated.'

Figure 1.5   Principles of Social Justice

(*Source*: Commission on Social Justice, 1993:(i))

principles of fairness could practically be translated into policy-making. To take forward this challenge, more than two decades later, the independent Commission on Social Justice was established (under the auspices of the Institute for Public Policy Research – IPPR), to document the extent of social inequality in Britain and to set out a vision of social justice. The Commission acknowledged that the term itself involved ideas about 'equality, need, entitlement, merit and desert', and that although most people said that they believed in social justice, their ideas were 'complex and indeterminate' (Commission on Social Justice (CSJ), 1993). It went on to outline some basic principles, which help to flesh out what social justice would actually mean at the levels of both the individual and wider society. These principles are summarised in Figure 1.5.

For many, these principles also underpin the condition and the existence of democracy itself. For example, in a series of contributions to the Madrid newspaper *Diario 16*, King Juan Carlos implicitly drew upon these principles in his analysis of Spain's transition to democracy:

> So long as poverty remains, so long as people who want to work are denied the opportunity to do so, so long as the development of some people means the smothering of others, so long as a single woman or man amongst us is not accorded the dignity that each and every human being needs and deserves, our transition to democracy has not been completed. (King Juan Carlos of Spain, quoted in Cook, 1997c)

Returning to the core aims of the CJS (outlined above), they too depend on similar foundations – the twin concepts of citizenship and legitimacy. Confidence in the CJS relies on citizens feeling that they are of equal worth and are treated as such, with dignity and respect: they need to trust that the law, and its implementation, is both *just and legitimate*. At the same time, equality before the law is a cornerstone of (civil) citizenship: if the law is perceived as unjust – either in its content or in the unequal ways in which it is applied (to some and not to others) – then both citizenship and legitimacy are threatened. In terms of the components identified in Figure 1.5, it is clear that *both* inequalities before the law *and* wider social inequalities serve to undermine social justice.

If a society cannot guarantee 'the equal worth of all citizens', mutual and self-respect and the meeting of basic needs, it cannot expect that all citizens will feel they have an equal stake in abiding by the law, and it cannot dispense justice fairly and enhance confidence in the law. In these respects, criminal and social justice are inseparable. One issue crucial to the sense of equal worth essential to citizenship is *recognition*, especially for those who suffer from identity-based forms of discrimination arising from a 'mis-recognition' of, for example, their sexuality, gender or 'race'. For the purpose of this book, the work of Nancy Fraser (2000), in attempting to engage with the politics of recognition *without* de-coupling identity-based issues from broader socio-economic ones, is important (and will be discussed further in Chapter 7).

Returning to the inseparability of criminal and social justice, there are differing views about precisely where to start in terms of working to reconcile these two spheres of justice. Rose (1996) focuses on criminal justice as the primary objective of policy in arguing that it offered a unique and, at the time of his writing[9], a timely point of intervention:

> The door is open to a new settlement between the State and the citizen. The institutions of policing, the courts and the prisons will never be a means of restoring an equitable society. But, at the same time, in the absence of criminal justice, social justice will be an impossible goal. (1996:336)

Conversely, Hudson (1987) focuses instead on social justice and recognises 'the impossibility of just legal punishments in an unjust society'. Nonetheless, she argues, 'we should scale down the level of our infliction of punishment rather than our search for justice' and strive for social justice whilst immediately concentrating on doing 'less harm' through the criminal justice and penal systems (Hudson, 1987:184). Of course, it is possible to envisage a response to reconciling criminal and social justice which would emanate from *both* ends of this two-way street.

7. Social Justice and 'Opportunities for All'

How is social justice being constructed in contemporary Britain? While the CSJ suggested that the principles of social justice rested on the foundations of 'the equal worth of all citizens', the primary thrust of British social policies since 1997 have interpreted that 'worth' in very specific ways. Increasingly an individual's **worth** has been seen in terms of their engagement in paid **work**. Citizenship has been seen as conditional upon the duty to be productive and economically active. A series of welfare benefit regimes and sanctions have therefore sought to 'restore work incentives', provide 'opportunities' and to put the poor to work (see Chapter 2 for a discussion of the historical themes underpinning such policies and Chapter 3 for an analysis of recent 'Third Way' politics). The discourse of responsibility has replaced that of citizenship rights and, in so doing, 'opportunity' has replaced 'justice'.

---

[9]With a general election looming in 1997.

In the political sphere much is said about 'opportunities for all' and this infinitely flexible phrase has not only formed the title of successive Annual Reports on the government's social inclusion strategy (SEU, 1999; DWP (Department for Work and Pensions), 2003), but is also associated with policy initiatives in a wide range of areas including: access to higher education; effective student learning in schools; and Department of Trade and Industry policy on 'enterprise, skills and innovation' (DTI, 2001). The meanings of this phrase – or mantra – are fluid, and shift according to its political contexts and imperatives. For example, in 2001 the then Secretary of State for Social Security, Alistair Darling, redefined opportunity in terms of making sure 'that everyone has the opportunity to contribute to building wealth, as well as sharing the benefits' (DSS Press Release, November 2001). This view is doubly problematic: firstly, it assumes that producing wealth is central to producing 'opportunity' and social justice, and secondly, that wealth is itself then 'shared'. Firstly, the equation of 'worth' with 'work' underlies Darling's statement: many would disagree, arguing that the goal of social justice and 'opportunity' entails far more than compulsion or incentives to paid work in order to generate personal and national wealth. Secondly, 'sharing the benefits' through a progressive and redistributive taxation system is, for the New Labour government, 'off message'. Not only does the UK have the most regressive personal tax regime in Europe, but it has a Prime Minister who is, at best, equivocal about the goal of redistribution and, at worst, dismissive of its implications. For example, when asked about the issue of higher rate taxation in an interview immediately before the 2001 election, Tony Blair stated that 'it is not a burning issue for me to make David Beckham earn less money'. Had he been serious about challenging inequality and promoting social justice, this is exactly what would be required – in both symbolic and fiscal terms. Two years on, when responding to the suggestion made (in June 2003), by his cabinet colleague Peter Hain, that tax rates (notably at the upper end of the scale) may need to be reviewed, the Prime Minister reiterated that his concern was not to take money from high earners. As the 2005 election campaign mounted, Blair responded to Liberal Democrat proposals for an increase in the top rate of income tax to 50% for those earning above £100,000 by dismissing them as 'economically wrong' (*BBC News*, 14 April 2005).

Tony Blair's approach to social justice and taxation is best understood in the context of his political critique of what he saw as the old left politics which he contended had:

> too readily downplayed its duty to promote a wide range of opportunities for individuals to advance themselves and their families. At worst, it has stifled opportunity in the name of abstract equality. (Tony Blair, 1998, quoted in Jackson and Segal, 2004:24)

The 'rubbishing' of egalitarianism had been an essential element in new right thinking since the 1970s and was central to the Thatcher governments' valorisation of individualism and wealth creation. It is not surprising that the famous 'tax giveaway' Budget of 1988 which saw the top rates of income tax reduced from 60%

to 40% was seen by Thatcher as 'the epitaph for socialism' (Hall, 1988). Tony Blair seems to share this perspective and with it, the view that the benefits of wealth are best shared through a 'trickledown' from the rich at the top to those at the base of the social pyramid.

While Blair rejects what he terms 'abstract equality', he privileges opportunity as a means of social mobility and sees this as preferable to pursuing greater 'equality of condition' between social classes and groups. But Richard Tawney's approach to egalitarian social justice (1931) had persuasively argued that material inequalities needed to be tackled because they prevented the realisation of equality of opportunity:

> ... it is only the presence of a high degree of practical equality which can diffuse and generalise the opportunities to rise. Their existence in fact, and not merely in form, depends, not only upon an open road, but upon an equal start. (1930:143)

Recent research supports this long-held contention that poverty is in itself a barrier to opportunity and mobility (Delorenzi et al., 2005). The pressing need not only for an open road (opportunity) but for an 'equal start' (practical equality) was nowhere more passionately articulated than in the 1987 speech by the then Labour Party leader, Neil Kinnock, who posed the question 'Why was I the first Kinnock in a thousand generations to be able to get to university?' His answer lay in the unfairness of Conservative policies which had denied generation after generation 'a platform upon which they could stand' (quoted in Jackson and Segal, 2004).

8. The State of Inequality

If, as Tawney in the 1930s, Kinnock and 'Old Labour' in the 1980s and the CSJ in the 1990s all suggested, social justice depends upon the elimination of **unjustified material inequalities**, then we need to examine the nature and extent of inequality in the UK today to assess the state of contemporary social justice. One striking feature of the period from 1980 to the early 1990s (the Thatcher/Major years) was a widening of income inequality in Britain and a deepening of poverty, and so it is important to see to what extent this has changed since the election in 1997 of a government committed to opportunity and, in theory, to enhancing social justice.

The most commonly used threshold of low income (often used to measure 'the poverty line') is 60% of median income. To put this into real terms, in 2003/4, this measure equated to:

- £200 per week before housing costs (BHC) for a couple with no children
- £118 for a single person
- £283 for a couple with two children
- £207 for a lone parent with two children.

(*Source*: Households Below Average Income, 2005)

If this is taken as the low income or poverty line, in 2003/4, 12.4 million people – 21% of the total population – were living on incomes below this threshold. This included 3.6 million children and 50% of all people in social housing, compared with one in six of those in other housing tenures. It is worth emphasising that figures monitoring poverty and social exclusion have shown some improvement in key indicators over the past two years (Palmer et al., 2003; JRF, 2004; Brewer et al., 2005), although the data do need to be set in the context of the 13% of the population who were on low incomes at the end of the Labour Callaghan administration and start of the first Thatcher government in 1979 (see Chapters 5 and 7).

There is still a long way to go if the Labour government is to fulfil the aims of its anti-poverty strategy, not least its ambitious 1999 *pledge to eliminate child poverty* 'within a generation'. The main drivers of this strategy are policies that focus not only on children themselves, but also encourage 'welfare to work' for their parent(s). The 2005 New Labour election manifesto continued to assert that 'work is the best anti-poverty strategy', although paid work is no guarantee of an escape from poverty: in 2004, two-fifths of people in low-income (working age) households had someone in paid work (JRF, 2004). While the establishment of a *national minimum wage* in 1998 (at the level of £3.60 per hour) did mark an important move in the government's drive to reduce poverty, many still slip through the net. In 2002 an estimated half a million young adults (aged 18–21) and one and a quarter million adults (aged 22 to retirement) were paid less than the then minimum wage of £4.50 per hour. In addition to reviewing the impact of the national minimum wage, the Low Pay Commission (LPC, 2005) also reports on relative pay levels and its most recent data reported that in 2003 a third of working women over 22 years and a sixth of working men were paid less than £6.50 per hour (with the national minimum wage from October 2004 standing at £4.85). In addition, more than three times as many people were in receipt of means-tested tax credits to supplement their wages in 2004 as had been in receipt of Family Credit a decade earlier. On the one hand, the latter can be seen as a positive development in that it shows take-up of means–tested benefits designed to support families living on low wages, but on the other hand it also signals the extent and persistence of the problem of low wages which is a major factor contributing to poverty. The latter view is supported by comparative research demonstrating that, despite the introduction of the minimum wage, Britain's competitive advantage in the EU is based on low wages within a de-regulated and flexible labour market (Daguerre, 2004:53). Moreover, to sustain such low wages, welfare benefit levels must be kept yet lower (as the discussion of the principle of less eligibility in the next chapter will show).

To summarise what we know of the state of inequality in contemporary Britain, we can draw on a wide range of research: for example, recent research by the Institute for Fiscal Studies (IFS) analysed income and expenditure inequality in the 1990s and 2000s (Goodman and Oldfield, 2004) and further IFS work offers a snapshot of poverty and inequality in Britain in 2004 (Brewer et al., 2004, 2005). An IPPR report on *The State of the Nation* provided an 'audit of injustice in the UK' ten years on from the Social Justice Commission (Paxton and Dixon, 2004). Taken together, the principle findings from these three pieces of research are summarised in Figure 1.6 (see page 27). This does not present an entirely positive picture of changes in patterns of poverty, income and wealth over the past decade.

Income inequality in 2002/3 stood at an historic 40 year high. Although New Labour's tax and social security policies had *slowed* down the rate of increase in income inequality, they had at that stage failed to either halt it or to reverse it. The richest 10% of earners held 28% of the total income share in 2002/3, while the poorest 10% held just 2.8%. Moreover, the top 1% of income earners massively increased their share of total income from 3.8% in 1980 to 5.8% in 2000.

Inequalities in the distribution of wealth are even more stark and have similarly widened, with the richest 10% owning 47% of wealth in 1980, but this had increased to 54% by 2000. By 2002, the wealthiest 1% of the population (around 500,000 people) owned 23% of the UK's marketable wealth, compared with 18% in 1990 (Social Trends, 2005). The results are even more skewed when the value of dwellings is excluded from the calculations, with the top 1% owning 35% of marketable wealth excluding housing in 2002: this contrasts very sharply with just 2% of marketable wealth (other than homes) owned by the least wealthy 50% of the population (ibid).

Ten years after the CSJ reported, research indicated that Britain remained divided on *income* lines from bottom to top in *a society split of '10-89-1'*, with the gap between the income of the bottom 10% and the top 1% increasing (Paxton and Dixon, 2004). By 2005 it was reported, in time for the May 2005 general election, that income inequality was being 'nudged down' as the tax and national insurance rises announced in the 2002 Budget (effective from April 2003) began to bite (IFS Press Release, 30 March 2005). These Budget measures included a 1% increase in national insurance contributions and a freeze on personal income tax allowances, bringing more people into the income tax 'net', and they led to the first drop in average take-home household income since the economic recession of the early 1990s (Brewer et al., 2005). While the 2003/4 figures do suggest a slight reduction in income inequality (as measured by the Gini co-efficient), it still remains marginally higher than the level which Labour inherited when it came to office in 1997. At the same time, the data indicates that some of the government's ambitious child poverty targets for 2004/5 may be missed.

Where *poverty* is concerned, the data summarised in Figure 1.6 may need explanation. Measurements of the percentages of a population in poverty may be expressed either *before or after housing costs* have been taken into account and this distinction is important, having different implications for different social groups. For example, where addressing child poverty is concerned, lone mothers and other poorer families often face uniquely high and variable housing costs which measurements of child poverty *before* housing costs (21%) fail to take into consideration. This effectively masks the extent of child poverty *after* housing costs are taken into account (28%), which is markedly higher. As Brewer notes, as significantly fewer children are poor under the BHC measure, this may reduce the cost to the government of meeting its child poverty target because 'a given percentage fall in poverty will require a smaller number of children to move out of poverty.' (Brewer et al., 2004:43).

- Income inequality (as measured by the Gini co-efficient) was higher in 2002/3 than it was in 1996/7 and stood at an historic 40 year high
- The top 1% of income earners (around half a million people) held a 3.5% share of total income in 1980; by 1990 their share had increased to 5.8%; and by the start of the 2000s the share of the top 1% had increased to 8%
- The richest 10% of the population held 28% of total income in 2002/3
- By contrast, the share of the bottom 10% decreased to just 2.8% of total income share
- Wealth distribution is more unequal than income distribution and is worsening: between 1990 and 2001 the percentage of wealth owned by the *wealthiest 10%* of the population had increased from 47% to 54%. Over the same period, the percentage of wealth owned by the *wealthiest 1%* of the population increased from 18% to 22%
- Between 1996/7 and 2000/1 the percentage of young people aged 16–24 with no savings remained constant at 56%
- In 2002/3, 12.4 million individuals (21.6% of the population) lived in households with incomes below 60% of the median wage (after housing costs) – often referred to as 'the poverty line'. In 2003/4 this decreased to 21%
- In 2002/3, child poverty stood at 3.6 million (after housing costs), which meant that around 28% of all children in the UK were in poverty. While 2003/4 saw a slight reduction of 100,000 this was not statistically significant
- Pensioner poverty, if measured before housing costs, remained unchanged from 1997 to 2002/3, but if measured after housing costs, fell by a quarter
- Poverty rates among the populations of working age without children (40% of all individuals) were higher in 2003/4 than when New Labour came to power
- Regional inequalities remain large: in the South East 17% of the population are in the poorest fifth of the population, compared with 26% of people in the North East
- Entry into higher education has increased from 19% in 1990 to 31% in 2000, but this has benefited the better off rather than the poor: in 2002, 40% of teenagers from higher professional backgrounds went to university compared with 11% from the lowest social class.

Figure 1.6 The State of Poverty and Inequality in the UK

(*Sources*: Brewer et al., 2004; Goodman and Oldfield, 2004; Paxton and Dixon, 2004; Brewer et al., 2005)

Where *older people* are concerned the data reflects the positive impact of the means-tested minimum income guarantee (MIG), leading to a marked reduction in pensioner poverty *after* housing costs since 1997, although poverty as measured *before* housing costs showed almost no change by 2002/3 (Brewer et al., 2004). Such disparities in before and after housing cost figures have led commentators and campaigning groups to argue for the retention of both measurements of poverty. But the government is moving towards the BHC measure, which will certainly smooth the way towards meeting its ambitious child poverty targets (Ambrose, 2004).

For older people, the introduction of the more generous pension credit (which replaced MIG in October 2003) should lead to further reductions in pensioner poverty in the coming years. However, the problem of enhancing *benefit take-up* is crucial if positive change is to take place: in 2002/3 it is estimated that pensioners failed to claim means-tested benefits worth £2.25 billion, half of that amount being attributable to non-take-up of MIG, with Council Tax Benefit also massively under-claimed (see http://www.poverty.org.uk). If anti-poverty strategies are to be successful, the problem of take-up must be addressed: latest figures indicate that for the main five income-related benefits paid by the Department of Work and Pensions (Income Support, MIG, Housing Benefit, Council Tax Benefit and Job Seekers Allowance), between 18% and 20% of those eligible for these benefits fail to claim them. Official estimates show that between £3300 million and £6260 million was left unclaimed in 2002/3 (DWP, 2005a).

Moving on from the data summarised in Figure 1.6, it is important to recall once again that poverty is a gendered experience (as Chapters 2 and 3 will go on to discuss) and that ethnic minority communities, too, continue to suffer disproportionately. For instance, three-quarters of Bangladeshi children were living in families in the bottom fifth of the income distribution at the turn of the new millennium (Platt, 2002). Nonetheless, the analysis presented by the Chancellor of the Exchequer, Gordon Brown, in successive Budgets, has suggested that Britain currently basks in the glow of economic prosperity. Not all UK citizens feel the warmth of this glow, and those who *do* may not feel it in equal measure. IPPR research has confirmed the growing income and wealth divide between people living in the North of England and those living in the South East, and between the homeowning majority and those who rent. They argue that the increase in the 'equity divide' has been the single greatest cause of inequality over the past 30 years: the value of the net equity of personally owned housing increased from £36 billion in 1970 to £1525 billion in 2001. While these figures of equity seem staggering, so do data relating to levels of *personal debt*, which send a chill wind of warning in indicating the following:

- In July 2004, personal debt in the UK broke through the £1 trillion barrier (£1,000,000,000,000) and is increasing at the rate of £1 million every four minutes
- In February 2005, total secured lending on homes was £887.8 billion
- In April 2005, the average household debt (excluding mortgages) was £7563
- Mortgage equality withdrawal (secured borrowing on homes that is not invested in the housing market) remained at less than 1% of post-tax income until 1999, but by the end of 2003 it accounted for 8.4% of total income
- By 2004, personal debt had grown twice as fast as income since the election of the first New Labour government in 1997
- Datamonitor figures show that consumer borrowing by UK adults (via credit cards, motor and retail finance, overdrafts and unsecured loans) has increased by 45% since 2000
- The amount of debt being chased by Britain's bailiffs increased by 70% over the two years from 2001–3, reaching £5 billion
- In 2001/2, 28% of households in the UK reported having no savings – working age, lone parent households were most likely to have none (67%)
- 12 million people are not saving enough towards their pensions and, of these, 60% are not contributing to a private pension at all
- One in six households in the UK with two children and one in three with four or more children are in credit arrears (with those renting twice as likely as homeowners to be in arrears).

(*Sources:* Credit Action, 2004, 2005; Social Trends, 2005)

The success of the British economy featured prominently as a theme in New Labour's 2005 election campaign, yet the data presented above shows that there is a potential personal debt 'time bomb' which threatens to shatter the UK's 'economic miracle' of the past eight years.

For the Chancellor, economic growth and prosperity fundamentally rests on the foundations of fiscal 'prudence' and a dynamic, flexible economy with (up)skilled workers. Much stress is placed on the role of *education and training* in creating 'opportunity for all'. To what extent does this hold true? Firstly, 12% of 16 year olds still obtain fewer than five GCSEs and 6% obtain no GCSEs at all – both of these figures are unchanged since 1998/9 (JRF, 2004). A quarter of young people at the ages of 11, 16 and 19 are still not reaching basic levels of educational attainment. Yet the consequences for poorer children who are seen to 'fail' are stark, with ever-narrowing options and life chances: people without qualifications are three times less likely to receive job-related training compared with those with some formal qualification (Palmer et al., 2003).

But qualifications are not equally vital for all: the founding father of British research on patterns of social mobility, John Goldthorpe, recently stressed the persistence of the advantages enjoyed by the relatively rich middle classes, despite their educational achievement (or lack of it). The 'soft skills' they acquire, such as sophisticated verbal and interpersonal skills and greater self-esteem at an earlier age, contribute to social and cultural capital which clearly 'pays off' for them:

> 'Tim nice but dim' and his sister 'Hattie sweet but scatty' who do not do very well at school rarely end up on the factory floor... instead one would expect to find them in upmarket hotels, restaurants and boutiques. (Goldthorpe, 2003)

Once again, it is clear that the relatively rich are able to benefit from opportunities that are denied to their poorer (and, particularly, minority ethnic) counterparts. Besides, there are few 'factory floors' remaining for less qualified young people to work on. Around half a million (10% of) young adults aged 16–24 were unemployed in 2003. Although numbers have halved since a decade ago, young adult unemployment rates remain two-and-a-half times higher than those for older workers. In addition, two-fifths of all those who did get a job in 2002/3 were out-of-work again within six months, raising doubts about the quality and sustainability of the work opportunities available (Palmer et al., 2003).

9. Just Talking

The final part of this chapter will move on from outlining conceptions of criminal and social justice and their 'state' in contemporary Britain, towards signalling some of the issues raised for those seeking to understand the relations between them. Some of the challenges and dilemmas for policy-makers seeking to reconcile criminal and social justice are signalled in this quotation from Andrew Rutherford:

Considerations regarding criminal policy closely intersect with broader ideas about citizenship (and the culture of rights and responsibilities), and the shaping of criminal justice arrangements *should* have the purpose of fostering social inclusion by, wherever possible, encouraging a rewarding and sustained membership within the wider community. Given the inherent tendencies of criminal justice towards social exclusion, this presents a daunting challenge to policy makers and practitioners. (2001:8, emphasis added)

For Rutherford, achieving criminal justice *should* foster social inclusion in the wider community but, at the same time, the CJS has deeply exclusionary tendencies. Criminal justice policies may therefore run counter to social policies that are seeking to promote social inclusion. To expand on this point, criminal justice can be seen as *excluding* in at least four ways: firstly, it casts the deviant as 'other' and thereby discursively sets them aside from 'normal' law-abiding citizens; secondly, many anti-social behaviours which fall short of 'crime' are increasingly leading to excluding consequences for the (predominantly) young people who engage in them (see Chapters 3 and 6 for discussion of Anti-Social Behaviour Orders); thirdly, the end point of the criminal justice system is imprisonment, which is by its very definition excluding; yet, fourthly, this is not the end of the excluding consequences of punishment as they extend beyond the prison walls (see Chapter 6). Having a criminal record does not only make it difficult to get a job, but also makes it difficult to open bank accounts, get a mortgage, credit and even home contents insurance (IPPR, 2002). As the Chief Executive of the National Association for the Care and Resettlement of Offenders (NACRO) stated, '... there is something fundamental about the need for a system which is claiming to be a system of justice to operate justly itself'. But not only is injustice evident in the operation of the CJS (as we have already seen), but in the 'double or triple punishment' inflicted on offenders after their sentence has been served (2002:20).

Given such excluding consequences, it is a paradox that policies to tackle crime and its (alleged) causes are frequently cited as those which are, at the same time, also promoting social inclusion. This is made particularly explicit in Figure 1.7, which is taken from a strategic policy document *Criminal Justice: The Way Ahead* (Home Office, 2001). Setting out New Labour's criminal justice policy for its second term, the policy 'wheel' in the diagram exemplifies the government's strategic, 'joined-up' approach to criminal and social justice. Here policies to tackle the alleged causes of crime (at the top half of the policy 'wheel') encompass policies in a range of 'social' fields including:

- The New Deal (employment and training)
- Surestart (education, childcare, health and development of young children)
- OfSTED (school inspection and education quality)
- The National Strategy for Neighbourhood Renewal
- The Anti-drugs Co-ordination Unit (headed by the Drugs Tzar).

At the same time, policies relating to the effective operation of the key components of the criminal justice system (in the lower half of the 'wheel') seek to be 'tough on crime'. These include:

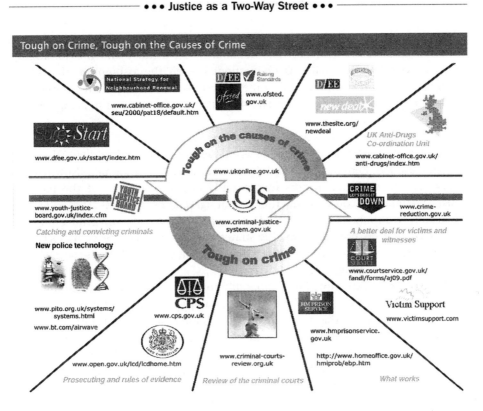

Figure 1.7   The Way Ahead?

(*Source*: 'Criminal Justice: The Way Ahead' (Home Office, 2001))

- Catching and convicting criminals (new Police technology)
- Prosecution and the rules of evidence (Crown Prosecution Service and the Police)
- Review of the Criminal Courts (Magistrates' and Crown Courts)
- What works (the prison service and probation service, now joined in the National Offender Management Service – NOMS)
- A better deal for victims and witnesses (The Court Service and Victim Support).

At the interface between addressing crime and its causes, and addressing both, lie the Youth Justice Board and Home Office Crime Reduction Programme.

The strategic overview represented in the diagram conveys a very particular, deterministic and managerialist view of policies and the relationships between them which, in turn, poses important questions about how criminal and social justice are (or are not) seen to be related here. We will return to the issue of managerialism, the politics of crime reduction and social inclusion in later chapters. But, at this point, it is essential to recognise that it is *politics* which shapes both the language and the visualisation of the links between criminal and social justice in *The Way Ahead* as it does in subsequent policy documents. Where this visualisation is concerned, the word 'justice' is conspicuous by its absence (except save for its coupling with 'criminal' in a website address). The desirability, the efficacy and the 'joining up' of all these spheres of policy is unquestioned (even the assumption that prison 'works'!), and the lexicon revealed in the diagram is one of 'deals', rules, inspection, co-ordination, efficiency and the technological fix to problems of policing. There is no real space for 'justice' here.

With the exception of Neighbourhood Renewal, all policies seeking to address the causes of crime that lie at the level of the individual and individual choices (Neighbourhood Renewal was and is an area-based programme). Nowhere are economic and structural factors incorporated into this analysis of the potential causes of crime, and consequently they do not figure in its solutions. The inequalities of income, wealth, housing, health, education and of 'race', age and gender described in this chapter do not factor in this strategy: while on the face of it, social and criminal justice are inter-linked in the wheel, fundamental problems for social justice are effectively de-coupled here.

This chapter has attempted to explore differing conceptions both of criminal and social justice and signal some of the possible relationship between them. But in order to better understand the ways in which criminal and social justice may be conceptualised (in theory) and reconciled (in theory, policy and practice) in the future, it is first necessary to address the legacy of the past – the continuities and the shifts that have shaped how we imagine criminal and social justice. This is the subject of the next chapter.

○ *two* ○ Constants and Dissonants in the Study of Criminal and Social Justice

---
Introduction

There is a saying that 'history repeats itself – it has to, because no-one listens'. We can certainly learn a great deal about contemporary attitudes towards criminal and social justice by examining our past. This chapter will identify those historical themes that continue to shape policies and discourses around criminal and social justice, even though they may have roots in past social, economic and material contexts and use different registers for their expression. But, in addition to analysing powerful historical themes, it is important to identify 'what's new' in terms of criminal and social justice, both in theory and in practice. This chapter therefore analyses both the continuities and shifts – the *constants* and the *dissonants* – which together contribute to our understanding of the relationships between criminal and social justice in twenty-first-century Britain. It will then go on to explore these understandings through a case study, which draws on issues of both criminal and social justice – the differential treatment of tax and benefit fraud.

---
1. The Deserving and the Undeserving Poor – the Legacy

Contemporary images and assumptions about poverty and crime, and about criminal and social justice, tap into a rich historical vein. From the 'dangerous classes' of the nineteenth century to the 'underclass' of the late twentieth, the poor have been portrayed as in essence criminogenic, posing a threat to both law and the social order (Williams, 1981). In this sense the discourses of poverty, pauperism, dishonesty and crime have long been interconnected. But, historically, the term 'poverty' did not possess a unified or clearly defined status and it's features were not *economic* alone: the factors that distinguished groups living in poverty were often *moral* ones. And so the ***'dangerous' and 'dishonest' poor*** were seen almost as a 'race apart' from the ***respectable working poor***. The former were not only distinguished by their economic dependency, but by the degrading lifestyle that was believed to accompany that dependency – a lifestyle that promoted habitual offending. According to Victorian social commentators such as Henry Mayhew the dishonest poor (man) was:

> distinguished from the civilised man by his repugnance to regular and continuous labour – by his want of providence in laying up a store for the future – by his inability to perceive consequences ever so slightly removed from immediate apprehensions – by his passion for stupefying herbs and roots and, where possible, for intoxicating fermented liquors. (Quoted in Murray, 1996:23)

More than a century later these themes resurfaced in the writings of the American guru of the 'underclass' Charles Murray as, for example, he spoke of his childhood in Iowa:

> There were two kinds of poor people. One class of people was never even called 'poor'. I came to understand that they simply lived on low incomes, as my own parents had done when they were young. There was another set of people, just a handful of them. These poor people didn't just lack money. They were defined by their behaviour. Their homes were littered and unkempt. The men in the family were unable to hold a job for more than a few weeks at a time. Drunkenness was common. The children grew up ill-schooled and ill-behaved and contributed a disproportionate share of the local juvenile delinquents. (1990:1)

For Murray the problem of poverty was not lack of (or low) income and the 'deserving' poor were therefore those whose behaviour remained respectable in the face of their adversity: the working poor, the elderly, the sick and children. By contrast, the 'undeserving' poor – primarily the 'able-bodied' who did not work – languished in a culture of dependency. As many nineteenth-century commentators had done before him, Murray characterised this culture as one of drunkenness, promiscuity, vices (such as prostitution and gambling) and crime.

In Britain, distinctions between deserving and undeserving poor had historically been sharpened in the Royal Commission on the Poor Law whose nineteenth-century architects believed that 'every penny bestowed upon the poor is a bounty on indolence and vice' (Fraser, 1973). They argued that the former Elizabethan system of supplementing the income of lowly paid men with families (known as 'outdoor' relief, financed by local parish rates) acted as an incentive to idleness and was a burden to the rate-payer. Consequently, for many social commentators, 'the problem', which they and society faced, was not defined in terms of poverty itself, but as ***pauperism***, which was poverty's visible form, and was regarded as both willful and sinful (Stedman-Jones, 1981).

In order to challenge and to deter pauperism, the 'New Poor Law' of 1834 was based on the twin principles of *less eligibility* and the **workhouse test**. The first ensured that incentives to paid work were maintained by setting levels of payment (relief) to the poor at levels below that of the lowest paid worker. This was put into practice through the 'workhouse test' as payment was only made to those living within the walls of the workhouse itself. Conditions here were so appalling that only the most desperate would enter, and yet those who were forced to enter included the old, infirm, women and children in addition to the able-bodied unemployed. The theory and the practical operation of less eligibility and the workhouse test therefore meant that Poor Law assistance was conditional not just on unemployment but on individual destitution (King, 1995).

As David Garland observed, the workhouse and the prison (the poor law and penality) framed a repressive disciplinary axis in mid-Victorian Britain which:

> attempted to dismantle the culture of immorality, intemperance and promiscuity which they recognized in the lower classes and to install in its place the values of self-help, sobriety, respectability and hard work. (1985:48)

This disciplinary axis still underpins in the workings of the criminal justice and welfare institutions, and notions of morality, less eligibility and work incentives continue to permeate welfare policy in twenty-first-century Britain. As we have seen, 'work' is largely equated with the 'worth' of citizens, for whom work is seen to have a moral as well as an economic imperative. In turn, 'work' is largely equated with full-time paid employment (Hirsch, 2002). The mantra which launched the New Labour government's welfare reform Green Paper in 1998 was 'work for those who can, security for those who cannot'. Although this statement has subsequently been 'watered down with the term "support" replacing "security" as the government's side of the bargain', it still forms the basis of current welfare policy (Walker, 2003:50). What remains beyond doubt is the centrality of the principle of **work for those who can**.

However, the demands of the global economy and flexible labour markets render the concept of 'work' as the basis for the welfare bargain far from straightforward. Work may be poorly paid, temporary, part time or casual and 'flexibility' itself does not make for individual or family stability. Engaging in paid work cannot (as we saw in Chapter 1) be assumed to offer financial security and keep families out of poverty. At the same time, the political messages about the priority and meaning of 'work' can seem paradoxical. For example, on the one hand the government seeks to enable and encourage lone parents, young people, disabled people, the long-term unemployed and the over 50s to enter and to stay in work. On the other hand, policies also stress the desirability of a 'work–life balance', the importance of meeting the needs of children and families and the value of being a 'carer' or a volunteer within the community.

So exactly who is regarded as a working, productive and deserving citizen, and who is seen as 'undeserving' of security and support, and why? The answer to these questions is a matter of degree and also relates to the issue of dependency: there are two key features of welfare policy that formally underpin the dichotomy between the status of working and not working. Firstly, the '16 hour rule', and secondly, the concept of availability for work (a 'work test'). If an individual works more than 16 hours they are considered part of the *employment system* and they can therefore claim benefits to top-up their wages through New Tax Credits.[1] But if they work less than 16 hours, they are considered part of the *benefit system* and are subject to its disciplinary regulations, and this includes the requirement to be demonstrably seeking paid employment (unless claimants are lone parents of small children, or exempted from seeking work through sickness or disability).

Welfare claimants may work part time (for less than 16 hours) to supplement their benefits. But for those who *do* work, all of their earnings above the threshold of a small amount of 'disregarded' earnings are deducted pound-for-pound from welfare benefits paid (Hirsch, 2003). Here the concept of incentives has perverse effects, which appear to penalise those constituted within the benefit system (working under the arbitrary 16 hours) while rewarding those who work more than 16 hours in the employment system by 'making work pay' (HM Treasury, 2000). This paradox reflects the legacy of the deserving–undeserving dichotomy as some individuals (in the employment system) are constituted as *givers to* and others (in the benefit system) *takers from* to the state. The ways in which work serves as a means of classifying and (re)constituting citizens as *workers* or *claimants* within such a restricted and inflexible welfare paradigm has profound implications for their lives and life chances (as we will see below). In many respects, therefore, the discursive schism between the deserving and undeserving poor remains as sharp in the twenty-first century as it was in the nineteenth.

--------------------------------------- **2. The Deserving and the Undeserving** ---------------------------------------
Poor – New Deals, New Subjects?

So 'what's new' in the construction of twenty-first-century British welfare? It is clearly not new that the principles of less eligibility underpin a social security system that is (still) being used as an incentive to full-time paid work – or at least to work amounting to over 16 hours per week. The first thing which *is* new is that the disciplinary mechanisms of the government's welfare to work strategy supporting this incentivisation are now being applied to people who would not previously have been regarded as 'undeserving' – such as disabled people and parents with childcare responsibilities.

---

[1]The **New Tax Credits** consist of: The **Child Tax Credit** introduced in 2003, which brought together the child elements of the Working Families Tax Credit (WFTC), Disabled Persons Tax Credit (DPTC), Income Support and income-based Job Seekers Allowance; the **Working Tax Credit** introduced at the same time which brought together the adult elements of WFTC, DPTC and Employment Credit which is part of the New Deal for those aged 50+ (Inland Revenue Cm 5706, 2003).

The government's flagship 'New Deal' policies for lone parents and disabled people were piloted in 1998 and launched in 2001 with the emphasis on one-to-one advisor support, which could be taken up voluntarily, and enhanced opportunities in terms of subsidised employment and/or education and training for these key groups.

But official data and evidence from a series of New Deal evaluations are far from positive. The statistical data produced by the Department for Work and Pensions (DWP) shows that around 52% of the lone parents and 40% of the disabled people taking up New Deal interviews subsequently left income support for employment – in other words, for almost half of lone parents and 60% of disabled people the New Deal did not lead to getting a job. Moreover, the numbers of those who *did* gain employment still includes those who, though working over 16 hours per week (often in unskilled poorly paid jobs), may still be claiming in-work benefits such as Working Tax Credit (Flaherty et al., 2004). The New Deal thus demonstrates a very particular (and paradoxical) conception of what constitutes benefit 'dependency', particularly for lone parents: for this (overwhelmingly female) group, their dependency on Tax Credits is apparently politically acceptable and desirable, even though they may be effectively undertaking state subsidised employment and leaving their children in state subsidised childcare. However, those lone parents who work less than 16 hours and/or look after their children at home while living on benefits are not accorded the same positive status (Grover and Stewart, 2000:248) as they are primarily regarded not as workers but as claimants depending on state benefits.

The success of New Deal for Lone Parents (NDLP) itself depends on the ***availability of appropriate and affordable childcare*** for all those parents who wish to work, but the delivery of the government's childcare vision is proving problematic. In terms of affordability, the Childcare Tax Credit covered only a quarter or less of typical childcare costs, ignored informal arrangements and, unsurprisingly, had a take-up rate of only 13% in 2002. Where availability is concerned the number of day nursery places per 1000 children in England in 2002 was 95, and was only 62.4 in Northern Ireland. Here, Horgan (2005) argues, high unemployment and low wages mean that welfare to work policies will almost certainly fail to eliminate child poverty. But the issue of appropriateness is also important: even if affordable childcare were to be available UK-wide, it would not be a sufficient condition for the success of the welfare to work strategy because, according to Duncan et al. (2003), the governments 'vision' for childcare makes what they call 'the rationality mistake'. Like Horgan, they see the strategy as labour-market driven, assuming that parents are driven primarily by economic rationales when making decisions around work and childcare. This fails to come to terms with the fact that there are those mothers who do not wish to, or cannot enter the workforce, or need extensive support to be able to, (Horgan, 2005). It also fails to acknowledge the wider social, moral and emotional factors around parenting and childcare, which may shape parents decisions and their preferences for informal childcare, by friends and family (Wheelock and Jones, 2002; Sipilä and Kröger, 2005). As is the case elsewhere in Europe, the UK welfare reform agenda in these respects fails to fully understand 'the difficulties described by families actually engaged in reconciling work and care' (Baldock and Hadlow, 2005:718).

The first New Deal initiative launched as part of the government's 'welfare to work' strategy was the New Deal for Young People (NDYP). Launched in 1998 it focused on those aged 18–24 years who had been unemployed for more than six months. As both 'able-bodied' and unemployed, this group would, historically, have fallen within the category of 'undeserving poor'. The success or otherwise of the NDYP has, however, proved difficult to measure with any precision: research evaluating its first 18 months of operation (Wilkinson, 2003) concluded that six months after qualifying for entry into the NDYP there was a reduction in unemployment of NDYP entrants of 30,000 to 40,000, although this reduction coincided with their moving from the initial six month 'gateway' phase to dedicated New Deal 'options' when their claims to benefits also ceased. But even this reduction in unemployment was eroded as time progressed: after one year the reduction in unemployment was more than halved. Moreover, most NDYP exits from unemployment were to undertake government supported training rather than to take on jobs.

A further problem for NDYP evaluations is that separating out the effects of NDYP and other 'employment effects' remains problematic: for instance, some of the young people entering new jobs may have done so even if the New Deal were not in place (these are termed 'deadweight' effects) and so these cannot be attributable to the success of the initiative. Looking back to the 1990s, the then 'Workstart' pilots experienced similar deadweight effects, which were estimated to account for 70% of job starts; meaning that only 30% of those jobs were net gains for the unemployed that resulted from the policy (Hasluck, 1999). A decade later the same may well hold for New Deal jobs. In addition, doubts also remain about the longer-term employment benefits of the NDYP which, it is suggested, are not sustainable over longer time periods (Wilkinson, 2003).

To briefly return to the imagery of the deserving and undeserving poor which opened this chapter, it could be argued that healthy, young people readily fit the caricature of the 'able-bodied' unemployed, and so could be constituted as undeserving of state support. The recent emphasis on the lone mother as a potential target for welfare to work intervention signals both an extension and a significant re-packaging of the discourse of the undeserving poor for the twentieth and twenty-first centuries. A crucial element of this re-packaging centres on the role of the lone mother as producer and reproducer of families that are seen to pose a problem for both the moral and social order.

3. 'Problem' Families

The notion of the ***problem family*** has long historical roots and has come to embody a worrying fusion of disparate discourses around morality, dependency and crime. There is a discursive continuum, of sorts, which runs from 'social problems' at one end to 'crime' at the other, and along which the boundaries between the two become blurred; causation is wrongly attributed, so that it is assumed these 'social problems' *cause* crime. Firstly, such assumptions completely fail to take into account that the most successful criminals (in terms of both the relative rewards of their crimes and their ability to escape punishment) are not the poor, but the rich: yet despite the divorce, lone parenthood, drunkenness and idleness of some of the 'rich', these attributes are not regarded as a 'social problem', a cause of crime or a predictor of their re-offending. So the 'problem family' is not rich, it is poor and, as such, is more likely to be headed by a female (Flaherty et al., 2004).

The essential ingredients of the stereotype are summarised in the following description of the 'underclass' by Charles Murray:

> Illegitimacy in the lower classes will continue to rise and, inevitably, life in lower class communities will continue to de-generate – more crime, more widespread drug and alcohol addiction, fewer marriages, more drop-out from work, more homelessness, more child neglect, fewer young people pulling themselves out of the slums, more young people tumbling in. (1994:18)

Murray's discussion of the characteristics and consequences of what he termed the 'New Rabble', echo the views expressed 20 years earlier in a speech by the then Secretary of State for Social Services, Sir Keith Joseph, whose call for 'the re-moralisation of public life' was uncomfortably dressed in the language of eugenics:

> The balance of our population, our human stock is threatened … a high and rising proportion of children are being born to mothers least fitted to bring children into the world. Many of these girls [from social classes 4 and 5] are unmarried, many are deserted or divorced or soon will be… They are producing problem children, the future unmarried mothers, delinquents, denizens of our borstals, sub-normal educational establishments, prisons, hostels for drifters. (19 October 1974)

Again, the poor are portrayed as a 'race apart', and they are responsible for breeding, quite literally, a plethora of social problems. At the forefront of these problems is crime, which is constituted as a core aspect of the lives of the poor: it is a problem that they are seen to reproduce, from one generation to the next, primarily through the medium of single-parent families. Not only do such discourses blame the poor for their own poverty, and thus for their own criminality, but in so doing they also effectively deny any structural or redistributive policy solutions to crime and its causes. There is no need to re-balance society or change the status quo if the fault lies within incorrigible individuals. At the same time, these individualised and 'victim-blaming' perspectives which allege causal links between poverty, morality and crime, fail to address the crimes of the rich and the powerful.

Discourses on crime, its causes and its perpetuation therefore frequently centre on the stereotype of the criminogenic nature of the female headed *lone-parent family*. The stigma associated with bearing children outside marriage has a long history in Britain, and these rich reservoirs were tapped in powerful discourses around lone mothers which (re)surfaced with a vengeance in the early 1990s. But not *all* lone mothers were seen to pose a problem: widows and divorcees whose husbands maintained them were not at issue because they were seen as deserving and posing no threat to the moral order. But at the 1992 Conservative Party Conference, the then Secretary of State for Social Security, Peter Lilley, drew laughter and much applause from the audience with his rhyming 'Little List' of benefit offenders who included:

> Young ladies who get pregnant just to join the housing list And Dad's who won't support the kids of ladies they have … Kissed. (Daily Mirror, 8 October 1992)

The rhetorical and policy onslaught against young, never-married lone mothers gathered pace as the following year the aspiring party leader and the then Welsh Secretary, John Redwood, recalled a visit to the St Mellons Estate in Cardiff and railed against the mothers who were 'married to the state'. In so doing he made the link with crime explicit declaring that 'six in ten children belong to unmarried mothers and crime is rife' (*Sunday Times*, 11 July 1993). It is not insignificant that cuts in lone-parent benefits followed in the later days of the Conservative government, and they were not immediately restored by the New Labour Chancellor, Gordon Brown on taking office in 1997.

Moving beyond the stereotypes, the evidential basis for associating female lone parenthood with criminal activity among their children remains questionable. Firstly, it is far more likely that it is the *poverty* disproportionately suffered by lone-parent families that is associated (though not necessarily causally) with crime, rather than the *type of family* formation in itself. Secondly, research does not support the simplistic causality of the lone parent family/crime link. But, as a note of caution, it is worth stressing that the kinds of positivistic research which test and allege causal links between various elements of individual and family pathology are highly con-tested. Constructivist criminologists, and others, would reject over-simplified expla-nations such as these in favour of more dynamic approaches that stress the complexities and contradictions of social phenomena – including crime. Nonetheless, research on crime and family formation (for what it is worth), has indicated that lone-parent families are not, by definition, more liable to produce habitual criminals than other forms of family arrangement. One recent longitudinal study of 'disrupted fam-ilies' concluded that the impact of family forms and relations on crime and deviance is far from simple:

> Some kinds of disrupted families are criminogenic (e.g. those where the boy does not remain with the mother), just as some kinds of intact families are criminogenic (e.g. those characterised by high parental conflict). Equally, some kinds of dis-rupted families (e.g. those where the boy remains with a lone mother) are no more criminogenic than intact harmonious families. (Juby and Farrington, 2001:37)

More recently, a similar study (Haas et al., 2004) concludes that 'the simple dichotomy of disrupted and intact families' is insufficient to account for the wide range of par-enting practices, forms of living arrangement, quality of relations between (each) par-ent and child, and factors such as being looked after in local authority care, all of which may have differing effects upon 'risks of delinquency'. There is, then, no straightforward positivistic relationship between crime and family formation itself, although lone parents (particularly mothers) continue to be constituted as a key element within the lexis and imagery of the criminogenic 'problem family'.

The 'problem family' is not only imagined – it is a product of distinct political and economic conditions and of welfare practices that have their origins in the emergence of modern industrial societies. Donzelot (1980) indicates the ways in which changes in the regulation of family affairs since the eighteenth century transformed the formerly private domain of the family into a space for public surveillance and intervention. A plethora of social practices and 'professional' discourses – such as philanthropy, social work, medicine, mass education and psychiatry – combined to effect the moralisation and normalisation of families.

Moralisation was not only achieved through the efforts of religious and charitable organisations, but was also effected by financial regulation as poor relief, and later 'welfare', sought to incentivise the poor to become honest, productive and thus deserving. Families were also liable to processes of *normalisation* as the particular forms of family living were disseminated through education and a range of welfare professionals. The 'scientific' knowledge to which these professions laid claim, and their increasing incorporation into the institutions of the state in the twentieth century, gave rise to their power to 'police' families (and they also gave rise to the 'new' science of criminology). Where processes of moralisation and normalisation did not achieve the desired results, Donzelot uses the notion of *tutelage* to describe the processes through which coercive and preventative actions could be taken to change families' behaviour and ways of living. However, such practices were both gendered and shaped by class relations, as philanthropists and state professionals alike related to middle-class and working-class mothers in very different ways (Donzelot, 1980; Swain, 1999).

Garland (1985) traced the transformations in both the penal and social realms from the onset of the twentieth century and goes on to describe the new strategies of regulation which emerged:

> The repressive language of oral distinction, 'desert' and 'worth', and the odious testing of the destitute were replaced by an administrative machinery and discourse quite separate from those of the hated poor law. Pensions were to be distributed through the Post Office; school meals, health care and insurance benefits provided without disenfranchisement; and if the worker was still forced to be responsible, regular and stable, then this force was discreetly contained in the automatic administrative decisions, not revealed in the mouths of 'philanthropists' and poor law officials. (1985:245)

But, as we have already seen, the repressive discourse of work and 'worth' is back again, with an added spin under New Labour and, as we will see in Chapter 3, the benign Post Office has been replaced by electronic methods of payment, which are themselves imbued with regulatory and disciplinary mechanisms. However, as Garland does go on to add, the *new* ideological revision which he describes (in the quotation above) was still predicated on the *old* notions of individual responsibility, thrift, self-help and the contractual nature of individual rights or entitlements. In this way, the apparatus and 'mode of address' in regulating the poor and poor families may have changed over the past century, but the overall aim remains the same – the effective regulation of an economically efficient and responsible population – and this starts with, and in, the family.

In the last quarter of the twentieth century, the family – whether 'problem' or not – has undergone changes in both its structure, and the nature and longevity of its relationships. These changes are regarded by some as positive, displaying diversity and increasing choice, particularly for women, while others grudgingly acknowledge the plurality in family forms, yet hark back to a mythical 'golden age' of the nuclear family (Halsey, 1992; Dennis and Erdos, 1993). But it is important to go beyond simplistic assertions of whether such changes are for 'better' or 'worse'. Alternatively, it is useful to emphasise the consequences of these changes in terms of the public–private dichotomy and the differential positions of men and women within the spheres of family, work and the state. These perspectives enable us to see that women are both gendered and racialised welfare and criminal justice subjects (Worrall, 1990; Lister, 2000). Where families are constituted as 'problems', the consequences for women may be dire as they are most often held to blame and may have most to lose in the wake of preventative or 'policing' interventions to restore what are seen as 'normal' family forms and behaviours.

What is relatively new here is that these interventions now also involve a wide range of non-state organisations who are increasingly engaged with families around issues including: health, parenting, training, skills and employment (of both parents and young people), offending and anti-social behaviour. At the same time, the 'policing' of and for the family is now often constituted in terms of interpersonal violence both within and outwith the family itself. Families are, at one and the same time, perpetrators and victims of violence.

The complexity and the extent of abuse (sexual, physical and emotional) of children and adults within families, has received greater recognition and policy attention in the past 20 years, yet the family is simultaneously idealised and demonised in contemporary criminal justice discourse. In relation to the latter, not only is the family a site of the victimisation of its own members but, at the same time, families are themselves targeted as the villains of the peace, as place-centred and media-fuelled myths around anti-social behaviour and 'neighbours from hell' raise the penal stakes ever higher. But, as recent research aptly notes, the consequences of 'tough' responses (such as Anti-Social Behaviour Orders – ASBOs) are that lone mothers disproportionately suffer the consequences – often eviction from their homes – when they find it impossible to control the behaviour of their teenage sons or their boyfriends (Hunter and Nixon, 2001). 'Problematising women' can also serve to transform the nature of the problem being addressed, according to Campbell, from the problem of a 'masculine response to an economic crisis, to the failure of mothers to manage the men' (1993:303).

In summary, the discourse of the 'problem families', which dominated both welfare and penal interventions in the 1970s, may often have invoked an assistantial response through the work of 'welfare' state professionals. Such responses were often disciplinary in nature and served to pathologise the family, but on the surface they aimed to understand and to 'help' (for example, through state sponsored social work). In New Labour's Britain, assistantialism has given way to a neo-conservative policy response with the concept of individual responsibility – or blame – unashamedly at its core. In these respects Blair's policies have echoed the perspectives of his Conservative predecessor and the current (at the time of writing) Conservative Party leader Michael Howard has stated in various speeches:

> You can argue forever about the causes of crime. My approach is based on some simple principles. That children – at home and at school – must be taught the difference between right and wrong. That criminals, and no one else – must be held responsible for their actions. (Then Conservative Home Secretary, October 1993)

> Families are the core of our society. They should teach right from wrong. They should be the first defence against anti-social behaviour. (Tony Blair, Labour Opposition Leader, April 1997)

Moreover, when as Prime Minister, in July 2004, Blair announced 'the end of the 1960s liberal consensus on law and order', he stole the very undergarments of his Conservative opposition as he blamed 'the sixties' for the law and order problems of twenty-first-century Britain (*Guardian*, 19 July 2004).

To sum up, where the twenty-first-century family is concerned, a range of discourses are available – both old and new – which may serve either to valorise or to penalise them. There is no one simple 'state' response to families – liberal, assistantial or otherwise – but a tapestry of overlapping, contradicting policy responses and modes of governance, which variously seek to modify, normalise, socialise and regulate not just families, but ultimately the (fragmented and diverse) places, spaces and communities within which they live their lives.

4. 'Problem' Places

The concept of the 'problem area' is a further historical theme that pervades contemporary understandings about poverty, crime, social and criminal justice and the relations between them. Latter twentieth-century British exposés of inner city deprivation (and depravity) retained many of the hallmarks of Mayhew's description of nineteenth-century Britain's criminal areas, the *rookeries*, which comprised squalid housing, overcrowding, gambling, vice (notably prostitution), drunkenness, petty theft and hardened criminals, together with a powerful sense of 'danger'.

But by the end of the twentieth century the lexicon of the problem area had dramatically shifted following the *riots* which occurred in several British cities in

1981, 1985 and 1991. One crucial dimension of the change in the conceptualisation of the criminal areas was the *racialisation* of the 'urban crisis'. Although keenly aware of the complexities involved in understanding the concepts of both 'race' and the 'city', Keith described the ways in which 'race' was systematically used 'to conjure up the urban crisis'. In general terms:

> Blackness... has come to play a cautionary role' which may be likened to the nineteenth century fears of the crowd and the dangerous classes. (Keith and Cross, 1993:10)

A prime example of this was evident in a speech made by the then Metropolitan Police Commissioner, Sir Kenneth Newman, in the wake of the 1981 inner city 'riots', where he coined the term *symbolic location* to describe what in essence were the (racialised) features of 'problem' areas:

> Throughout London there are locations where unemployed youth – often black youths – congregate; where the sale and purchase of drugs, the exchange of stolen property and illegal drinking and gaming is not uncommon. The youths regard these locations as their territory. Police are viewed as intruders, the symbol of authority – largely white authority – in a society that is responsible for all their grievances about unemployment, prejudice and discrimination. They equate closely with criminal 'rookeries' of Dickensian London... If allowed to continue, locations with these characteristics assume symbolic importance and negative symbolism of the inability of the police to maintain order. Their existence encourages law-breaking elsewhere, affects public perceptions of police effectiveness, heightens fear of crime and reinforces a phenomenon of urban decay. (Quoted in Gilroy and Sim, 1985)

The policy response of the then Secretary of State for the Environment, Michael Heseltine, to these 'riots' (or uprisings, depending on your perspective) in the Toxteth area of Liverpool, was to host a garden festival in the city. For many, this confirmed a political intention to address the outward manifestations of urban decline without addressing its root causes.

Two decades after Newman's infamous pronouncement on race, territoriality and disorder, his views still resonate in popular and political discourses, and all despite the fact that it had become apparent, in 1991, that 'race' could not explain why riots erupted in predominantly white and/or 'suburban' localities such as Blackbird Leys, Oxford and Scotswood, Meadowell Tyneside (Campbell, 1993). As Campbell indicated, the problem of the architecture and the residents who inhabited 'problem areas' was becoming inseparable:

> The theory of the underclass entered the vernacular together with the image of the estate. The two became synonymous in Britain. (1993:314)

She goes on to summarise how the *spatialisation* of crime had changed by the 1990s:

> The collective gaze was directed at localities rather than, for example, the grandiose corporate frauds which vexed, and ultimately exhausted, the judicial system... the 'symbolic locations' shifted from... the inner city... to the edge of the city... These were places that were part of a mass landscape in Britain, *estates* were everywhere. But in the Nineties, estates came to mean crime. (ibid:317, original emphasis)

Crime was now conceived as a 'mass' phenomenon, not confined to the inner city, but in estates everywhere and anywhere. Paradoxically, though, the flight of people and of capital out of certain localities has intensified the spatial divisions between rich and poor. The term 'fortress Britain' has become a description for a landscape where the well-off live separately from their poorer counterparts, surrounded by high walls, private CCTV and security systems which, at the same time, fuel their anxieties (and those of 'middle England' in general) about their security and the 'otherness' of the problem neighbourhoods that often surround them.

This spatial bifurcation has been compounded and complicated by the ways in which the 'racialisation of the urban crisis' took on a very different form with the events in Bradford, Burnley and Oldham in 2001 (see further discussion in Chapter 6). These events signified a range of concerns – on the part of the 'rioters' and middle England – over the meanings of 'Britishness', cultural identities, racism, housing policy, poverty and inequality. Following 9/11, the nature and objects of racialisation shifted dramatically once again: the racialisation of the urban crisis has given way to more complex and insidious forms of discrimination and oppression based not on place and visibility but on religious difference. The burgeoning phenomenon of Islamophobia exists independently of 'race', skin colour, place of birth, citizenship status, residence and place. Nonetheless, the *places* where Muslims live, meet, work and worship are, in the post-9/11 siege mentality, defined as 'problematic' for law, order and security.

Despite historical shifts and seismic shocks, contemporary criminal justice and social policy still remains focused on the 'problem neighbourhood'. What is new is that both policies deploy the language of *social inclusion* and *neighbourhood renewal* as key means of addressing crime – notably through the allegedly 'joined-up' work of community safety strategies and the Neighbourhood Renewal Unit. As we have seen, the soft vocabulary of 'social exclusion' has replaced the hard 'p' word – poverty – where, under New Labour, its usage is almost entirely confined to child and pensioner poverty. At the same time, the lexicon of crime now encompasses a range of (non-criminal) activities under the umbrella of *anti-social behaviour* (to be discussed in more depth in Chapter 6). The blurring of boundaries between the criminal and the social has implications for how crime is to be addressed. While criminal justice and social policies have been 'shackled' together, it is notable that a higher degree of influence is accorded 'to crime prevention – as opposed to poverty prevention' (Crawford, 1998:121). It is within such problematic contexts – social, cultural, political and spatial – that we need to examine the interface between criminal and social justice in contemporary Britain.

5. Responses to Tax and Benefit Fraud – A Case of Rich Law, Poor Law?

So far, this chapter has looked at the ways in which, historically, certain individuals, groups, spaces, behaviours and lifestyles have come to be regarded as 'a problem' in terms of crime and/or a threat to the social order. While there are some distinctive continuities, there are also historical shifts and breaks in the discourses and practices through which such 'problems' are articulated and constructed. This section will take the analysis a stage further by applying it in more depth to one issue – the concept of the 'undeserving poor' – and examine how this has shaped the regulation and criminalisation of the relatively poor who commit (or are suspected of) benefit fraud. In order to assess the implications this holds for social justice, the experience of the relatively rich who similarly defraud the public purse (through tax evasion) will provide an initial and comparative basis for the analysis. By examining attitudes towards these frauds and the policies and practices used to regulate them it is possible to offer an answer to the question: *When it comes to fiddling the state, is there one law for the (relatively) rich and another for the poor in contemporary Britain?*

Death and taxes

In Chapter 1 it was suggested that the rich benefited more from the 'citizenship deal' than the poor in three key respects: firstly, by paying less into this 'deal'; secondly, by having less demanded of them in terms of their active citizenship; and thirdly, by attracting less censure and moral approbation when they breach the law or their citizenship obligations. This section will explore how these three propositions have historically been interconnected around the issue of social, political, legal and public responses to tax and social security fraud. In Britain, taxation has historically been regarded as an 'intolerable inquisition' upon hard pressed taxpayers. The US statesman and father of the US constitution – Benjamin Franklin – famously commented in 1789 that 'in this world nothing can be said to be certain, except death and taxes', an observation which also typifies the British traditional hatred of paying personal taxes.

In twentieth-century Britain a 'new' approach to the role of taxation became evident after the First World War as Lloyd George's 'Peoples Budget' introduced Land Duty, Capital Gains Tax, death duties and progressive personal taxes. In so doing he clearly signalled that this was 'a War Budget... for raising money to wage implacable warfare against poverty and squalidness' (quoted in Fraser, 1973). The progressive and galvanising effect of war on social and fiscal policy, epitomised by the slogan 'we're all in it together', was once again evident after the Second World War as the Pay As You Earn (PAYE) means of tax collection was introduced. The Wilson Labour governments of the 1960s and 1970s briefly returned to highly progressive rates of taxation which, in the words of its Labour Chancellor, Denis Healey, would 'squeeze the rich until the pips squeak', although the government of the day was reviled for doing so.

Taxation has long been represented in political and popular discourse as stifling enterprise and a disincentive to effort – a view that was particularly evident following the relatively high progressive rates of tax under Harold Wilson's Labour governments of the 1960s and 1970s. In the 1980s, the Conservative 'new right' government of Margaret Thatcher sought to 'roll back' the frontiers of the state, and that meant rolling back taxes. She embraced the values of the *enterprise culture*, which allegedly depended on the financial incentives that high taxes were seen to stifle. At the same time she denounced the evils of the *dependency culture*, which was seen to be associated with the unemployed and undeserving poor languishing at the tax-payers expense. But when enterprising folk broke the law by evading taxes, Thatcher was far from censorious about their actions: in an infamous comment on the 'black' (or hidden) economy, she proclaimed that it was 'big, flourishing, thriving' and evidenced that 'the enterprise is still there' (ITV *Weekend World*, 17 November 1985). But, as we will see below, the same political enthusiasm for 'enterprise' was not evident when this involved the poor engaging in the 'thriving' hidden economy while claiming welfare benefits from the state.

The taxpayer has historically been valorised as a law-abiding and productive citizen, and a *giver* of revenue for state services, including welfare. By contrast, the welfare claimant is a *taker* from the state (and thus from the honest taxpayer). In this way, the taxpayer and the benefit claimant represent both elements of the twentieth-century mythological 'Robin Hood' state in action – taking from the rich and giving to the poor (Cook, 1989:173). The ways in which taxpayers have been constituted as givers and benefit claimants as takers from the state, serve to shape very different social, political, judicial and public responses to the (relatively) rich and the poor when they breach citizenship 'rules' and/or the law.

Responses to tax offences

To take tax evasion first, it is important at the outset to define precisely what the term means. According to Kirschler et al. (2002) evasion is one of at least three ways of reducing the taxes an individual or business pays:

1. **Tax avoidance** – which attempts to reduce payments by legal means (such as exploiting loopholes)
2. **Tax flight** – which involves the relocation of business to save taxes (for instance to offshore tax havens)
3. **Tax evasion** – which involves the illegal reduction in taxes paid by under-reporting income or over-stating allowable reductions.

All these activities have the same negative effects on revenue yields, but only the third – evasion – is illegal. But legal actions can have damaging consequences: for example, tax flight and the use of off-shore havens threatens both democracy and economic development as states compete with each other to offer tax exemptions to capital. As a result:

tax havens grow more numerous, the world's richest financial centres get even richer, taxes paid by large corporations fall, and ordinary citizens bear the cost. (Tax Justice Network, 2003)

Where (illegal) tax evasion is concerned, the primary means of evading taxes is by under-reporting income and this often involves engaging in activity within the 'hidden economy'. The hidden, or informal, economy was defined in an influential report by Lord Grabiner in the following way:

> [it] is usually taken to mean any undeclared economic activity. It covers tax evasion of all kinds, ranging from casual moonlighting and work paid cash-in-hand through to organised crime. Some of the informal economy is truly 'hidden' (for example firms that are not registered with any government agency); much of it, though, consists of undeclared profits from known businesses. (2000:1.1)

This makes it clear, then, that tax evasion is also committed by known, legitimate businesses and this muddies the waters where the imposition of censure and punishment are concerned (as we will see later). It is notable that the word 'crime' is rarely associated with tax evasion. Rather, it is couched in terms of its polar opposite – *compliance* with the law. Thus, by discursive sleight of hand, illegality is transformed into a mere failure to comply with tax law (but the same linguistic tricks are not available to cloak the crimes of the poor). It is significant that recent research (Ortivska and Hudson, 2002) indicates that an individual's income level is negatively correlated with their compliance with tax laws – in other words, the higher an individual's income, the less likely they are to comply with tax law (and more likely to engage in illegal evasion). Even when the better off do comply with the law, their compliance may involve 'creative' practices (McBarnett, 2001) whereby they find ways to comply with the letter of the law while undermining its spirit and the policy behind its words.

The scale of the problem of tax evasion is immense, although it is inevitably hidden and immeasurable. Lord Grabiner's report avoided providing any estimate, but instead concluded that the hidden economy was 'a major problem involving billions of pounds' (2000:3). Looking beyond the UK and to the UK for comparisons, tax evasion is widespread: in 1998 it was estimated that over 25% of taxpayers in the US underpaid their taxes by $1500 or more. Tax evasion in 'developed' countries is often estimated at about 20% of revenue yielded, with the problem worsening in 'less developed' nations, such as the Philippines, where the loss is estimated at 50% of revenue (Ortivska and Hudson, 2002).

Where the UK is concerned, research findings have resonance for issues of citizenship and social as well as criminal justice. Firstly, Ortivska and Hudson found that tax evasion declines with *age*: this could be result of 'ageing' itself, or it may indicate longer-term generational differences in attitudes, which could have damaging effects on revenue collection and good government in the UK in future, as the young are less likely to pay their taxes fully than the generations before them. Secondly, *education* is also a significant factor: not only do the most educated disapprove *least* of evasion, but a 'greater level of education tends to reduce law abidance' and is associated with

Activity or scenario	Seeing it as 'wrong' (%)	Seeing it as 'seriously wrong' (%)
VAT evasion	32.8	7.7
Tax evasion	44.1	8.8
Benefit fraud	51.2	23.5

Figure 2.1   Public Perceptions of Revenue and Benefit Fraud
(*Source*: Ortivska and Hudson, 2002)

tax evasion. Thirdly, the research indicated that the more educated signalled their commitment to *civic duty* (in terms of believing that everyone should do voluntary work), but while they may 'talk the talk' on civic duty, they are least law-abiding when it comes to paying their taxes. Fourthly, there were significant differences in *public perceptions* of various 'scenarios' involving VAT evasion, tax evasion and benefit fraud: as indicated in Figure 2.1, VAT evasion was seen as 'wrong' by 32.8% of respondents and 'seriously wrong' by only 7.7%. Evading tax was regarded as wrong by 44.1% and seriously wrong by 8.8%. By contrast, benefit fraud was regarded far more negatively with 51.2% of respondents seeing it as wrong and 23.5% as seriously wrong.

A more recent survey has suggested even harsher attitudes towards benefit fraud with 94% of respondents regarding 'stopping benefit cheats' as extremely or very important (DWP Press Release, 15 June 2004).

Taken together, these findings signal that the better-off and the educated are the groups most likely to break the law by evading taxes, but that public attitudes to different types of fraud can underpin very unequal strategies for addressing tax and benefit fraud. The subsequent differential prosecution and criminalisation of social security and tax fraud has long been an issue of concern for social policy commentators and campaigners. For instance, in 1984 the National Association for the Care and Resettlement of Offenders (NACRO) stated that the ratio of prosecutions brought by the Inland Revenue in 1984 for tax fraud, and the Department of Health and Social Security (DHSS) for benefit fraud was 1:30 (1986:70). As Figures 2.2 and 2.3 indicate (overleaf and page 56), 20 years on, this ratio has dramatically increased to around one Revenue prosecution for every 215 by the Department for Work and Pensions (and this for income support and JSA fraud only – not including Council Tax and Housing Benefit Fraud). Such a disparity is worrying for all those concerned with social and criminal justice. But the story does not end here.

Compliance and costs

In recent years, 'what's new' in relation to responses to tax fraud is not only a plummeting in the *number* of prosecutions mounted by the Inland Revenue, but also a decrease in the cash *yield* arising from their tax investigation and compliance work.

YEAR	1993/4	1994/5	1995/6	1996/7	1997/8	1998/9	1999/2000	2000/1	2001/2	2002/3	2003/4
Tax prosecutions[a]	216 (17)	356 (25)	177 (11)	167 (13)	116 (17)	32 (2)	37 (10)	54 (7)	30 (5)	43 (4)	43 (5)
WFTC prosecutions	–	–	–	–	–	–	–	2	28	34 (1)	56 (1)
Compliance: tax yield (£billions)	4.69	6.11	5.2	4.31	3.93	4	5.44	4.49	3.8	4.3	4.6
Total net revenue receipts (£billions)	77.62	87.3	97	103.7	117	128	197[b]	211	214	212.7	230.8

[a]Figures given are for successful prosecutions, with figures for acquittals then given in parentheses.
[b]Figures from 1999/2000 onward include receipts and costs for National Insurance Contributions and payments and costs for Tax Credits.

Figure 2.2 Revenue Receipts, Yields from Compliance Work and Prosecutions: 1993/4 to 2002/3

(*Sources*: Board of Inland Revenue Annual Reports for the years ending 31 March 1998 to 31 March 2002; Report of the Commissioners of Her Majesty's Inland Revenue for the year ending 31 March 2003)

Figure 2.2 shows that in 1994/5 and 1995/6 the yields achieved from compliance work had been impressive, totalling £6.11 billion, whereas the total for the most recent three years shows a reduction to £3.8 billion in 2001/2 followed by increases to £4.3 billion in 2002/3 and £4.6 billion in 2003/4. Tax yields from compliance work have therefore decreased in absolute terms by 30% since their peak in 1994/5 (the gap in relative terms, allowing for inflation, would be even greater).

This dramatic reduction in the yields from investigation work also needs to be set in the context of increases in the net taxes and duties *received* over the same period: in 1994/5 net receipts from taxes and duties collected by the Inland Revenue (excluding National Insurance contributions) were £87.3 billion, in 2001/2 it was £167 billion and by 2003/4 the comparable figure was £159 billion. Much revenue received since 1997 has come from indirect taxes and duties (such as VAT, fuel duty and so on) and this may partly explain the higher levels of taxes and duties collected. The decline in investigation and compliance yield over the same period therefore indicates a substantial weakening of the Revenue's investigatory and compliance work in the New Labour years. This analysis was confirmed in critical comments made by the Public Accounts Committee (PAC) in 2003:

> The low number of fraud investigations and prosecutions is not commensurate with the potential sums at stake in lost revenue. Nor has the overall scale of work kept pace with the expansion of the Revenue's business. Investigation work on tax fraud seems to have reduced as work on tax credit fraud has increased... [Though] the financial returns on investigations suggest that it would be cost effective to do many more. (2003:6)

The issue of tax credits is indeed noteworthy. Firstly, the cost of administering tax credits is relatively high, when compared with the costs of collecting taxes. The costs of administering WFTC and DPTC were: 2.53 pence for every pound in 2001/2, increasing to 4.58 pence in 2002/3 (Inland Revenue, 2003). But, secondly, investigatory efforts and prosecutions in this new 'giving' area of Inland Revenue work is now beginning to outstrip that of prosecutions relating to their core business of 'taking' (collecting taxes). Interestingly these changes are set in the context of a government commitment to fiscal 'prudence' and the over-arching modernisation agenda, but they are far from consistent with these priorities. The costs of collecting government revenues were, overall, 1.41 pence per pound when New Labour came to power in 1997 and while this had been reduced to 1.16 in 2001/2, these advances have been slow and rather faltering. Moreover, as we have seen, the costs of administering tax credits are becoming worryingly high (see Chapter 4 for discussion of the information technology issues which have contributed to these costs) and a recent report indicates that the system is near collapse (Citizens Advice, 2005). This hardly signals the fulfilment of New Labour's promise of massive strides in public sector efficiency and modernisation. In addition, their failure to tackle tax fraud has led to missed opportunities to yield more than – or even come close to matching – the tax revenue from compliance achieved in the Thatcher/Major years. This does not represent either prudence or efficiency in gathering tax revenues.

Compliance and justice

One long standing justification for the sparing use of prosecution in tax fraud cases was the difficulty involved in proving guilt: the burden of proof in often complex tax fraud cases was heavy and additional difficulties in gathering evidence (usually held by the suspect) led to the Revenue often seeking 'private justice' and financial settlement instead (Uglow, 1984; Cook, 1989). Nonetheless, despite such difficulties, the Revenue's 'selective prosecution' policy is officially committed to taking proceedings forward in the following types of cases:

- The most 'heinous cases'
- 'Status prosecutions' where accountants and/or tax advisers have been involved (thereby harming trust)
- Cases where taxpayers have already enjoyed a negotiated (private) settlement and have re-offended
- Where taxpayers have failed to make a full disclosure during an investigation.

It therefore beggars belief that, given this formal policy commitment, a mere 48 Revenue prosecutions were mounted in 2003/4, with five cases being acquitted. Of just 43 successful prosecutions, 15 referred to internal frauds involving Revenue staff and accomplices and so this leaves a grand total of just 28 successful prosecutions for tax evasion in 2003/4.

It is telling that there has been no independent review of core issues of tax evasion and the hidden economy since Lord Keith of Kinkell's report[2] on the enforcement powers of the Inland Revenue in 1983. A review of the informal economy (Grabiner, 2000) and organised benefit fraud (Scampion Report, 2000) have been undertaken under New Labour, but 20 years on from Keith, a thorough review of Inland Revenue enforcement and compliance activities remains long overdue. Changes in the law have, however, taken place that should have led to an easing of the evidential and prosecutorial burdens in many tax evasion cases. For example, in 2001 the Revenue received £2 million funding to pay for extra staff to conduct investigations and apply the new criminal offence of 'being knowingly concerned in the fraudulent evasion of income tax'. This offence can be tried in Magistrates' Courts and should allow the Revenue to mount more prosecutions, particularly in relation to the informal or shadow economy (PAC, 2003). But the PAC noted, with some disappointment, that results so far were 'limited'.

It is rather surprising, then, that the Grabiner Report had concluded in 2000 that 'for tax evasion, the current system seems to work well'. Indeed, it does seem to work well – for the tax fraudster. However, the report did acknowledge that such a selective prosecution policy (and only prosecuting in cases where amounts evaded were large) did give rise to a risk of inconsistency with other departments. But this inconsistency

---

[2]The Report of the Committee on the Enforcement Powers of the Revenue Departments (CMND 8822, 1983).

does not only relate to the *numbers* if prosecutions mounted and the size of the *sums* defrauded, but also to *who* was involved in the fraud: for example, Grabiner astutely notes that a collusive employer operating in the informal economy would be regarded *very* seriously by Inland Revenue, but *not* so by the then Department of Social Security (DSS), even though the amount of illegal gain from tax evasion may be far greater than most social security frauds. The DWP, like its predecessor department (the DSS), is less interested in collusive employers than individual benefit claimants, whose removal from the benefit rolls contributes to meeting government anti-fraud targets. And it is to the issue of benefit fraud that we now turn.

The politics of benefit fraud

The preceding discussion of tax fraud has been underpinned by an analysis of data provided in a range of official documents, principally Inland Revenue Annual Reports and Public Accounts Committee reports. Where benefit fraud is concerned, there are long standing issues around the accuracy and accessibility of data on fraud and prosecutions. Before its abolition in 1980, the then Supplementary Benefits Commission produced annual reports which gave this kind of information. However, for the past 20 years, it has become increasingly difficult to access reliable and consistent information on benefit fraud and then to interpret it. This may be part and parcel of the politicisation of benefit fraud, which has gathered pace since the 1970s.

Moral panics over 'scroungers' or rogues are not new, building as they do on historical constructions of the undeserving poor: for example, mid-twentieth-century versions include the post-war 'spivs' who lived off the 'black market' (Deacon, 1980). But it was the 1970s and the successful rise of Thatcherism, channelling an anti-permissive backlash against the Labour governments of the 1960s and early 1970s, that signalled a step change and *scroungermania* was born. By 1997 *The Times* observed that there was 'a widespread belief in this country that many people receiving social security payments are scrounging off the state' (*The Times*, 8 December 1977).

The years immediately following the election of the first Thatcher government in 1979 saw major changes in the estimation, investigation and policing of benefit fraud. The official estimate of the extent of benefit fraud increased from £4 million to £200 million and staffing for investigation work increased accordingly (Spicker, 1998). Benefit fraud prosecutions had reached their peak in 1980/1 when 20,105 supplementary benefit claimants were prosecuted through the criminal courts. But the Rayner enquiry (held in the same year) advocated a more 'cost-effective' approach involving 'non-prosecution interviews', which would lead to benefit savings without the costs of mounting a formal prosecution. This approach was pursued vigorously by new Special Claims Control Units (SCCU), established to undertake unannounced 'blitzes' on target groups of claimants (notably the unemployed and single mothers) in target areas (of highest poverty and unemployment). Their techniques were oppressive and their goals were to persuade claimants to withdraw their claims. Clearly the so called 'super-snoopers' 'chased people off the books' (*The Times*, 4 August 1980) but their estimates of the benefits saved as a result of their efforts were viewed very sceptically by many. Benefit savings calculations then involved multiplying the weekly benefit paid out by a factor of up to 52, dubiously assuming: firstly, that the claim was fraudulent; and secondly that it would have continued for up to another year were it not for the investigation (Cook, 1989:127). An important consequence of these new policies was to *inflate* the estimates of benefits saved through SCCU activities, thereby inflating the scale of the problem of fraud, ratcheting up the political and public response still further.

The SCCU, blitz tactics and 'Dolebusters' of the 1980s were supplemented by 'Spotlight' Campaigns and the introduction of 'Shop a Cheat' hotlines in the 1990s.

When New Labour came to power the power of the scrounger discourse proved irresistible and the Conservative policies targeting benefit fraud were continued and intensified. Press, television and the Internet all now offer citizens the opportunity to give anonymous tip-offs about scroungers they know. Twenty-first-century campaigns including the 'Targeting Fraud' campaigns are glossy, professional and stir up images of benefit claimants as, among other things, attractive shopaholic hairdressers, whose penchant for fashion is funded by benefit fraud. A more recent campaign attempted to inject a more intimidating and threatening tone to anti-fraud drives, by using the voice of a celebrity villain:

> Hard hitting adverts, featuring former Bond villain Stephen Berkoff, leave listeners in not doubt that the DWP is cracking down on cheats. (DWP Press Release, 28 June 2004)

The anti-fraud Minister Chris Pond launched the campaign by saying:

> The adverts are hard hitting and so is our attitude to cheats who steal taxpayers money. That money should be spent on schools, hospitals and other public services. (ibid)

The cheats and scroungers are here presented as 'the enemy within' who are stealing cash meant for hospitals, schools and services. But the same tone and argument are not being deployed where tax evaders are concerned, although their activities are far more costly to law-abiding taxpayers and, many would argue, more prevalent. The only Inland Revenue advertising campaigns seek to humorously reassure us that 'tax does not have to be taxing' in an effort to encourage us to get our tax returns in on time. Tax evasion has never been the subject of publicity campaigns (Grabiner, 2000), which is in itself an indication of very unequal political responses to frauds that both 'steal' from the public purse.

Guesstimating and prosecuting benefit fraud

Both media-fuelled 'moral panic' and political hype have had an impact on the calculation and dissemination of estimates of benefit fraud over the past 25 years. As we have seen, estimates of benefit fraud rose from £4 million to £200 million when the Thatcher government took power in 1979. This was largely due to the use of multipliers to calculate **benefit savings** thereafter used as the basis for estimate of the extent of fraud (Cook, 1989). Although the New Labour government ceased to use multipliers, it nonetheless pedalled some dubious fraud estimates. For instance, its 1998 Green Paper on Social Security Fraud (entitled *Beating Fraud is Everybody's Business*) began with the widely-publicised estimate that 7% of claims were fraudulent. But, on closer inspection, this assertion concealed that the estimate of 7% was calculated by adding up three different elements:

- 2% of fraud which was estimated as having been 'established'
- A further 3%, based on 'strong suspicions'
- A 'lower suspicion' which was said to exist in a further 2% of cases.

In the case of the latter, 'low suspicion' may arise from a claimant's spending appearing to outstrip their means. Nonetheless, this type of suspicion will be included in fraud estimates 'on the balance of probabilities' and without any formal evidence of fraud taking place. These dubious methods of calculating the extent of benefit fraud, which conflate suspicion with proven cases, are themselves highly 'suspect'. (Sainsbury, 2001).

The DWP continues to pursue a policy which, like the Inland Revenue, seeks only selective prosecution. In addition it favours cautions, withdrawal of benefit, with possibilities for additional penalties and sanction. Yet, as Figure 2.3 on page 56 indicates, the DWP *still* prosecuted 9270 income support and jobseekers allowance claimants in 2002/3, a year in which *only* 43 people were successfully prosecuted in relation to tax offences. The data and the extensive 'notes'[3] accompanying it provided by the DWP (see Figure 2.4, page 57) demonstrate the complexities and the duplicities involved in compiling data on 'detected' benefit fraud. The limitations of the data evident in the DWP's own notes, summarised in Figure 2.4 and the inconsistencies with other data sources (indicated in the author's footnotes) should make any reader extremely cautious about the completeness, accuracy and comparability of the data year-on-year.

There are further issues that also shape 'guesstimates' of the scale of benefit fraud. Firstly, benefit prosecutions may be mounted by *different agencies*: the DWP, Local Authorities (LAs) (in relation to Council Tax or Housing Benefit fraud) or joint prosecutions by both. Significantly, the Anti-Fraud Minister, Chris Pond, when asked how many joint prosecutions had been undertaken by DWP with LAs responded that 'the information is not available' (Hansard, 23 February 2004, Col. 305W). All three types of investigation – DWP, LA and joint – may be conflated where media coverage of fraud is concerned, with a consequent amplification of the scale and threat of the perceived problem of benefit 'scrounging.'(e.g. DWP Press Releases, 15 and 28 June 2004).

Secondly, prosecutions are supplemented by alternative regulatory responses which 'count' where calculations of the scale of detected fraud are concerned. It has

---

[3]These notes were supplied by the DWP (2004) to accompany the more recent data.

Year	Successful prosecutions		Cautions and administrative penalties		
	DWP (formerly DSS)	Local authority	DWP	Local authority	TOTAL
1993/4	7645	–	–	–	
1994/5	9546	–	–	–	
1995/6	10,677	–	–	–	
1996/7	11,000[a]	–	–	–	
1997/8	11,380	700	–	–	12,080
1998/9	9970	800	–	–	10,770[b]
1999/2000	9130	860	11,030	390	21,410
2000/1	11,400	1100	15,560	550	28,610
2001/2	11,180[c]	1700	13,550	2600	29,030
2002/3	9270	2503	14,270	6001	32,044

[a]*A New Contract for Welfare: Safeguarding Social Security* CM4276 (1999) http://www.dwp. gov.uk/publications/dss/1999/fraud/pdfs/safegrd.pdf
[b]But the figure cited in Social Security Departmental Report (2001) Cm 5115 p. 47 is 14,000 prosecuted or sanctioned.
[c]HC 488 (2003) PAC Report cites 11,183 prosecutions, of which 98% were successful and 646 resulted in a custodial sentence and 175 in suspended custodial sentences.

Figure 2.3 Benefit Fraud Prosecutions, Cautions and Penalties for Those Claiming Supplementary Benefit/Income Support or Jobseekers Allowance 1993/4 – 2002/3

(*Sources*: DWP Personal Communication, 19 July 2004; Cook, 1997; DWP, 1999; DWP Departmental Report, 2001; PAC, 2003)

always been the norm to seek repayment of benefit overpaid to individuals after an admission of (or proof of) fraud. Additionally, the Social Security Administration (Fraud) Act (1997) introduced *cautions* (followed by withdrawal and repayment of benefits) and additional *administrative penalties*. Recent research reviewing the benefit fraud sanctions scheme (SPARK, 2004) found some inconsistency in the application of sanctions and drew attention to the impact of the scheme on claimants who had been overpaid benefit and were sanctioned despite asserting that they had no intention to defraud. This group, termed 'incogniscant fraudsters', admitted their guilt and gained a criminal record by accepting a caution, but 'found the sanction harsh because they did not agree that they had *intended* to defraud the system' (ibid:79, emphasis added).

1. An effective benefit case is defined as an investigation that results in an adjustment of the current rate of benefit, an overpayment or an underpayment or the person ceasing their claim to benefit. There is a significant reduction in effective cases from April 1999 following the introduction of a new measurement regime allowing only immediate interventions to be counted.

2. Administrative penalties, as an alternative to prosecution, were introduced by the Social Security Administration (Fraud) Act (1997) with effect from December 1998. Cautions were made available to local authorities as a sanction from the start of 2001/2.

3. Figures for financial years 1997/8 to 2000/1 are taken from local authority management information returns. It is possible that there could be some double counting with DWP data if there were cases which involved a joint prosecution.

4. Management information data for financial years 1997/8 to 2000/1 is not available for all local authorities. The total for Great Britain includes estimates for local authorities that have not responded. These estimates are based on historical and regional data. This type of estimate is standard practice in reporting totals where there have been non-respondents. The figures for financial years 1997/8 to 2000/1 have been rounded to two significant figures.

5. Information for 2001/2 is from a count of prosecutions and sanctions completed by all local authorities; this data is collected from local authority subsidy returns. Subsidy data may differ from management information data (shown for financial years 1997/8 to 2000/1) at local authority level; however, analysis shows a high level of consistency between the two data sources at national level.

6. The DWP figures are from the Fraud Information By Sector database, which shows completed cases commenced in the relevant period. Due to the elapsed time between commencement of an investigation and completion of a prosecution there are cases that are inserted into previously completed data for earlier periods. All DWP totals are therefore correct at the time when quoted but subject to adjustment at a later date.

7. In accordance with National Statistics Guidelines all DWP figures are rounded to the nearest 10. Due to rounding process totals may not agree.

Figure 2.4   DWP Notes Relating to Fraud Data
(*Source*: DWP, 2004)

The Social Security Fraud Act (2001), following on from the 1997 Act, strengthened departmental powers to uncover fraud by means such as information sharing with a range of government and other (notably credit rating) agencies. But its critics argue that the Act:

> Threatens too many innocent people's privacy; and giving the DSS more power to define for themselves the types of people who are 'more likely' to commit offences could well prove discriminatory in effect. (James Welch, legal director of Liberty, 19 December 2000)

In addition, and in line with US inspired policies on 'persistent offenders' in other crime domains, the DWP has, since April 2002, been able to *suspend benefits* for 13 weeks if an individual is convicted of committing benefit fraud twice in three years (the 'two strikes' penalty). Though rarely used so far, the fact that this penalty exists is of concern to poverty campaigners and civil libertarians alike, who would argue that: it denies any notion of 'rights' to benefits and a minimum income; such penalties will have unjust impacts on other members of the family, including children; and that they take no account of the reasons that propel some to commit fraud in the first place – poverty, and an inability to make ends meet on benefits. Ironically, Lord Grabiner (2000) argued that, in relation to 'smaller' tax offences in the hidden economy, 'a person's means to pay is key – where there are "no means" to pay, the tax is written off as irrecoverable'. A lack of means to pay does not similarly apply to benefit fraudsters and for them recovery, not write-off, is the norm.

Thirdly, it is crucial to recognise the discursive contexts within which benefit fraud data are constructed. Official estimates of benefit fraud are not only flawed in terms of the inclusion of 'suspicious' cases, as already discussed. But in addition, frequent reference is made – in policy documents, political speeches and press releases – to *fraud and error*. This conflates the illegal and the erroneous, and also conceals the fact that benefit losses may be due to errors by the department rather than the claimant. Nonetheless, government targets for anti-fraud work are couched in terms of percentage reductions in fraud and error, although errors may be nothing whatever to do with fraud. For example, with a baseline of 1997/8, the most recent report on *Fraud and Error in Income Support and Jobseekers Allowance from April 2002 – March 2003* confirms the Departmental target to:

> achieve a 10% reduction by March 2002, a 25% reduction by March 2004 and a 50% reduction by March 2006. (DWP, 2004a)

It states that the amount of benefit overpaid due to fraud and error on IS and JSA in 2002/3 as 6.3% of the total benefit paid. But the tables within the report indicate the following breakdown:

- Fraud – 3.6%
- Customer error – 1.1%
- Official error – 1.7%.
(ibid:5)

If the department does indeed meet its targets, this will partly be a product of reductions in its own errors and those of claimants, although the media tale will not report this detail: it will inevitably concentrate on the highlights and so will once again amplify the scale of fraud and accentuate the moral panic around it. The conflation of JSA, IS, Council Tax and Housing Benefit fraud (evident in Figure 2.3 on page 56) achieves a similar end.

The benefit fraud agenda

The ingredients of one recent press release from the DWP shows the ways in which all the statistical and discursive tricks discussed so far can come together to justify and to drive social and criminal justice policy against benefit fraud. In this example, benefit fraudsters are constituted as both cheats and thieves (from the honest tax-payer) and are juxtaposed with 'genuine' claimants and honest taxpayers who are encouraged to report anyone they 'suspect' of committing fraud. Here also prosecutions by the DWP and LA (for housing benefit fraud) are added together, as are prosecutions and lesser sanctions, thereby increasing the *number* reported and, with it, the perceived *scale* of benefit fraud itself:

> ... the public are fed up with cheats who steal money from the taxpayer that should go to people in genuine need of help...
> And the public have supported our campaign by contacting us if they suspect someone they know of committing fraud...
>
> [The] DWP, in partnership with local authorities, is carrying out more prosecutions and sanctions then ever before – in 2002/3 there were over 32,000 prosecutions and sanctions. (DWP Press Release, 15 June 2004)

A final word on the context of the recording, reporting and construction of the 'problem' of benefit fraud. With such a myopic political and public focus on benefits *overpaid*, one missing element is that of **benefits underpaid**. It has long been accepted that benefit fraud campaigns are counter-productive where benefit take-up is concerned: older people, in particular, are reluctant to be seen as 'scrounging' from the state by claiming the benefits to which they are legally entitled. As we saw in Chapter 1, one in five people who could claim one of the five main means-tested benefits (Income Support, Minimum Income Guarantee, Housing Benefit, Council Tax Benefit and Jobseekers Allowance) is not doing so and is suffering accordingly. Most worrying was the low take-up of MIG by pensioners, which ranged between only 63% and 72%. Campaigning groups have long been concerned about the overall and specific impact of low benefit take-up for claimant groups:

> ... the role of benefits in maximising income is fundamental to the relief of income poverty for families with children. (Child Poverty Action Group, Press Release, 4 March 2004)

The stigma attached to claiming benefits acts as a powerful deterrent to claiming, as one cancer charity indicates:

> More than half of people with cancer (83,000) who die each year (154,000) do not claim their entitled disability benefits. Lindsay Baker, 37... who was recently diagnosed said 'I found claiming benefits more stressful than having cancer itself.' (Macmillan Cancer Relief, 22 June 2004)

Any government genuinely committed to social justice would be addressing benefit underpayments in, at the very least, equal measure to fraud and overpayments of benefit. While some publicity campaigns have been mounted to encourage take-up (for example, of Pensioner Credits), low take-up of many means-tested benefits persists. At the same time, social justice would involve ensuring parity of responses to individual citizens who defraud the state whether by tax evasion or by benefit fraud, and this is very far from the case in contemporary Britain. To return to the question posed at the beginning of this section, it does indeed appear there is 'one law for the rich and another for the poor'. This disparity can be understood both in terms of the continuity of historical themes (notably the notion of the undeserving poor, and a traditional hatred of personal taxation), and shifts in policy, notably agency investigation and prosecution policies and broader political priorities designed to appeal to middle England (see Chapter 6). The next chapter will go on to set the theoretical and political context for developing an understanding of such disparities.

○ *three* ○ **Signs, Posts and the Third Way**

Introduction

Everything is 'post'. We have become used to post-industrialism now for some time, and we can still more or less make sense of it. With post-modernism things began to get blurred. The concept of post-enlightenment is so dark even a cat would hesitate to venture in. (Beck, 1992:9)

Ulrich Beck's classic work *Risk Society: towards a new modernity* addresses the concerns and transformations of societies which have been variously described as: post-Fordist, post-Enlightenment, post-welfare, late-twentieth century modernity and postmodern. The quotation above, taken from its preface, captures some of the difficulties faced by academics, students, politicians, practitioners and public alike in finding ways to name, to understand and to theorise the dramatic changes and upheavals that transformed (formerly) modern, industrial societies in the latter part of the twentieth century. As the title of this chapter suggests, the signs and the 'posts' facing those attempting to examine the relations between criminal and social justice in such societies are confusing and do not point in any clear direction. It is little wonder, then, that those seeking to reconcile these two key aspects of policy often get lost along the way. The aim of this chapter is to drop markers in order to help those trying to navigate through the theoretical and policy spaces in which contemporary 'justice' – criminal and social – is constituted. In so doing, it will also build upon the historical themes in criminal and social justice – both the constants and dissonants – which were discussed in the previous chapter.

---
1. Postmodern Confusion

As David Garland (2001) observes, the major changes which swept across modern societies in the latter half of the twentieth century were, at the same time, economic, social, cultural and political. Over the past 20 years academics have struggled to theorise the dynamic, diverse and complex sets of changes which have questioned 'modern' taken-for-granted assumptions about the nature of social, economic, cultural, gender, class and international relations. A full discussion of all of these changes is clearly beyond the scope of this book but, following Garland, they may be briefly summarised as consisting of:

- The unfolding **dynamic of capitalist production** and market exchange, and corresponding changes in technology, mass production, consumption, transport and communications
- The **restructuring of the family** and the household: smaller households with fewer children, women entering the workforce in greater numbers and alternative family formations
- Changes in the **social ecology of cities and suburbs**: with car ownership and mass transport leading to suburbanisation (of employment and residence) and parallel urban decline
- The **rise of the electronic mass media**, giving nation-wide information, displaying consumption patterns and 'lifestyles' previously beyond the reach of many social groups
- The **democratisation of social and cultural life**: following struggles for civil rights for a range of groups (black, gay, (dis)abled, mentally ill people and women), enhanced citizenship, political pluralism and challenge, and a shift from 'communities of fate' to individualism and 'communities of choice'.

One important consequence of these changes was a dissolving of the *grand narratives* which had previously sought to explain social political, economic and cultural life. The competing grand narratives of 'modernism' – Marxism, democratic socialism and neo-liberalism – all seemed incapable of adequately addressing the complexities of late modernity and the diversity of interpretations and responses to them. Concepts such as 'class' and 'the market' were rendered ineffectual by a postmodern stance which unpackaged grand narratives revealing the insecurities and 'unknowables' which accompany an increasingly 'reflexive' approach to apprehending and understanding a dynamic world. Broadly, what had been typified as *industrial society* structured through social class, gave way to a highly individualised *risk society* and, at the same time, concerns about the distribution of *goods* shifted to concerns about the distribution of the *bads* (Beck, 1992:3).

Where the 'bads' were concerned, challenges to science and to scientific/professional expertise grew as the technology and science of late modernity proved to be evermore fallible and risky. The 1980s saw two horrendous examples of this: in December 1984 a discharge of poisonous gas from the Union Carbide pesticide plant killed more than 6300 people in Bhopal, India; and in April 1986 the nuclear reactor disaster at Chernobyl, Ukraine, exposed 1.7 million people to radiation. The invisibility (and yet ubiquity) of the toxins released in both cases gave testimony to the truly 'global' nature of the risks unleashed by, and acutely felt in, late modernity. Proximity (physical or cultural) was no longer a defining issue where such risks were concerned – anyone, anywhere could be at risk. Moreover, as Beck persuasively argues, if people *say* they experience risks as real to them, then they *are* indeed real, and when their concerns are met with denial by 'the experts', then trust in those experts diminishes further. Lack of trust and the demystification of expertise and scientific knowledge are crucial to the reflexivity of postmodern society. In such societies the process of ***reflexive modernisation*** involves individuals making critical evaluations and decisions about a bewildering array of life choices – where to live, where is safe to work and travel to, what to eat, whether to immunise infants and so on – in order to minimise the perceived risks for themselves and their loved ones. However, risks are not experienced or perceived alike by all social groups: for example, 'there is more apprehension among working-class people about social change and about the greater choice with which they believe they are presented.' (Taylor-Gooby, 2001:205). The contradictory messages sent out in risk societies can, therefore, be perplexing and unequally experienced: the dangers of MMR vaccinations, CJD and hospital 'superbugs' have all been 'scares' of national concern, but we are reassured not to be *too* worried about them; the threat of weapons of mass destruction was imminent, but this was de-bunked (when none were found following the invasion of Iraq); and the very real scare for us all is the omnipresent fear of 'terrorists'. Terrorist attacks have taken place which have killed and maimed thousands (in Bali, Egypt, Iraq, London, New York and Turkey, for example). But it is nonetheless important to recognise the confusing (and sometimes reactionary) effects of the perpetual state of anxiety that characterises postmodern societies. This state of 'high anxiety' is captured, albeit with irony and humour, in the cartoon overleaf (Figure 3.1).

In the sphere of welfare policy, the perceived collapse of other grand narratives – not least social democracy and 'the welfare state' in Britain – has also led to a quest for new ways to cope with the challenges of postmodern societies. In the US and the UK the free market philosophies of the (1980s) new right administrations of Ronald Reagan and Margaret Thatcher were characterised by: antipathy to 'big government'; a consequent desire to 'roll back the frontiers of the state'; economic individualism; free market principles; and a belief in a strong (moral) civil society. The Keynesian demand-side economic approach and pursuit of policies geared to greater equality, which had dominated the so-called post-war 'welfare settlement', became fundamentally unsettled as the twentieth century drew to a close (Clarke, 2004b). The fall of old style communism in Europe and the former Soviet Union was signalled by the literal collapse of the wall dividing communist East Berlin from the democratic West of the city in 1989, and with it the face of international politics and global economic relations also changed: the old adversaries in the cold war of the 1950s (the states comprising the former Soviet Union, most notably Russia) were no longer enemies of the West. At the same time, the challenges posed by globalisation (of production, markets, consumption, culture and risk) also provoked a re-appraisal of social and economic policy as the 'tiger economies' of the far east presented a challenge to the former leading economies of the US and western Europe. It is within this dynamic, fluid and insecure context that US, UK and European attentions turned to seeking out a 'Third Way' – both at home and abroad.

Figure 3.1   Postmodern Confusion

(*Source*: Martin Rowson. Reproduced with permission of the *Guardian*)

2. 'Thinking in Thirds' and the Narrowness of the Third Way

The concept of third space is not new and not restricted to politics. For instance, in the field of modern geography:

> ... Thirdspace is a purposefully tentative and flexible term that attempts to capture what is actually a constantly shifting and changing milieu of ideas, events, appearances and meanings. (Soja, 1996, quoted in Haylett, 2001:43)

The words 'tentative' and 'flexible' are very telling when this concept is applied in the context of New Labour's much vaunted Third Way 'project'. As I will go on to explain, many regard the Third Way as more about antithesis than thesis, more about opposition than proposition, and more about pragmatism than politics. But let us start by examining how the Third Way is described and understood by its two leading proponents – Tony Blair and the man often referred to as his 'guru', Anthony Giddens.

According to Giddens:

> The overall aim of the third way in politics should be to help citizens pilot their way through the major revolutions of our time: globalization, transformations in personal life and our relationships to nature. (1998:64)

He goes on to outline what he sees as core Third Way values which will make this navigation possible:

1. Equality – defined here as 'inclusion'
2. Protection of the vulnerable
3. Freedom with autonomy
4. No rights without responsibilities
5. No authority without democracy
6. Cosmopolitan pluralism – as a means of regenerating solidarity in the face of globalization and rapid social change
7. Philosophic conservatism – a pragmatic approach to coping with change and sustaining continuity in family life.

(ibid:66)

These values, in turn, translate into a 'project' which situates itself between 'old' left and new right, while purporting to be a radical alternative to both. For example, in 1998 the then Secretary of State for Education, David Blunkett, stated that the *Third Way* was 'an alternative between old Labour welfarism and the rampant individualism of the Right' (quoted in Haylett, 2001:46). The alternative positioning of the Third Way is demonstrated in Figure 3.2 which summarises Giddens' views on the key dimensions of these three distinct political, economic and social philosophies. The Third Way is literally betwixt – in the space that separates – the old left and the new right. But when set against one another, it becomes apparent that the Third Way is clearer about what it *is against* than what it *is for* – more antithesis than thesis.

The Third Way thesis, such as it is, depends on language and concepts which are deliberately fluid and slippery so that they may cover the exigencies of a globalised, shifting and risky social and economic world. But in so doing, I would argue, what they offer can only be a potential coping strategy rather than a positive 'way forward' based upon a clear vision of political and ideological goals. In this respect the Third Way is more about the journey than the destination, more about the *means* of getting there than the *ends* to be achieved, more about power and governance than politics and values.

Tony Blair not only implicitly accepts this interpretation, but on taking power he positively celebrated it:

> We will be a radical government. But the definition of radicalism will not be that of doctrine, whether left or right, but of achievement. New Labour is a party of ideas and ideals but not of outdated ideology. What counts is what works. (Tony Blair, 1998, quoted in Powell, 1999)

'What works' will be the subject of the next chapter, but here it is important to recognise the centrality of *pragmatism* – and getting (re)elected – to New Labour and the Third Way project.

Area of political philosophy	The 'old left' classical social democracy	The Third Way 'project'	Thatcherism or neo-liberalism (the 'new right')
The state and society	Pervasive state involvement in social and economic life. State dominates over civil society. Collectivism.	The radical centre. The new democratic state (the state without enemies). Active civil society.	Minimal government. Autonomous civil society. Market fundamentalism.
Economic relations	Keynesian demand management, plus corporatism. Confined role for markets: the mixed or social economy. Full employment.	The democratic family. The new mixed economy.	Moral authoritarianism, plus strong economic individualism. Labour market clears like any other.
Social and welfare relations	Strong egalitarianism. Comprehensive welfare state 'from cradle to grave'.	Equality as inclusion. Positive welfare. The social investment state.	Acceptance of inequality. Welfare state as safety net.
Global relations	Linear modernisation. Low ecological consciousness. Internationalism. Belongs to bi-polar world.	The cosmopolitan nation. Cosmopolitan democracy.	Linear modernization. Low ecological consciousness. Traditional nationalism. Realist theory of international order. Belongs to bi-polar world.

Figure 3.2 The Third Way Project: Betwixt Left and Right
(*Source*: Adapted from Giddens, 1998)

Days after Tony Blair's first landslide election victory in 1997, an 'old Labour' elder statesman and former part Deputy Leader, Roy Hattersley, expressed doubts about the unashamed pragmatism of New Labour. He argued that sooner or later the British electorate would need 'an ideal to live by' but felt that Blair had 'built a government which is untainted by dogma. He is taking the politics out of politics.' The apparently fluid policy stance of the Third Way therefore posed fundamental questions because, as Hattersley perceptively noted, the problem with pragmatism is that 'nobody ever died for it' (*Guardian*, 14 May 1997).[1]

The Third Way presents itself as a modern, pragmatic approach to addressing challenges in ***delivering*** as well as re-shaping social and criminal justice policies. The rise

---

[1]Ironically, eight years on from this observation, there are tens of thousands who have died in pursing the Blair's government's policies (most notably in Iraq), but many critics – including this author – would argue that they have died *because of*, and not *for*, the politics of Blair's Third Way.

of New Labour coincided with an acknowledgement that there were a raft of new, complex, **wicked issues** (such as crime, drugs, environmental issues) that defied resolution under traditional government's 'silo' approach to departmental policy-making and delivery. According to Clarke and Stewart (1997) these 'wicked issues' needed:

- Holistic, not linear, partial thinking to address complex problems which could not be addressed by a single agency
- A capacity to work across and between organisational boundaries (multi-agency and partnership working)
- The positive engagement of the public in developing appropriate responses (challenging top-down government, and the dispersal of power)
- A willingness to think and work in different ways, and to pursue the radical
- A new style of governing for a learning society, challenging fragmentation and bureaucracy.

(Taken from: Ling, 2002:622)

The Third Way response to the complex challenges of such issues was couched in terms of: modernisation, democratisation and governance, all of which were symbolised in the notion of **joined-up government** (JUG). Ling argues that JUG cannot be understood merely as the 'administrative corollary of the politics of the Third Way.' (2002:639). As we will see in Chapter 4, making policies 'work' is far from an exact science and different departments (for instance the Treasury, Home Office and Cabinet Office) conceive the relative importance of managerial targets, organisational culture change and public participation in very different ways.

Alongside (and integral to) its emphasis on the need for holistic, multi-agency, democratised responses to key policy challenges, the politics of the Third Way engages with a range of agencies beyond the public state sector. But it is important to recognise that the beginnings of this shift – referred to by Clarke (2004a) as the **dissolution of the public realm** – were evident more than 20 years ago with new right policies of privatisation and the contracting out of formerly public sector services, most notably in the sphere of health. The dissolution continued through the 1980s and 1990s as public responsibilities for the care of elderly, disabled and mentally ill people were transformed into 'community care' strategies and, in the field of education, responsibilisation strategies shifted the emphasis from the state to parents (Clarke, 2004a). The Third Way has continued and accelerated this trend with the development of its private finance initiatives (PFI) and public–private partnerships (PPPs). But many former state functions have not only been commercialised but also voluntarised: in the field of criminal justice, in particular, key functions around the support and care of victims of crime, and the 'treatment' of offenders are frequently conducted not by the state's criminal justice agencies, but by volunteers (Cook and Vallely, 2003; Cook and Lyle, 2004). While, in theory, New Labour is committed to less 'big government' (on the part of the state), it has nonetheless presided over the development of different and more complex forms of **governance** which are more penetrating than ever before and so there is 'less government, but more governance' (Clarke, 2004a:480).

In summary, the flexibility of Third Way politics means that it may appear all things to all people and, as such, may at first sight seem to present a very broad path. But the range of policy options it countenances is relatively narrow and limited in three key respects. Firstly, it is invariably *relative* to those philosophies and policies which it is cast in opposition to – the old left and new right. In this sense, the Third Way is a rhetorical device for the positioning of pragmatic policy responses rather than a genuinely value-led political philosophy. This view is supported by frequent references to the Third Way or New Labour as a *project*: a project is, by definition, a scheme, a plan or 'contrivance', but it is not a political philosophy. This characteristic clearly limits the Third Way's potential as a purposeful, radical driver for change. Secondly, those policies which were seen to be potential electoral liabilities for an emergent New Labour government (including raising higher rate taxes) were 'ruled out' well before the 1997 election, narrowing the Third Way still further (Lister, 2001). Thirdly, it is premised on the twin concepts of *modernisation and globalisation* which are seen as 'inescapable forces' that proffer just one (restricted) model of social development:

> The singular and unified status politically granted to that model is its most powerful ally, allowing no alternatives to be brokered, quashing other social and economic imaginaries and ways of living with its material and symbolic weight. (Haylett, 2001:52)

But for some critics the third way is materially and symbolically a far 'lighter' phenomenon, as Calum Paton observed in 1999:

> The 'Third Way' is mostly rhetoric. Almost all New Labour policies are announced as a 'third way'; but you must look at the particular context to see which two alternatives the alleged 'third way' is coming between. On the economy generally, it appears to be between *laissez-faire* capitalism and redistributive welfare capitalism, with the 'Third Way' being a limited supply-side tinkering. On welfare reform, it is between collectivism in financing and universalism in provision on the one hand, and pure individualism on the other. (1999:74)

For those concurring with his view, the Third Way may be interpreted as signalling the 'end of ideology' and the end of political dogma, which Blair may well see as cause for celebration. Such a perspective would render redundant the concern of many critics that New Labour lacks a 'big idea' – the lack of a big idea would not in itself pose any problem. Fundamentally, then, it could be argued that New Labour's big idea is that, now, *there is no* big idea.

---

3. New Labour, 'Social Justice' and Inequality

To be able to assess the extent to which the Third Way politics of New Labour are capable of reconciling criminal and social justice in contemporary Britain, we first need to examine how social justice has been constituted in Third Way discourse, and how it has (or has not) been subsequently realised in New Labour social and economic policies. According to Blair, New Labour was and is:

> … a left of centre party, pursuing economic prosperity and social justice as partners and not as opposites. (Quoted in the *Guardian*, 11 September 2001)

And, as Alan Deacon goes on to argue,

> According to Blair, the third way does not just split the difference between the old left and the right. Indeed, the defining feature of third way politics is that it 'reconciles' themes which in the past have been wrongly regarded as antagonistic. It does not see a contradiction between the creation of wealth and the pursuit of social justice. It seeks both to promote enterprise and to attack poverty and discrimination. (2002:104)

In short, it is argued that we *can* have it all ways via the Third Way, providing that compromise is sought and deals are struck to 'reconcile' what was previously seen as irreconcilable by both the old left and the new right.

But precisely what do advocates of the Third Way mean by 'social justice'? Firstly, social justice for them is located in the context of a vision of equality that is rooted in *equality of opportunity*. The Chancellor, Gordon Brown, has articulated this in terms of Christian Socialism and focuses on education as the key mechanism for its transmission: for Brown, equality of opportunity is not only valued on ethical grounds, but the education and skills which drive it are good for the economy too (Deacon, 2002:112). This conception of equality *as* opportunity links with a dominant feature of the Third Way's 'social investment state… the investment in the child as citizen-worker-of-the-future' (Williams, 2004:408). But even its investment in children is limited: while Tony Blair proclaims in the forword to the government Green Paper on reforming statutory services for children (*Every Child Matters*), that 'our children are everything to us: our hopes, our ambitions, our future', no commitment is made to increase expenditure in order to meet their needs (Williams, 2004). Moreover, equality of opportunity, as measured by levels of social mobility from one generation to the next, is moving in a negative direction under New Labour: recent research for the Sutton Trust on international patterns of social mobility reveals that educational opportunities are still primarily shaped by class and family. As a result:

> intergenerational mobility has declined in Britain at a time of increasing income inequality. The strength of the relationship between educational attainment and family income, especially for access to higher education, lies at the heart of Britian's low mobility culture. (Blanden, 2005:3)

Secondly, the Third Way defines *equality as inclusion* and *inequality as exclusion* (Giddens, 1998:102). This represents a 'paradigm shift from concerns of equality to inclusion and opportunity, with which comes responsibility' (Lister, 2001:431), and a policy focus which effectively displaces concerns about social and economic inequality, which remain 'off' the agenda.

Thirdly, the term 'social justice' is itself liable to many interpretations in Third Way politics, but these are not related back to structural or systemic inequalities in income and wealth in wider society. It is significant that social justice is effectively de-coupled from issues of income inequality in Third Way discourse, as the following extract from a lecture by the then Home Secretary David Blunkett shows:

> The distribution of assets, rather than simple income, is increasingly important to how we understand equality in life chances. Other assets such as educational attainment are also crucial… I believe we also need a benchmark equality of opportunity by reference to the experience of crime and anti-social behaviour, which is a major determinant of social outcomes and quality of life. (2003:21)

This statement raises two further themes in Third Way discourse: one is the conflation of the criminal and the social (which we will return to below), the second is the *lexicon of finance* – social capital, the investment state, individual and community assets – which permeates New Labour political discourse on what is constituted as 'social justice'. Paradoxically, the words 'income' and 'wealth' and 'inequality' are conspicuous by their absence. In this way, the Third Way financial lexis through which notions of social justice are constructed and articulated is almost wholly devoid of the grubby idea of real 'money'.[2] As mentioned in Chapter 2, the 'p' word – poverty – was largely absent from New Labour's first term in office, only being deployed in the context of New Labour's 1999 commitment to ending *child poverty* within a generation. In its second term, Gordon Brown pledged in 2002 to end pensioner poverty, although no specific targets or deadlines were set. Adult poverty is not a pressing issue for the New Labour project, although adult *responsibility* (to support themselves and their families), *inclusion* (in the civil society) and *engagement* (in a renewed, community and partnership-based democracy) all are.

Back in 1994, while Shadow Chancellor, Gordon Brown articulated his vision of social justice in terms of building:

> a fair society in which all people, regardless of class, race or gender have available to them the widest choice of options and opportunities to enhance their earning power and fulfil their true potential. (Brown, quoted in Prideaux, 2001:89)

---

[2]But one classic policy initiative which has involved money – in the context of addressing child poverty through 'asset based' welfare – is the Children's Trust Fund. This will provide all children born after September 2002 with a £250 initial bond, topped up to £500 for those children in families receiving maximum Child Tax Credit. It also allows for further investment of sums up to £1200 per year on behalf of the child. The Fund is accessible at the age of 18, by which time better off children whose parents and families are able to make further annual investments will benefit most. At the same time, government has failed to review the cash limited Social Fund, which help the most vulnerable families meet essential one-off and lump sum costs (Child Poverty Action Group, Newsletter Issue 30: December 2003).

On gaining office in 1997 he therefore developed policies that aimed to provide *'pathways' of opportunity* from welfare-to-work and out of unemployment, poverty and crime too. The difficulty was that these policies involved using resources to provide 'opportunities' (notably through New Deal programmes) and did not involve spending more resources on individuals themselves. As already discussed, paid work became synonymous with inclusion, and the Third Way defines equality and social justice in terms of inclusion. Social justice is, therefore, seen as a product of engagement with paid work and maximising the opportunities for advancement which it offers. This limited conception of the constituents of social justice serves to displace alternative concerns about: the adequacy or incomes (both earned and in terms of welfare benefits), redistributive taxation and the vast inequalities in the distribution of income and wealth which have thus far characterised the first eight New Labour years.

Blairite policies envisage no contradictions between promoting the goals of enterprise and pursuing social justice, but the evidence presented in Chapter 1 suggested that an adequate balance has not been struck between these two policy aims. There is evidence that dramatic increases in 'executive pay' have played a part in widening inequality, even though the relationship between that pay and individual success or 'enterprise' remains unproven. By 2000 the richest 1% of the population (around half a million people) received 8% of total income while the share of the poorest 10% declined through the 1990s and by 2002/3 stood at just 2.8% of total income. Put simply, the rich have got richer and the poor have got poorer still under New Labour (Goodman and Oldfield, 2004). The Third Way discourse of 'equality as inclusion' forestalls any discussion of resource redistribution and, at the same time, it is coupled with an emphasis on *rights and responsibilities* which may also include concerns around social justice. The relationship between rights and responsibilities is grounded in communitarian thinking which seeks to balance universal rights and the common good, and self with community. This is best achieved through norms and values which are shared and internalised:

> For a social order to be able to rely heavily upon normative means requires that most members of the society, most of the time, share a commitment to a core set of values, and that most members, most of the time, will abide by the behavioural implications of these values because they believe in them, rather than being forced to comply with them.' (Etzioni, 1997, quoted in Deacon, 2002:70)

Within communitarian discourse, work is still seen both as a means of personal fulfilment and as the key 'passport back into the accepted norms of society' (Prideaux, 2001:97). The communitarian understanding of social justice is thus constituted in terms of *reciprocity*, with rights conferred conditional on obligations owed. More broadly still, communitarian thinking also engages with a further theme within Third Way discourse – that of *community and partnership* (Taylor-Gooby, 2001). It is through community-based partnerships that *both* democratic self-government *and* crime reduction policies are to be realised (see Chapter 5 for a fuller discussion of partnership working). The notion of 'community' as used by New Labour does not merely involve the bemoaning of the passing of a 'golden age' of community. Rather, it is seen as a means of restoring order and disciplined personal behaviour and is thus a crucial element of Third Way politics.

Discipline is also a key theme where welfare policy is concerned. The Third Way focuses on what it terms *positive welfare*, which is seen to involve 'attacking problems of poverty, isolation and lack of self-fulfilment wherever they arise' (Giddens, 2000:166). But the ways in which these problems are to be 'attacked' is at the level of the individual – her or his responsibilities, behaviours and motivations – and so invariably fails to address systemic or structural issues. Consequently, poverty per se is not the problem, but:

> It is poverty of ambition and poverty of expectation that is debilitating – if you are going to crack that you have to confront it and do some things which people think are tough. (Alistair Darling, Secretary of Sate for Social Security, in the *Guardian*, 11 February 1999)

Positive welfare may therefore involve the equivalent of 'tough love', coupled with regulation and compulsion. The view that 'rights entail responsibilities' and the other Third Way catchphrase 'work for those who can, security for those who cannot' evidences this approach, as does the following statement by Chancellor Gordon Brown:

> Full employment is not just about the right to work, but where there are jobs, the responsibility and the requirement to work. (Brown, 2000:16, emphasis added)

This vision of welfare subjects here is far from 'positive' as it is assumed they are in need of policing, management and control to ensure they fulfil their responsibilities in terms of paid work. This is to be accomplished by a thoroughly modern welfare state:

> I believe you cannot have a modern Britain without a modern welfare state – empowering, clear on priorities, realistic about human nature, tough on fraud, using the best modern technology in delivering services. (Darling, quoted in Haylett, 2001:50)

The prioritising of the benefit fraud issue has already been discussed and more will be said about issues of 'modern technology' (below) and empowerment (Chapter 5). But the comments of both Brown and Darling indicate that the modernisation agenda has taken a cultural turn where welfare is concerned, by deploying the notion of the 'undeserving poor' where those who *can* work fail to do so. (It is no accident of policy, therefore, that those who are of working age and have no children are poorer under New Labour than before they came to power – see Figure 1.6 (on page 27). The welfare recipient – unless a child or a pensioner – is thus cast as 'other', in need of management, regulation and inclusion, for their own and society's good.

There are are, however, alternative perspectives which challenge Third Way welfare politics and offer an alternative vision of how welfare may be re-ordered to address the challenges of modernity. For example, Fiona Williams (2000: 675–84) proposed what she has termed seven 'good enough' principles for the re-ordering of social welfare relations:

1. **Interdependence**: in a rejection of the centrality of paid work and the dependency/ independence dichotomy, this principle acknowledges the range of emotional, material, reciprocal networks which make autonomy possible, through collective effort.
2. **Care**: the ethic of care 'presumes relationships which are bounded by mutual interdependence'.
3. **Intimacy**: intimate relationships are more about commitment and trust than duty and tradition. This principle also focuses on democratised gender and parent-child relations.
4. **Bodily integrity**: welfare interventions have traditionally been based on healthy/ productive, unhealthy/unproductive dichotomies. This principle sees the body as a site of control and resistance (e.g. for reproductive rights, challenging certain medical treatments, campaigning against sexual abuse), arguing that 'respect for the integrity of the body is fundamental to the integrity of the welfare citizen'.
5. **Identity**: recognition is central to gaining a sense of self and belonging. This principle suggests that New Labour's focus on 'family, community and nation' as the bases for solidarity is simplistic and insufficient, given the complexities and diversities which cut across the monoliths of family, community and nation.
6. **Transnational welfare**: nationality as the basis of welfare is increasingly being challenged by shifting national boundaries and increasing numbers of people crossing those boundaries (e.g. migrants, refugees, asylum seekers). This principle argues for a move towards 'post-national citizenship'.
7. **Voice**: this principle runs through all of the above and stresses the value of 'lay' in addition to 'expert' knowledge. Based on radical, pluralist notions of democracy, this poses an alternative version of 'active citizenship'. It would also recognise the need for greater equality and entail struggles for redistribution of resources.

These values suggest an alternative 'active welfare subject' who differs radically from those constituted within and through Third Way welfare politics. For Williams, this subject is neither an exerciser of choice in the welfare market nor simply pursuing family and community responsibilities through engaging in paid work. S/he is not driven by incentives, duty and responsibility alone. Rather, these welfare subjects are pursuing 'the recognition of moral worth... [through] new social movements and user groups' (Williams, 2000), and are sustained through interdependence, mutual recognition and security and tolerance (ibid). The Third Way ethic of paid work is balanced here by the ethics of interdependence and care in global as well as mutual, family and community contexts.

The core values behind these principles are also evident in Ruth Lister's work which offered a 'compass to guide New Labour towards a more progressive second term' (Lister, 2001). However, the extent to which the compass she provided has been utilised as a guide along the (Third) way is highly debateable. Yet without commitment and adherence to such principles it is difficult to see how genuine progress towards social justice can be made in contemporary Britain or, indeed, globally.

4. The Third Way, Crime and Justice

Having suggested that social justice remains an ill-defined and illusory goal in New Labour's Third Way politics, this section will address issues of *criminal justice*. Firstly, however, it is necessary to build upon the issues raised in Chapter 2 by locating Third Way criminal justice policies in their appropriate historical, social, economic and cultural contexts. This involves revisiting the politics of Thatcherism.

As already suggested, the rise of Thatcherism in Britain in the 1970s marked a significant break with the past, in terms of both economic and social policies. In sharp contrast with the previous decade, Britain in the mid-1970s was beset by a deepening economic and industrial relations crisis coupled with a conservative 'backlash' against what had come to be seen as the 'permissive' cultural climate of the 1960s. A vital component of this backlash was a powerful appeal to *Law and Order* which served to bridge both sets of concerns – the economic and the social.

This fusion – of economic and social concerns – in law and order discourse was particularly evident in relation to crime and 'trades union power', which were frequently referred to within the same breath: for example, in 1979 Margaret Thatcher spoke of the 'vandals on the picket lines and muggers on the streets' (Hale, 1989). In this way appeals to 'Law and Order' became unifying and populist themes which encapsulated a range of social anxieties of the day:

> The Tory Party was able to present a coherent framework in which to tackle problems in both the economy and social life. The debate as they defined it had recurring themes: welfare scroungers, stand on your own two feet, the need to break the dependency culture, trades unions operating outside the law, moral decline, personal discipline and personal responsibility. (Hale, 1989:344)

Law and order proved to be the decisive factor in the Conservative election victory in 1979 which brought Margaret Thatcher to power. In relation to this dominant agenda, 'the mugger on the street' had become a particularly powerful symbol of Britain's economic and social decline in the mid-1970s, although the term 'mugging' itself, and the moral panic it generated, had been imported from the US (Hall et al., 1978). Public fears about mugging in the UK were, therefore, largely shaped by the US experience and were distinctly racialised. The *racialisation* of the law and order discourse (indicated in Chapter 2) continued in to the 1980s as Britain witnessed a shift in concern from 'crime' as such to a wider concern over social disorder following the 'riots' (or 'disturbances' or 'uprisings', depending on your perspective) in British cities during 1980/1 and 1985. Despite evidence to the contrary, the events in Brixton (London), Handsworth (Birmingham), Toxteth (Liverpool) and Mosside (Manchester) were defined as 'race riots' and so the threat posed to social order was once again seen as a racialised one (Solomos, 1993:129).

The policy responses to the law and order 'crisis' of the 1970s and 1980s were essentially punitive: criminal justice and penal policies were primarily concerned with the apprehension and punishment of offenders, rather than with their rehabilitation or the prevention of their offending. What crime prevention there was during the 1980s was *situational* rather than *social* – it involved locks, bolts and 'target hardening' rather than seeking to address the social conditions which were regarded by many as the source of crime (as will be discussed further in Chapter 4). The emphasis, then, was on crime as the product of individual 'wickedness' and there was little political truck with social explanations. For instance, the then Conservative Home Secretary, Douglas Hurd's, response to the 1985 disturbances in Handsworth was that the events marked 'not a cry for help, but a cry for loot'. Inflammatory tabloid headlines including 'Hate of the Black Bomber' (*Sun*), 'Bloodlust' (*Daily Mail*) and 'War on the Streets' (*Mirror*) focused on the allegedly linked issues of race and criminality. The tabloid press ignored, however, the social problems of racism and the apparent breakdown of community policing in Handsworth which many felt to be at the heart of the problem.

Looking back at the list of social and economic problems, identified by Hale above, which the Conservatives highlighted in 1979, we could, 25 years on, beg the question 'What has changed?' With the notable exception of the 'problem' of powerful trades unions, which (after repressive legislation in the 1980s and decimation of Britain's industrial base over the past 25 years) is no longer an issue, the remaining concerns around welfare dependency, personal and moral responsibility are all echoed in the New Labour agenda of Tony Blair. His 'moral crusade', which marched on into the twenty-first century, has now been accompanied by a rejection of the 1960s 'liberal consensus on law and order' (*Guardian*, 19 July, 2004), which was as powerful a denunciation of the era as that mounted by Margaret Thatcher a quarter of a century ago.

The law and order agenda has remained a vital electioneering platform since 1979, when Margaret Thatcher fused her key economic and social policies in one key phrase:

> What the country needs is less tax and more law and order. (Margaret Thatcher, 1979, quoted in Charman and Savage, 1999:193)

Following on from the ousting of Thatcher in 1991, the new Shadow Home Secretary, Tony Blair, was determined to challenge the Conservative party as the 'natural' party of law and order. His famous soundbite of 1993 that a Labour government would be 'tough on crime, tough on the causes of crime' enabled the Third Way to distance itself from the old left who had traditionally been seen to be 'soft' where issues of law and order were concerned. It also captured the hostile public mood following the murder of Liverpool toddler, Jamie Bulger, by two other children in February 1993.

'A hard core of persistent young offenders commit a disproportionate number of crimes. They offend again and again, laughing at the law and making their neighbours' lives a misery.'
(Conservative Party general Election Manifesto, 2001)

'[We will] take further action to focus on the 100,000 most persistent offenders. They are responsible for half of all crime. They are the core of the crime problem in this country.'
(Tony Blair, Prime Minister, 2001)

'Conservatives will stand up for the silent, law-abiding majority who play by the rules and pay their dues. The clear distinction between right and wrong has been lost in sociological mumbo-jumbo and politically correct nonsense.'
(Michael Howard, Conservative Party Leader, 2004).

'[People] want a society of responsibility. They want a community where the decent law-abiding majority are in charge; where those that play by the rules do well and those that don't get punished.'
(Tony Blair, Prime Minister, 2004).

Figure 3.3 Tough Crime Talk 2001–2004

Since that time both major parties have vied to 'out-tough' one another, thereby ratcheting the penal stakes still higher and so the following themes have remained at the core of both New Labour and Conservative criminal justice policy:

- The difference between right and wrong
- Standing up for the law-abiding citizen (and victims)
- Standing against the anti-social
- No-nonsense sentencing and punishment
- Prison works (and its use fully justified)
- Common sense (not liberal political correctness).

Taking the Third Way has led to a growing convergence in political discourses in recent years, and this is particularly evident in relation to 'tough' talking about crime as the quotations in Figure 3.3 show.

The consequences of tough talk such as this were clearly acknowledged by Blair:

> But as fast as we act, as tough as it seems compared to the 1970s or 1980s, for the public it is not fast or tough enough. (Tony Blair, 2004)

Blair is quite correct: New Labour's bid to develop its Third Way politics and in so doing to distance itself from its predecessors (by being seen to be tough on crime, law and order), is bound to fall short: the hyper-politicisation of the crime issue, and an often hysterical media, fuels a spiral of anxiety, fear and anger wherein the public will never believe that anything is ever tough enough. This does, however, have serious consequences for the direction of future policy, as Michael Tonry observes:

> People who are constantly reminded that they should be fearful and protect themselves from criminals become fearful; and that may make them more likely

to be more mistrustful and more receptive to populist anti-crime appeals. And having, through assiduous crime-prevention programmes created a more fearful populace, England is now busily expanding its criminal justice system to address those fears. (Tonry, 2004:6)

In government, New Labour policy responses to their tough promise has indeed involved expansion of the criminal justice systems (in particular imprisonment – see Chapter 5). Broadly, its approach has been twofold: firstly, a populist penal strategy which is indistinguishable from that which it inherited from Conservative Home Secretary Michael Howard. Secondly, a community safety strategy, implemented at a local level, which adopts a twin track approach – reducing the problems of crime and disorder, while addressing the perceived causes of crime within those localities. The community safety approach (to be discussed in detail in Chapter 5) also seeks to tackle the problem of the insecurity and anxiety which crime engenders. Much anxiety is spatially experienced: individuals are fearful of places and neighbourhoods, and it is to this level of concern that community safety strategies are also addressed. There is therefore a vicious circle (or spiral of decline) whereby crime and environmental decay are seen to be mutually reinforcing, as the one is cited as evidence of (and explanation for) the other, very often in the context of 'sink' housing estates (as described in Chapter 2). But, at the same time, crime and environmental decay are both seen to be associated with deeply rooted social and cultural changes – epitomised by the notion of the 'loss of community':

> With the collapse of local communities there is less stigma attached to criminality, the informal sanctions and expressions of disapproval which offenders fear are no longer there; and they have little reason to empathize with their victims. There are fewer inbuilt deterrents and greater incentives to criminal behaviour. (Hutton, 1995, quoted in Worrall, 1997:49)

However, for political commentator Will Hutton, community breakdown and crime are not the products of individual inadequacies, but are the logical consequences of the economic and social policies of the last 20 years. These policies have resulted in what he sees as an obsession with short-term profits; lack of investment; unemployment; insecurity; and impoverishment and social exclusion, particularly of the young. This view echoes earlier analyses in the US which similarly argued that urban communities blighted by such *capital disinvestment* became associated with a *recapitalisation* around illegal activities – notably drugs and crime. Although, particularly for the young, crime may bring short-term gains, the long-term consequences are significantly diminished life chances, and a spiral of decline prolonged into adulthood (Hagan, 1994:93).

While the Third Way focuses on community as *social* – a source of solidarity, reciprocity, empowerment and social capital – it has yet to demonstrate that it grasps the macro and micro-*economic* conditions and the political 'givens' that curtail the capacity of individuals within those communities to respond in such positive, civic ways (this theme will be explored further in Chapters 5 and 6). It is necessary, then, to engage with theory at a range of levels in order to grasp the constraints, complexities and local struggles within communities which shape the ways in which issues of crime and disorder are interrelated and responded to in local social/economic/cultural environments. In other words, this engagement involves not only analysing formal crime reduction and community safety policies, but also involves developing 'a *local politics of crime control*' which is informed by local sensibilities about place (Stenson and Crawford, 2001). This process would also entail a critical appreciation of the ways in which New Labour criminal justice and social policies have served to blur the boundaries between the criminal and the social: this blurring is particularly evident, at the local level, at the interface between community safety and social inclusion strategies.

5. Criminalising the Social

> Community safety is perhaps best seen as an aspect of 'quality of life' in which people individually and collectively, are protected as far as possible from the hazards or threats that result from the criminal or anti-social behaviour of others, and are equipped or helped to cope with those they do experience. It should enable them to pursue, and obtain fullest benefits from, their social and economic lives without fear or hindrance from crime and disorder. (Ekblom, 1998:8)

This extract, from a Home Office publication, exemplifies the overlapping nature of the criminal and the social within community safety discourse. Here crime and disorder are conceived as essentially 'quality of life' problems and, on the face of it, this seemed to mark a shift towards a 'socialising' of the problem of crime. In a briefing tellingly titled *Reducing Crime and Tackling its Causes*, the then Home Secretary, Jack Straw, announced the £250 million *Crime Reduction Programme* (CRP), which was ambitiously geared to securing a reversal in the long-term rise in crime and achieving a corresponding reduction in the fear of crime. The stated goals of the CRP are explicitly linked with broader *social aims* to 'add value to every aspect of life, enhance liberty and revitalise our communities' (Home Office, 1999:2). These goals also tie in with the remit of the government's overarching Social Exclusion Unit (SEU), set up in 1997, to:

> develop integrated and sustainable approaches to the problems of the worst housing estates, including crime, drugs, unemployment, community breakdown and bad schools etc. (SEU, 1998)

The first SEU Report *Bringing Britain Together – a National Framework for Neighbourhood Renewal* outlined the goals and plans of the 18 separate (but 'joined-up') Policy Action Teams operating within the SEU framework with the fourfold goals of achieving:

- Lower long-term unemployment and worklessness
- Less crime

- Better health
- Better qualifications.

The SEU sought to succeed, where other policy initiatives since the 1960s had failed, 'in setting in motion a virtuous circle of regeneration, with improvements in jobs, crime, education, health and housing all reinforcing each other' (SEU, 1998:9). Clearly, then, the problem of crime under New Labour was part and parcel of the broader problem of *social exclusion*. Consequently, the policy goals of both crime reduction and community regeneration strategies were seen as inextricably linked, as 'the fight against crime is at the centre of this Government's commitment to make Britain a better place to live' (Home Office, 1999:2). Crime, 'disorder' and social exclusion are all fused within such discourses. Not only are the criminal justice and social *policies* intertwined, but so are the *objects* of those policies: the lexicon of criminal justice, crime reduction and community safety policies have effectively been extended to encompass a range of (non-criminal) activities under the umbrellas of *disorder* and '*anti-social behaviour*'. However, these terms are (perhaps deliberately) imprecise and may be used to cover a multitude of sins.

There is no single definition of anti-social behaviour, although section 19(1) of the Crime and Disorder Act (1998) defines it as: 'that which causes or is likely to cause alarm or distress to one or more persons not of the same household'. The SEU nevertheless acknowledged potential ambiguities and difficulties in operationalising the term in its observation that:

> Anti-social behaviour covers a wide range of behaviour, from the clearly criminal to that causing lifestyle clashes. Activities that are criminal are defined by law. Defining other behaviour as anti-social is more difficult. Behaviour regarded as acceptable by some can be completely unacceptable to others. Acceptable behaviour to a young person can be difficult for an elderly person to tolerate. (SEU, 2000:para 1.1)

The recognition that 'lifestyle clashes' may lead to behaviour being interpreted and labelled as 'anti-social' is very significant, as is the acknowledgement that age and tolerance thresholds play a part in how behaviours are interpreted. But these issues are swept aside in political discourses and policy-making which is geared to appeal to those demanding 'toughness' on crime and disorder. For example, locating his 'stand against' anti-social behaviour within the Third Way politics of responsibility, duty and active citizenship, the Home Secretary, in his Ministerial foreword to the White Paper *Respect and Responsibility – Taking a Stand Against Anti-Social Behaviour*, framed new legislation in the following way:

> Our aim is a 'something for something society' where we treat one another with respect and where we all share responsibility for taking a stand against what is unacceptable... We must be much tougher about forcing people to not behave anti-socially. When people break the rules, there must be consequences for them: consequences that are swift, proportionate and that change the pattern of their

behaviour. And where those who are responsible for tackling anti-social behaviour fail to do so, we must intervene. (David Blunkett in Home Office, 2003b)

This suggests that part of the community citizenship deal involves 'taking a stand against' what is unacceptable, although there is no clear idea of *who* defines acceptability and in line with *whose* political and cultural norms it is defined. This is not only insufficient but also very worrying, not least because the full force of the law (civil and criminal) may be brought to bear on those who engage in behaviours which are, in their very essence, both contentious and contested. There is a good deal of slippage from what is seen by some to constitute the **unacceptable** to the **anti-social** to the **criminal** and yet all are fused together in a disciplinary continuum which reflects the hyper-politicisation of law and order (McLaughlin, 2002). The issue of anti-social behaviour and policy responses to it will be discussed in more depth in Chapter 6. But, for the time being, it stands as a worrying example of the 'criminalising of the social' within Third Way criminal justice discourse.

At a broader level, criminal justice discourses under New Labour also reflect the power and significance of the multi-layered relationship between the media and policy-makers, which generates a state of 'permanent campaign' (24 hours a day, seven days a week), in which governments are pushed to evidence, again and again, their ever-tougher approach to crime (Garland, 2001; McLaughlin, 2002; Tonry, 2004). If they are seen to fail, as they invariably must, their response is often denial. As already noted, professional and expert denial may contribute to growing mistrust of those experts and a disengagement from them. It is to the problematic issue of trust in Third Way politics that we now turn.

6. The Vexed Issue of Trust

Now, at the beginning of the twenty-first century, it is commonplace to speak of a ***trust deficit***. The risk society has significantly undermined trust, whether this is trust in politicians, banks, insurers, pension providers, judges, police officers, doctors, big businesses or their products. As Skidmore and Harkin (2003) note, 'trust is a way of coping with complexity rather than being paralysed by it'. Inimical feelings of anxiety and trust are therefore central to the ways in which we all try to 'cope' with a dynamic, uncertain world: but they are also vital for politicians who seek to gain and hold on to power. However, after the events of 9/11 in New York, fear has further corroded feelings of security and trust – not only in the US but globally. In the UK the *trust deficit* has been increasingly evident in a series of opinion polls over the past 15 years which showed, for example, that non-expert opinions are often seen as more trustworthy than those of either scientists, 'experts' or politicians. When asked who they would trust most to tell the truth about risks of pollution: 61% favoured pressure groups; 5% private companies; and only 4% trusted politicians (ibid). Government decision-making on policies ranging from genetically modified crops to MMR immunisation for infants have led to similar expressions of public mistrust of politicians and 'experts'.

In the UK in the 1990s, the problem of trust in public life most often referred to the problem of 'sleaze' and corruption in business and politics. A series of scandals around allegations of political bribery and MPs being offered 'cash for questions' dogged the Conservative government of John Major and, in part, led to its downfall. Under New Labour the twenty-first-century manifestation of the trust deficit is different, but it also encompasses concerns about the 'truthfulness' of politicians, and this has profound implications for public participation and democracy. In both respects the government's controversial decision to invade Iraq in 2003 has been of immense significance in the wake of BBC-aired allegations that the evidence upon which the decision to go to war was taken had been 'sexed up'. Following on from the suicide of the man held to be the main source of the BBC story (Dr David Kelly), a series of Parliamentary Inquiries (under Lord Hutton and Lord Butler) sought to restore trust. But public disquiet remained over the truthfulness of the reasons given to parliament (and to the public) for going to war, particularly as the weapons of mass destruction, which were the primary justification for the war, have never been found.

But, even before the invasion of Iraq, there was a problem of trust in UK politics. A MORI survey conducted in 2002 showed that:

- 91% of those surveyed would trust doctors to tell them the truth
- 85% would trust teachers
- 25% business leaders
- only 19% would trust politicians to tell them the truth.

(Quoted in Skidmore and Harkin, 2003:9)

The research authors stress that 'trust must be earned – but it must also be learned' and, they suggest, learned in new ways. The tired and discredited strategies of reputation management, 'spin', audits and inspections cannot restore what they term 'grown up trust'. Yet these strategies do seem to remain at the heart of Third Way approaches to trust. If we take the example of New Labour's second term mantra of 'delivery, delivery, delivery', the implication here was that if performance management and targets work, if they *did* deliver the enhanced public services promised in the second-term manifesto, then the public would recognise this and trust would be restored. However, this simplistic view fails to recognise that a downward spiral of mistrust is hard to break. For example, politicians may claim that child poverty is being gradually eliminated, school performance enhanced or that hospital waiting lists are being greatly reduced, but faith and trust in politics and politicians is far from restored by graphs, statistics and good news stories.

By the time of the 2005 general election, trust had been very far from won by New Labour in general and by Tony Blair in particular, and the issue dominated much of the campaign. Nonetheless, New Labour responses to the trust deficit continue to depend on performance management, reputation and news management, while at the same time attempting to engage the public through enhanced forms of consultation, community engagement and participative democracy (Blunkett, 2003). As we will see in Chapter 5, community consultation and empowerment for the most part remain a matter of rhetoric rather than reality (although there are opportunities for challenge and for positive change).

The Third Way democratisation project, like the welfare project, is also mired in the language of finance and management with talk of *social capital* and *co-production* as essential components of trust and positive political, economic and social engagement. The concept of 'co-production' rests on the notion that public goods, such as health and education, are not produced and delivered by state, but produced with the consent and active participation of all citizens and, hence:

> Active citizenship. Community engagement. Co-production between providers and users. These are the modern routes to social justice. (Milburn, 2004)

Once again, *active citizenship* (through engaged communities) is lauded as a means of fostering new forms of trusted governance, which lie beyond the realm of the public state. Here, too, the notion of 'social justice' (albeit a very partial one) is portrayed as the end point of the route to democratisation and 'co-production' in contemporary Britain. But there are clear limits which bound relations of co-production: the political realities of New Labour mean that central control by the state – most importantly in terms of Treasury support and decisions as to whether certain policy options are 'on' or 'off' the national agenda – is still very much alive and kicking. While both modernisation and democratisation promise a new localism to provide 'local solutions to local problems', there are distinct limits to localism: firstly, central government (Treasury) resources are not made available to put desired solutions in place; and secondly, those locally suggested solutions which are regarded as 'off message' (and not reflected in centrally defined performance targets – see Chapter 4) are highly unlikely to be taken forward. And so while the new localism may offer possibilities for challenge and change (Hughes, 2004b; and Chapter 5), the gulf between its promise and its reality leave further space for public disillusionment and the erosion of trust. One (Third) way to address the trust deficit is by attempting to restore the bonds of trust that are a core element of the concept of social capital.

7. Social Capital – A Third Way Policy Panacea?

The Third Way conceptions of community, participation, trust and active citizenship could be seen to coalesce around the core notion of *social capital*. As we have seen, the election of the New Labour government in 1997 saw the establishment of the cross-departmental SEU in 1999, signalling the government's intention to deploy the concept of social capital in the policy arena to address a range of social ills including poor health, low educational attainment, crime and unemployment. However, social capital still remains an elusive concept which is hard to pin down in 'the real world' (Roche, 2004a).

The genesis of the concept can be traced back to US sociologist James Coleman (1990) and political scientists Francis Fukuyama and Robert Putnam who, in the

1990s, attributed the social ills of the US to a deterioration in community life to the erosion of social capital. They envisaged social capital as being:

> a range of social structures and relations which acted as a form of 'social glue', facilitating human interaction within communities. (Roche, 2004a:98)

The processes at work in generating social capital are acknowledged to be complex. They involve, at the same, three levels or dimensions:

1. **Relations of social capital** (trust, expectations, obligations, sanctions), which may operate through...
2. **Structures of social capital** (society, regions, communities, families), both of which may relate to, or be shaped by...
3. **Ideologies of social capital** (altruism and notions of 'the public good') which can be manifested at the levels of individuals, groups or more widely in communities.

These processes are represented diagrammatically in Figure 3.4.

Where UK policy is concerned, social capital has traditionally focused a relatively narrow range of issues centring on the social and economic *benefits* of increasing participation (within communities and social networks), trust, shared expectations, reciprocity and altruism. In the UK the most frequently utilised interpretation of social capital – that put forward by Giddens – defines it in terms of 'trust networks that individuals can draw on for social support, just as financial capital can be drawn upon to be used for investment' (Giddens, 2000:78). The benefits of social capital are therefore seen in terms of its ability to harness community networks to help address

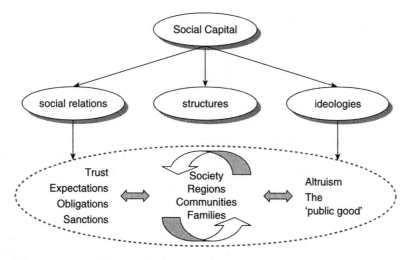

Figure 3.4   Defining Social Capital
(*Source*: Roberts and Roche (2001))

the problems of under-employment, crime and disorder and to enhance health and well-being (Campbell et al., 1999; Lederman et al., 2002).

The relations and structures of social capital are viewed, by Giddens, through the lens of 'active citizenship'. Such networks can range from leisure centres, job clubs, churches and faith groups to credit unions and neighbourhood watch schemes. But, for its critics, social capital may also have negative consequences, such as sectarianism and corruption. As Putnam (1993) acknowledges, examples of social capital in action may well include choral societies, bowling leagues, trades unions and faith groups, but may also include organised criminal gangs and right-wing militias. The networks and relations of social capital may therefore not always be directed to lawful and positive civic ends.

For some commentators, the speed with which the concept of social capital has gained ascendancy across a range of disciplines reflects the political and intellectual vacuum which the concept is seen to fill by offering a *Third Way* between economic interventions and political interventions and so seeking 'to connect "the economic" with "the social" (beyond market and state) in new ways' (Mayer, 2004:113). But Mayer contends that social capital cannot escape its fundamentally economic roots and herein lie many criticisms. She persuasively argues that in urban settings, social capital deals largely with 'excluded' and poorer groups and the tapestries of 'third sector' (not-for-profit, voluntary and community sector) initiatives that aim to achieve the inclusion of the poor and marginalised into a harmonious, civil society. This focus effectively filters out any adversarial movements and so prevents challenges to the capitalist economic orthodoxy that underpins the concept of social capital itself. As a result, a failure to ask the key question *social capital for whom and to what end?* can lead to a narrowed set of aims, and policy goals defined as 'inclusion' and not the reduction of inequality. These 'blind spots', which Mayer observes in the theories and policies of social capital, limit the possibilities for radical community and group movements in deprived urban areas. At the same time, they can put pressure on those who may be striving for fundamental change: for instance, many of those working with grassroots initiatives may be either 'too busy working with the poor to join coalitions against poverty' or are so under-funded and under-staffed that they exhaust themselves trying to achieve the competing aims of (largely economic) inclusion and genuine empowerment and 'mobilisation from below' (Mayer, 2004:113).

Having established that there are problems in the definition of social capital and a lack of critical engagement with its negative features, we now turn to one of the key difficulties that the concept poses for policy-makers and analysis – how to *measure* social capital and its consequences (either positive or negative). If it is a critical element in New Labour policies geared to health, safety and inclusion, we need to be able to evaluate the success (or otherwise) of policies which seek to develop social capital and networks. Methods used to assess the extent and effects of social capital, usually in deprived communities, have often depended on large-scale survey methods, which explore questions related to the key 'domains' of social capital – *sociability, participation, trust and altruism*. But quantitative methods have proved to be blunt instruments for assessing the complex and slippery concept of social capital and its impact in the 'real world' (Roche, 2004a).

Despite problems of definition, scope, usage and measurement, a great deal of *political capital* has been invested in social capital in recent years, both in the US and the UK. As we have seen, it has been seized upon by Third Way advocates as a policy panacea for a range of social ills and 'wicked problems' in the UK, and is frequently invoked by politicians as a means of (re)building community:

> Building social capital is the pre-condition for tackling problems of urban decay, crime-ridden streets, educational failure. (Milburn, 2004)

> It gives concrete empirical and theoretical content to ideas about community networks, the bonds of trust and belonging, and shared values amongst families, friends and communities. (Blunkett, 2003:26)

Social capital is presented here as a 'good thing' which is associated *with* community, bonds, trust, family and friends, and seen as *against* 'bad things' such as urban decay, crime and educational failure. In short, it is sold as a policy cure-all. The usage of the concept in this unfocused way poses the rhetorical question 'Who can argue with that?' There is a feel-good factor embedded in the discourse of social capital – encompassing community, participation, trust, bonds, altruism and the public good – that is seductive. Mayer argues that in appearing to connect the *capital* with the *social*, this concept gains a potentially attractive force. It also offers politicians a 'non-economic (low-cost) solutions to social problems' (Mayer, 2004:115). The attraction of the low-cost solution is evident in the work of Charles Leadbeater who identifies the pivotal role of the *social entrepreneurs* who can:

> set in motion a virtuous circle... They help communities to build social capital which gives them a better chance of standing on their own two feet. (Leadbetter, 1997:9–10)

Building social capital therefore depends on members of communities helping themselves and, ultimately, having only themselves to blame if they fail to 'invest' sufficiently to improve their own quality of life and life chances. In this sense the policy panacea of social capital is closely allied to notions of active citizenship and positive welfare. But, for many sceptics, it remains a concept bereft of real substance and ill-equipped to address the multi-faceted and structurally rooted problems facing postmodern societies.

8. Social and Criminal Justice – The Technological Fix

This section will go on to look at another key element of Third Way political discourse – information and communications technology (ICT) – which is, like social capital, often held out as a 'policy panacea' for a range of complex and intractable problems. Moreover, leading proponents of the Third Way have made explicit connections between the relations and structures of social capital and developments in ICT:

> the cultivation of social capital is integral to the knowledge economy because while innovation in the 'old' economies was based on research and development, innovation in 'new' knowledge-based economies derives from networks and collaborations. (Giddens, 2000:78)

Therefore networks and collaborative ventures are seen as the basis of social (as well as financial) capital in postmodern knowledge-based economies.

Broadening the survey one finds the epochal shifts that Third Way politics are fundamentally concerned with that centre on *globalisation* and the *information revolution*. Consequently, for Giddens, responding to these challenges involves 'a commitment to modernisation – to shape the future by embracing change not seeking to defy it' (Giddens, 2000:32). ICT lies at the heart of the New Labour modernisation project and is fundamental to a range of social policies including education, training, enhanced citizen and community participation, the modernisation of local democracy, and the management and delivery of a range of health, welfare and criminal justice services (to name but a few). But faith in 'new technologies' has taken on a particular resonance for Tony Blair's government. Just as politicians in the Victorian Age wished to be associated with the then 'new' technologies of the railway, and as Harold Wilson seized upon and valorised the 'white heat of technology' in the 1960s, Tony Blair embraced ICT in the 1990s (Geoghegen, 2004).[3]

For New Labour, ICT offers the radical prospect of changing the way companies do business and the way citizens gain access to goods and services (Cabinet Office, 2000). Discussion of the extent to which ICT based solutions 'work' in these and other respects will follow in Chapter 4, but regardless of whether it 'works' or not, there remains a firm *faith* in the capacity of ICT to provide access to information for all, a source of empowerment and route for new forms of democratic governance. Consequently, the government's ambitious *e-government* strategy (Cabinet Office, 2004) promised that all citizens would have electronic access to all government services, through their own home computers or through community access points, by 2005. The e-government strategy is lead by the governments 'e-envoy', Departmental Information Age Government Champions (IAGC) and the Central IT Unit (CITU) in the Cabinet Office (ibid). But despite the impressive array of acronyms, institutional changes and the 'feverish outpouring of policy papers' that have accompanied the strategy (Hudson, J., 2003), grave doubts still remain about whether this 100% access target is achievable and, moreover, whether meeting it would achieve the overarching

---

[3]However, Luke Geoghegen argues that New Labour's emphasis is less on the *information* and *communication* aspects of ICT than the potential offered by the new *technologies* themselves.

inclusive, democratising, empowering, enabling and efficiency aims sought. For the strategy to be successful, everyone who wants to use the Internet must have not only access to it, but also the skills to use it (Hudson, J., 2003). As a result, the *digital divide* between information 'haves and have-nots' remains a crucial issue for the legitimacy of e-government and the government's social inclusion strategy: there are dangers that lack of access and skills for ICT will reinforce rather than reduce social disadvantage and exclusion (ibid).

To shed light on the relative success of ICT in enabling public sector reform, we can usefully turn to the work of Richard Heeks (1999). He offers a chronology of approaches to ICT, which governments, and the senior officials who develop and implement policy, may adopt: as the summary in Figure 3.5 shows, these approaches can range from the tendency to 'ignore' ICT to a recognition of the need to 'integrate' ICT into all policy reform and delivery processes. A cursory glance at Britain in 2005 suggests we remain at the intermediate 'idolise' stage, with ICT seen as an 'end' and a policy centrepiece rather than a crucial 'means' of working towards genuinely integrated policy solutions. 'Over-awareness' of ICT and misplaced faith in its potential to fix problems and transform government could be illustrated with reference to a number of policy spheres, but the research-based examples[4] chosen for brief discussion here are: firstly, shared information regarding vulnerable young people; and secondly, ICT and information exchange in the criminal justice system.

- **Ignore**: Out of ignorance, public officials include neither ICT nor information in plans for reform
- **Isolate**: Public officials lack computer literacy and an understanding of the power of information, yet are aware of ICT and its potential. Investment in computing is therefore included in reforms, but as a preserve of 'ICT experts', not as a systematic component of the reform process
- **Idolise**: Public officials are often semi-literate. They are over-aware of ICT's potential, and believe it can transform government (or at least transform their careers), so ICT becomes the centrepiece of all changes
- **Integrate**: Public officials have become information-literate. They recognise information as a resource central to all public sector functions. ICT is relegated to a secondary role as a valuable means to achieve certain reform ends, not as an end in itself. Re-engineering of information systems and introduction of ICT are now fully integrated into the change and reform process.

Figure 3.5 'The Four Is': A Chronology of Approaches to the Use of ICT in Enabling Public Sector Reform

(*Source*: Heeks, 1999)

---

[4]See research project reports: Cook and Roberts (2001) www.wlv.ac.uk/pri. Cook and Vallely (2003) www.wlv.ac.uk/pri and Cook, Burton, Robinson and Vallely (2004) www.eps.gov.uk/publications/docs/ specialistdvcourts.pdf

Vulnerable young people and information sharing

The vulnerability of young people and need for effective systems to ensure child protection have long been an important policy issue. There have been over 70 public inquiries into severe child abuse in Britain and the majority of these were worryingly similar, centring on children killed after months of torture and neglect. The first of these inquiries, held in 1945, following the death of 13 year old Denis O'Neill led to a new Children Act and to the creation of local children's committees. But little appeared to change and almost 30 years later (in 1974) the report following on from the death of seven year old Maria Colwell led to further significant reform creating local committees to co-ordinate child protection. 30 years on from Maria's death, the Laming enquiry into the torture and death of Victoria Climbié found a similar catalogue of failings in relation to poor communication and co-ordination between agencies, bad practice and inadequate supervision of social workers.

The Green Paper, *Every Child Matters*, was published following the Laming enquiry into the death of eight year old Victoria at the hands of her aunt and her aunt's boyfriend. The enquiry revealed a catalogue of professional and bureaucratic mistakes and failures in decision-making and inter-agency communication. In response the Green Paper proposed to introduce electronic dossiers for all children in order to minimise future mistakes and enhance child protection. These electronic dossiers would hold information for *all* children on, for instance, school exclusions and whether they are 'known' to agencies including Youth Offending Teams (YOTs), the police, mental health and social services. But critics cast doubt on how the dossiers can be implemented and managed as the Green paper had envisaged: for Williams (2004) the paper's proposals seek a technological fix for problems which involve deep-seated issues around agency trust, accountability and clashes of (multi-)organisational cultures. Research on ways of linking information on vulnerable young people supports the view that organisations including the police, social services, YOTs, Connexions,[5] Primary Care Trusts (PCTs) and voluntary and community sector agencies may work to very different organisational goals and targets (Cook and Roberts, 2001; Green et al., 2001). These studies suggest that if those working with vulnerable children and young people are to adopt a genuinely multi-agency and holistic approach, then all available information needs to be synthesised in an agreed and structured format in databases held by all the key agencies (health, social services, YOTs and so on). But information sharing at this level presents a number of problems, including:

- **Technical challenges:** ensuring consistency across multiple databases. Agencies frequently use different ICT systems which are often not compatible with each other

---

[5]Connexions is the government's support service for young people aged 13–19 in England. The service aims to provide integrated advice, guidance and access to personal development opportunities and help the transition to adulthood and working life. Connexions joins up the work of six government departments and their agencies and organisations on the ground, together with private and voluntary sector groups and youth and careers services.

and do not enable the speedy transfer or sharing of data between agencies (Cook and Roberts, 2001)

- **Legal barriers**: ensuring compliance with the provisions of the Data Protection Act and the European Convention on Human Rights is often cited as a major problem facing multi-agency partners. However, these principles may for some agencies be a 'shield behind which to hide' if they are reluctant to share information (Green et al., 2001)
- **Cultural barriers**: are as important as technical ones. The creation of a culture of information sharing that recognises the enhanced decision-making capability that better information provides an essential precondition for success
- **Geographical barriers**: different agencies often work to different spatial boundaries: the operational boundaries of YOTs, health services (PCTs) and social services may not be coterminous. Some may be 'borough-wide', others 'county-wide' and some work to historical divisions which cut across both of these. This poses challenges for effective cross-border working and permeability of these boundaries for real multi-agency planning and service delivery (Cook and Roberts, 2001).

Recalling Heeks' chronology, an *integrated* approach is needed to address these problems, but this would require that public officials are 'information literate' and recognise ICT as a valuable means to achieve policy ends. This also involves several other important developments in relation to organisations' attitudes to ICT and partnership working which, arguably, have not yet taken place. Firstly, such integrated approaches would require a *culture change* within organisations to shift from a concentration on their internal priorities and targets towards 'joined-up' multi-agency goals. Secondly, they need *hybrid managers* who understand both ICT and policy issues and are in a position to offer a balanced (not idolised) view and to manage systems effectively towards agreed policy ends (Heeks, 1999). Thirdly, there is a need for agencies to be *open* and willing to respond positively to, and not hide behind, the frameworks provided by Data Protection and Human Rights legislation (Green et al., 2001). Fourthly, a strategic and well-managed approach to *commissioning* public sector ICT projects is crucial. Fifth and finally, there is a requirement for *resources* – in terms of money and skilled staff – to provide an adequate and planned infrastructure for all of the above. In relation to the last two issues, the second example to be discussed here – ICT for the criminal justice system – is particularly relevant.

ICT for the criminal justice system

As in other policy spheres, criminal justice reforms depend on effective communication and use of ICT. A key weakness within the CJS is that its lead agencies – police, courts and CPS – all have differing ICT systems. Moreover, the 43 police forces in England and Wales differ from one another too and the difficulties involved in the exchange of information and intelligence between police forces in England and Wales was highlighted in the high profile case of the Soham murders. Where the CPS is concerned, the introduction of their new COMPASS ICT system in May 2003 may have helped to improve their internal communications, but it will still not interface with the Magistrates' Court's Libra system or many of the police systems. This, in turn, has a

Effective information exchange is a key requirement for joining up the operation of the CJS, including by:

- Providing more up-to-date criminal records for all who use them, improving bail, charging and other decisions
- Improving the information available to victims and witnesses and reducing the time they spend at court, thereby improving the quality of service to them
- Better use of court time and a reduction in discontinued trials through more immediate access to court lists and better information
- Enabling end-to-end process management and innovation
- Reducing the costs that currently result from duplicating information input. We are committed to major improvements in the sharing of case information between criminal justice agencies by 2005. During 2002/3 work was undertaken on the options and funding of £1.2 bn over the next three years secured for investment in infrastructure, linked case management systems and supporting services. This funding is ring-fenced and subject to the joint control of Home Office, LCD[b] and CPS Ministers, and the Director General CJS IT. Priorities include:

  - Modernising the ICT infrastructure within agencies and enabling them to securely e-mail each other and partners, such as Youth Offending Teams and defence solicitors;
  - Establishing linked case management systems to ensure that up to date case information is available to those who need it and that resources are not wasted; and...
  - Providing a 'one stop shop' for victims who will be able to track the progress of their cases on-line.

[a]Home Office Departmental Report 2003 Cm5908 (2003).
[b]Now Department for Constitutional Affairs – DCA.

Figure 3.6   ICT in the Criminal Justice System[a]

(*Source*: http://www.homeoffice.gov.uk/docs2/annexrep2003)

negative impact on attempts to more effectively co-ordinate criminal justice services for victims: the differing ICT systems of the different CJS agencies therefore remain unable to 'talk to' one another and so the police, CPS, Probation and Court staff, some of whom may be working in shared offices, are still often unable to transfer case-related information to one another even if they work in the same room (Cook and Vallely, 2003; Cook, Burton, Robinson and Vallely, 2004). And so, while the intentions of the Home Office ICT strategy (reproduced in Figure 3.6) are clearly stated, the practical means and resources to deliver them remain unclear.

The dangers of over-'idolising' ICT and over-reliance on it as a policy panacea are evident in the final elements of the strategy which refer to linked case management systems and the ability of victims to track the progress of their case on-line, both by 2005. This ability is, at the time of writing, a very long way off for victims and those who engage with them. While there are examples of innovative 'information portals' (such as the Warwickshire Victim Information Portal – VIP) being developed by multi-agency partnerships, these are often funded as Home Office pilot projects and remain the exception rather than the rule. Research undertaken in 2003/4 found that case tracking remained a key problem for staff within the CJS, with evidence that it was not the use of ICT but the actions of committed staff – from the CJS and voluntary and community sector support groups – using word of mouth and telephones that provided the basis for most case tracking and updating to victims (Cook and Vallely, 2003; Cook et al., 2004). The technical fix promised in the CJS ICT strategy by the end of 2005 therefore appears a very long way off.

Finally, it is worth emphasising that Third Way faith in ICT has often gone hand in hand with (often misplaced) faith in the private suppliers of ICT infrastructure, systems and services. Where the Magistrates' Courts are concerned, the consequences have been disastrous. A common ICT strategy for all courts had been called for since the 1980s and, after two failed projects in the early 1990s, the Lord Chancellor's Department (now the Department for Constitutional Affairs) procured a PFI contract in 1996. By 1998 only one bidder for the contract remained – ICL (now called Fujitsu Services) – and a deal was struck with them later that year for *The Libra Project*. Five years on, the PAC (2003) castigated the project as 'one of the worst PFI deals we have ever seen'. The original *bid* in May 1998 estimated total costs of £156 million for an 11 year project; by the time the contract was *signed* in December 1998 the costs had risen to £194 million for a ten and a half year project. By July 2002, the costs of the project had soared to £390 million over a reduced term of eight and a half years (ibid). There remain serious reservations about the fitness for purpose of the system with many experts believing that business systems should have been redesigned before the new ICT system, and others stating that 'Fujitsu had "run rings" around officials' (*Computer Weekly*, 30 January 2003).

As the first section of this chapter demonstrated, the belief that the UK economy and society is undergoing an inevitable 'ICT-driven transformation' is central to the political discourse of the Third Way. There are important debates and questions to be posed around the nature, limits, meanings, consequences and 'inevitability' of those transformations. For this discussion of criminal and social justice it is important to recognise the significance of the concept of the 'information society' in driving (and justifying) Third Way policies. ICT in particular is re-shaping issues of welfare and social equality in very specific ways as 'it allows New Labour to craft a narrative that presents the abandonment of traditional egalitarian policies as a necessary modernization of values' and the only viable basis for egalitarianism in the new world order (Hudson, J., 2003:281).

Hudson signifies this important shift through the motif of *e-galitarianism* which usefully conveys three themes connecting ICT with Third Way conceptions of equality:

- The centrality of the ICT revolution for New Labour (through the '*e*' prefix)
- A clear break with the 'old' past and traditional *egalitarian* values
- And a reduced (– minus) version of the former Labour vision of egalitarianism.

(ibid:284)

Having examined some of the 'signs' and 'posts' along the Third Way it is clear that in terms of both ideas and policies much has been abandoned and much re-branded to meet the perceived challenges of postmodernity.

9. More Than Just Words

In this chapter we have seen how and why in 1990s Britain, the Third Way marked a significant departure from the language and politics of both the 'old left' and the 'new right'. Where the former is concerned, the Third Way departure from the language of class and conflict was clearly a crucial element in its wider aims, or 'project':

> The simultaneous reform of welfare and Labour party principles is a re-structuring project which starts as a language and a set of ideas: the 'third way' is a discourse through which restructuring is proceeding, through which the meanings of welfare, work and Labour are being remade. (Haylett, 2001:14)

In this process of 'remaking' the political values of Labour, the Third Way rhetoric of *inclusion* is very significant. Many feel that this is serving to displace more radical concerns over socio-economic inequality and polarisation (Lister, 2000). At the same time, the (cultural) use of the term inclusion implicitly identifies those who do not 'fit' with the new demands of the modern and globalised economic order. It constructs an 'exclusive' version of citizenship which centres on paid work, and in which equality and justice are re-defined in terms of 'equality of opportunity'. Moreover, the concept of inclusion itself presumes that there is consensus about what exactly it is we are being included into. In so doing it side-steps struggles and conflicts over values and politics and generates a 'non-conflictual, non-targetable, procedural form of politics', which acts as a persuasive and potent strategy for power (Haylett, 2001:53). This politics is dominated not by ideals and ideologies but by pragmatism and what works.

But the importance of the language that shapes the parameters as well as the expression of politics needs to be emphasised because, in politics, words are not just words but are powerful tools for, and engineers of, change. The former Republican Speaker of the US House of Representatives, Newt Gingrich, acknowledged this when he asserted that:

> The real breaking point is when you find yourself having a whole new debate, with new terms. That's more important than legislative achievements. (Quoted in Peck, 1998:135)

Whether Third Way political philosophy is seen as insubstantial or not, it has certainly changed the language and parameters of debate across British politics and so, taking on board Gingrich's argument, this is indeed a breakthrough. However, in attempting to present a non-conflictual Third Way, New Labour has astutely succeeded in occupying a political centre-space against which competing politics (from the left or the right) will inevitably be presented as 'extreme'. In this way the Third Way rejects the bi-polarity of the old order and takes the imagined position of 'middle England' as its political benchmark (see Chapter 6 for a fuller discussion). But this position is far from a politically neutral one: for example, in her discussion of social capital Mayer (2003) expressed concern at the dominance of 'less conflictive civil society groups' at the expense of political and oppositional movements. For her, as for other critics, binary politics and conflicts over values and political priorities can be healthy and productive for democracy. It is to these conflicts and challenges and the possibilities they hold for enhancing and reconciling criminal and social justice that we will return in the final chapter of this book.

○ *four* ○ 'What Works' and Criminal and Social Justice

For his first major speech as Prime Minister, Tony Blair chose the run-down Aylesbury estate in Southwark, London, to set out his political priorities for the first New Labour term. In this speech Blair established his firm commitment to pragmatism and to finding out (and funding) 'what works' across all spheres of policy:

> Unless government is pragmatic and rigorous about what does and does not work, it will not spend money wisely or gain the trust of the public... We will find out what works, and we will support the successes and stop the failures. We will back anyone – from a multinational company to a community association – if they can deliver the goods. We will evaluate our policies – and improve them if they need to be improved. And where appropriate we will run pilots, testing out ideas so that we can be sure that every pound we spend is well spent. (Tony Blair, speech at the Aylesbury Estate, Southwark, 2 June 1997)

This speech marked a departure from the political values of the old left and the new right, which were seen to have hampered the development, design and delivery of effective (and cost effective) policies in the past. The new approach indicated in the Southwark speech was therefore not just pragmatic but it was anti-ideological too (Solesbury, 2001): reacting against previous government policy-making, which was seen as driven by political 'dogma', New Labour instead advocated the 'objective' and efficient processes of audit, inspection and evaluation. What mattered for Blair and New Labour was not that policies were driven by political ideals, but that they 'delivered the goods', and it did not matter who delivered them – whether the public, private or voluntary and community sector.

The 'objective and efficient' managerial processes to be taken forward by New Labour had first been set in train in the 1980s with the Thatcher governments' drive to bring private sector business practices into the state realm, notably through the tools of performance management. But these processes were, and are, very far from objective and value free: critics of what they came to signify (New Public Sector Management – NPSM) located the development of the management tools of audit, inspection and evaluation in the context of the rise of new, more penetrating, forms of regulation and governance (Daly, 2003; Clarke, 2004a). Where New Labour departed from its Conservative predecessors was not in their use of such techniques but in their motivation for adopting them: rather than seeing them as essentially 'a good thing', chiming with their (Conservative) ideological beliefs in the primacy of the market, New Labour was interested only in what was effective – what worked, in practice. Crucially, for New Labour, this key aim was underpinned by a belief in the value of *research and evidence* as the objective basis for policy choices and interventions, whether in the fields of health care, welfare or criminal justice.

The relationships between research, 'evidence' and policy development are complex and highly contested, and nowhere more so than in the fields of criminal justice and social policies. Moreover, the sheer scope indicated by the title of this chapter could merit at least one book in its own right. But for the purposes of *this* book, an inevitably limited and summary approach will have to be taken to accomplish three broad aims. The first aim is to outline the *rise of evidence-based policy (EBP) and the 'what works' paradigm*, which lies at the heart of post-1997 welfare and criminal justice policies. Secondly, the chapter will explore *theoretical and practical problems associated with 'what works'*. Thirdly, it will examine examples of *the use, or misuse, of 'what works'* in the fields of criminal justice and social policies. Finally, while addressing these three aims, the chapter will seek throughout to critically appraise what works in the context of the rise of new forms of *governance* which are shaping the contours and the limits of criminal and social justice.

1. Evidence-based Policy and the Rise of the 'What Works' Paradigm

In popular terms the word 'evidence' is often associated with forensic science and the investigators who use evidence as the basis for solving crimes. Similarly, medical and scientific models of enquiry are based on the objective collection and analysis of data (evidence) in order to support or reject the hypothesis or theory the investigator is testing. It is important to recognise that the emergence of the 'what works' paradigm in the 1990s was not an entirely new phenomenon, but signalled a re-emergence and re-shaping of a long-standing positivist approach in which scientific research had long been seen to hold the key for explaining (and thereafter changing) human and social conduct (Sebba, 2001).

Where crime and criminal justice were concerned the earlier positivistic view had been challenged from a range of perspectives: Marxist approaches argued that 'crime' itself was defined by the ruling capitalist elites and that punishment and the process of criminalisation constituted part of a repressive social apparatus. Postmodernist and interpretivist approaches to crime and justice also rejected positivism, but for different reasons, arguing that using pseudo-scientific tools in the search for universal 'truths' or generalisations in dynamic, contested, *social* spheres was not only futile, but was an ideological enterprise in itself. Particularly notable in undermining scientific and positivistic approaches were the reviews of penal policies and interventions conducted during the early 1970s, the most notable being Robert Martinson's work, which concluded that community corrections were no better or worse than incarceration and that, in short, *'nothing works'*. This stance paved the way for a rejection of the rehabilitative ideal in favour of a 'just deserts' approach to penal policy (Hudson, 1987).

But the impossibilism inherent in the 'nothing works' stance would not prevail for long, not least because it ran counter to political imperatives that demanded that *'something* should be done' about crime, law and order. Subsequently, reviews of preventative and correctional interventions returned to predominantly scientific/medical models of research and evaluation and suggested that some things did indeed work and that it was, after all, possible to assess what works, what does not work, and what is 'promising' in anti-crime interventions (for instance, see Sherman et al., 1997). Government funded research by, for example, the Department of Justice in the US, the Home Office for England and Wales and the Ministry of Justice in the Netherlands, all gave a renewed impetus and a veneer of legitimacy to quantitative, evidence-based research (Sebba, 2001).

Where the development and 'testing' of *social policy* solutions are concerned, issues of evidence and evaluation have only come to such prominence relatively recently. To some extent they can be traced back to movements towards greater consumer choice and the 'Citizens Charters', which were led by Conservative Prime Minister John Major in the early 1990s and have been adopted since then by successive governments. According to this view of *citizens as consumers*, it was clear that if citizens were to have 'choice' (in education, health care, housing, pension provision, transport and so on) then they needed the evidence upon which to base their choices. If they were to receive the rights that their 'Charter' guaranteed, then the services they received would need to be evaluated against the Charter's promises. In these two key respects, evidence and evaluation were therefore, in the 1990s, becoming influential in the development, choice and delivery of policies in a range of fields.

At the same time, universities became increasingly involved in gathering and disseminating the research base for EBP. But this role was (and still is) not without its tensions and ambiguities: for example, the conventions of writing up research findings for academic journals invariably leads to an editing down of much rich contextual information and may also lead to a reluctance to give entirely honest accounts of research or programme failure (Pawson, 2001). The demands of academic performance may also militate against 'take risks' with innovative or controversial research findings (Crawford, 1998). In addition, the pressure on university research centres to generate external income may lead to their trying too hard to please research funders by giving them 'what they want' rather than opening up spaces for dialogue and critique.

Early academic/practitioner collaborations around EBP included: the Evidence for Policy and Practice Information and Co-ordinating Centre (EPPI-Centre) based at the University of London, established in 1993 to address the need for a systematic approach to evidence-based work on social interventions; the Centre for Evidence Based Social Services (CEBSS – a partnership comprising the Department of Health, Social Services Departments in the South West of England and the University of Exeter), established in 1997 with the main aim of ensuring that decisions taken at all levels in social services were 'informed by trends from good-quality research'. More recently, the collaborative National Institute for Clinical Excellence (NICE) was established by New Labour in 1999 to bring together researchers and practitioners and to promote and disseminate evidence of good practice in the sphere of health. At the same time, National Service Frameworks drawing on research evidence were developed to provide templates of 'what worked best' in organising and delivering health and social care services. Where social care was concerned, the children's charity Barnardo's also committed itself to 'what works' in arguing, quite rightly, that it was the right of every child 'to expect that professionals intervening on their lives do so on the basis of the best available knowledge' (Jackson and Thomas, 1999).

2. 'What Works' – Theoretical and Practical Issues

One key issue at the heart of the what works paradigm is how to determine exactly what *is* the 'best available knowledge' for guiding interventions. The means by which this is established is not a neutral process as it involves decisions about what constitutes robust, ethical, relevant and 'good' research. By definition, finding out 'what works' also involves judging the cause and effects of interventions in the social world, but the means to accomplish this are often drawn from the philosophy and methods of the natural sciences.

Deciding what works

In the fields of medicine and health care, international networks have been established to use 'scientific' methods to produce robust evidence of what works for policy-makers: for instance, the Cochrane Collaboration (established in 1993) seeks to produce evidence which has been '*systematically* searched, critically appraised and rigorously analysed according to transparent criteria' (Davies, 2004:7 original emphasis). The same basic principles for establishing what works are also adopted by the Campbell Collaboration (C2) network, which covers research in social and educational interventions. For these (and other) networks, the *single* research study is seen often to lack methodological rigour and is not 'sample-specific, time-specific and context-specific' (ibid). By contrast, engaging in *systematic reviews and meta-analyses* can lead to an *accumulation* of evidence collected from those single studies which are deemed eligible for inclusion according to clear sample, time, context and quality criteria. In this way, the selection of which studies are appropriate and included in reviews is crucial to the subsequent analysis which, in theory, should then offer more than the sum of its parts.

When deciding on the inclusion criteria for systematic review, such networks see the random controlled trial (RCT) of medical research as the methodological 'gold standard', but many argue that systematic review and meta-analyses are inappropriate for the complex analysis of cause and effect in the social realm. Moreover, the processes for judging what evidence qualifies for inclusion in reviews is seen by some as a highly selective and limiting process:

> These services, while valuable, are dominated by peer reviewed journal papers, with variable and usually limited coverage of the wealth of social science research, policy and practice information that appears in government reports, independent research institutes and think tank publications, academic working paper, other grey literature and books. (Gomersall, 2005:127)

Where social issues and interventions are concerned, recent moves to develop merged, databases which would incorporate these 'grey' sources may begin to address some of the problems raised by systematic review (ibid). Nonetheless, there remain profound theoretical problems in adopting the *scientific realism* they imply. Firstly, within the social realm there are difficulties in establishing exactly what is a 'programme' for the purposes of comparative research and systematic review. For instance, programmes addressing teen pregnancy may be defined by their *goals* or by the *elements* that constitute them: the goal of reducing pregnancies may be achieved through 'programmes' stressing abstinence, or those promoting contraception and these are by no means comparable (Cottingham et al., 2004). Secondly, there is a risk that scientific realism may descend into *scientific reductionism*, so 'rendering complex social world simple and governable' (Gadd, 2004). David Gadd's work (on cognitive behaviour programmes for perpetrators of domestic violence) makes it clear that, in this field, dubious evidence of programme 'success' has nonetheless been used to justify certain (preferred) policy options (Gadd, 2004). Recent regionally-based research on voluntary domestic violence perpetrators' programmes similarly revealed concerns around the policy orthodoxy of the cognitive behavioural approach in general, and the Duluth model in particular (Cook and Lyle, 2004). What emerged from our analysis of international and UK studies, and our own empirical research, was that there was *no clear evidence* that voluntary perpetrator programmes (or, indeed, court mandated programmes) had a positive effect on perpetrator attitudes, re-offending patterns or victim safety. In short, we were unable to propose a 'model' which could be adjudged to 'work' in these crucial respects.

But certain orthodoxies are hard to shift, particularly when they have acquired 'scientific' kudos, however dubious. Home Office research published in 1997 had already acknowledged the difficulties in 'scientifically' assessing the effectiveness of programmes based on the cognitive behavioural approach and, moreover, went on to cast doubt on the value of systematic review and meta-analyses in assessing what does and what does not work to reduce offending (Vennard et al., 1997). However, in respect of domestic violence offenders, government policy appears to be shackled to perpetrator programmes based on the cognitive behavioural approach, despite significant problems in implementation and little, if any, robust evidence that they actually work to reduce offending and enhance the safety of victims and their families.

The evidence-based policy (EBP) agenda

The EBP movement has in recent years been intimately linked with the New Labour government's modernisation agenda, as the following quote from the 1999 White Paper, *Modernising Government* shows:

> [Government should] produce policies that really deal with problems; that are forward looking and shaped by the evidence rather than a response to short-term pressures; that tackle causes not symptoms. (Cabinet Office, 1999)

Finding out and supporting 'what works' based on the core principle of 'building initiatives by learning from past successes and failures' is a commendable aim (Pawson, 2001). But, while there is widespread support for drawing on robust research evidence to *inform* decisions about policy and practice, 'the evidence-*led* agenda promises too strong a role for evidence' (Tilley, 2001:96). Rather, Tilley advocates a rational, reflective and *generative* approach to what works, which rightly acknowledges that it is not *programmes* that work, but the underlying reasons or resources that they offer which work to generate change. The CEBSS adopts a complementary stance in its stress on the importance of professional and personal contexts and argues that 'what works' *alone* is not a sufficient basis for policy: research evidence needs to be used 'in combination with the preferences of clients, and the judgement and experience of professionals' (http://www.ex.ac.uk/cebss/evidence_based_practice.html). These are important qualifying additions to the what works paradigm which taken together confirm that:

- Evidence in itself should *not determine* policy – it is not *just* what works that matters
- A thoughtful and *generative approach* needs to be taken to assessing the benefits, changes or failures of policy interventions
- *Practitioners and service users* also have a vital role to play in shaping the policy process.

As already indicated, the rise and use, of EBP and 'what works' has been particularly notable in relation to crime and criminal justice policy over the past two decades. In England and Wales this work has broadly consisted of two strands. The first is evident in the work of the Home Office Crime Prevention Unit, set up in 1983 to address *situational crime prevention* measures. These measures have developed, over time, from 'locks and bolts', to include a range of more complex techniques. Situational crime prevention measures currently consist of those geared to: increase the effort required to commit crime (car immobilisers, anti-robbery screens in banks, gating alleys); increasing the risks of crime (better street lighting, CCTV, neighbourhood watch); reducing the rewards of crime (property marking, merchandise tagging); and, more recently, 'reducing provocations and removing excuses' (for instance, reducing crowds, installing breathalysers in pubs) (www.crimereduction.gov.uk).

Secondly, the *psychological approach* to crime is also a significant interest among Home Office researchers, for instance, the use of cognitive behavioural approaches to changing offenders' behaviour (Home Office, 1997). Evaluation research conducted within the what works paradigm – whether situational or individual in focus – is invariably limited to the parameters of the intervention being studied: this means that the wider context in which the intervention takes place is seen as beyond the scope of the research. Critics have argued, therefore, that where 'official' Home Office research on crime is concerned, the twin focus on situational measures and individual psychology has served to displace broader concerns with the economic and social relationships and structures that shape the contexts of, and motivations for, crime (Stenson and Edwards, 2004).

Where economic and social relations were concerned, a tranche of high-profile centrally funded programmes launched in the term of the first New Labour government (1997–2001) explicitly set out to address the *causes of crime*: among others, the flagship New Deal for Communities, Surestart and Connexions programmes were all seen as *The Way Ahead* in tackling the causes of crime (as indicated in Figure 1.7 earlier (see page 31)). But these programmes remained somewhat separated from those Home Office initiatives geared to *tackling crime* itself: these were based on measures involving situational crime prevention, enhanced law enforcement and more effective administration of justice. Therefore, despite the rhetoric of joined-up policy, 'crime reduction is separate and relatively disconnected from strategies to deal with the deeper causes of crime' (Stenson and Edwards, 2004:226). This is particularly evident when these strategies come together in local contexts, as we will see in the discussion of partnership, social inclusion and community safety strategies in the next chapter.

What works and governance

Researching within a 'what works' paradigm has practical, theoretical and ethical implications for researchers engaged in it: for those of us with experience of community-based and evaluative research, it is clear that inherent within the paradigm is a higher than ever degree of *client control and prescription*. For example, research sponsors have the power to identify, adopt and fund the policy intervention that is being studied in the first place (and this will inevitably have involved the exclusion of alternative interventions); they pose the research aims and questions to be answered (ruling out of order more radical research questions); they frequently set the criteria against which projects are to be evaluated (often in terms of internal organisational goals, targets, and cost effectiveness criteria); closely define research parameters (with no-go areas or themes for research); and, on some occasions, seek to restrict the dissemination of 'unpopular' research findings. Many of these constraints have always applied to social research but, above and beyond this, what is distinctive about 'what works' is the driving force of its managerial logic and its subsequent role in constituting and justifying new forms of *governance*. As Peter Raynor observed (in relation to Probation Pathfinder evaluative research),

> Detailed ideas about the methodology of evaluations were developed in RDS [the Home Office Research and Statistics Directorate] before invitations to tender were issued... the scope was limited by the fact that budgets had been provisionally determined on the base of the methodology already devised within RDS... the process of tendering and contracting felt more like becoming a subcontractor of RDS than receiving a research grant. (2004:314)

Raynor's comments on the extensive accountability requirements of the HO as research funders (for instance, frequent progress reports and steering group meetings), chime with my own experience and, I am sure, are typical of the experience of many researchers working with government departments and public bodies. Academics working within such tight managerial constraints (even to the point of the funder attempting to re-work or ignore unpalatable research findings – see Hope, 2004) find the experience not only frustrating but a threat to ethical and robust research practice.

As a consequence, some (though not all) research conducted within the what works paradigm can be conceptualised as part of a constrained, controlled and managed process for the selection and validation of particular policy options. It is not surprising, then, that many doubt the value and ethics of much officially sponsored policy research in the what works mould, and that research conducted by and on behalf of the Home Office has come in for particular criticism (Hope, 2002; McLaughlin, 2002). Critics see researching what works in the sphere of crime and criminal justice largely as a limiting and self-referential exercise, which is part and parcel of a wider process of governance and policy legitimisation. This process effectively constitutes 'governing at a distance' and is partly accomplished through the discursive and working practices that operate through the what works paradigm: these practices serve to manage research in ways that effectively 'bracket out' the complex politics and conflicts around crime reduction – at national and local levels. Consequently, McLaughlin contends that:

> ... the excessive focus on demonstrating the relentless march of the 'what works' programme flattens New Labour's criminal justice project into a non-descript, uninflected narrative devoid of complexity, tensions and contradictions. This account has no use for letting the different facets of the government's crime reduction agenda 'breathe' and no interest in exploring the social and political overtones and undertones of policy, practice and discourse. (2002:48)

The same criticisms can be made of what works research in other areas – such as social exclusion (see also Chapter 5). The paradigm itself displays what McLaughlin terms a 'high modernist' faith in administrative efficiency, science and technology to reduce crime and to solve social problems. (This is a theme we will return to in the discussion of the Crime Reduction Programme below.)

Realistic evaluation – in theory and practice

There have, however, been attempts to develop EB research in ways that would raise more important questions that *just* 'what works'? For instance, the principles of *realistic evaluation* seek to avoid some of the pitfalls of a 'flattened', narrow 'what works' approach (Pawson and Tilley, 1997). Instead, it seeks to develop theorising which is based on contexts, mechanisms and the (sometimes unintended) outcomes of interventions, which are not predictable or generalisable. Instead of the medical model's RCT as a gold standard for evidence-based research, the goal of realistic evaluation research is conceived as:

> a tested theory or set of theories that provides an improved grasp of what worked, how and with whom within the programme. (Tilley, 2001:94)

Realistic evaluation, rooted as it is in a 'middle range scientific realism', is far from 'sexy' and, as Tilley puts it:

> 'What works for whom and in what circumstances' is hardly a rallying cry. It calls for patient analysis and hard thought. It eschews the undifferentiated, blanket response. (2002:79)

For crime reduction and criminal justice research, then, what works is being slowly refined and developed through the principles of realistic evaluation and problem-solving approaches to research and policy. But in practice these refinements are not easy to take forward on the ground within agencies and partnerships. The reasons for this are due in part to the *cultures* of crime reduction organisations and partly due to issues of *resources*. In relation to the former, many of those working in crime reduction and in community safety partnerships may feel constrained by their organisational roles and are understandably reluctant to be critical of what works (officially) and to pose creative alternatives (Gilling and Hughes, 2002). In relation to the issue of resources, Read and Tilley (2000) in a paper suitably titled *Not Rocket Science? Problem-solving and crime reduction*, examined police approaches to crime reduction through problem-solving. They found that despite two years of a high profile policy drive from the Home Office, high quality problem-solving remained 'exceptional' as police forces continued to focus on the 'sharp end' of policing and on offenders. They went on to observe that:

> data are weak, and routine aggregate data sharing is exceptional and problematic. Analysts are thin on the ground, often used mechanically and for processing management information, and tend to be inexperienced, poorly paid, and with few qualifications for preventive analysis. (2000:vii)

Two years on from Read and Tilley's observation on the lack of staff, skills and ICT resources to make what works *really* work, very similar problems resurfaced in a further Home Office sponsored report that sought to develop a framework for police and local partnerships to address crime and disorder problems more effectively (Tilley and Laycock, 2002). In line with what works principles (and based on US and UK research), the authors identified six key principles which would underpin successful, EBP namely:

1. **Aims** – knowing what you aspire to do
2. **Problem specification** – having a detailed and evidenced statement of the aim
3. **Tactics** – what will actually be done to tackle the problem
4. **Mechanisms** – ways in which these tactics will bring about change
5. **Context** – the time, place, social organisation in which the tactics will activate the mechanisms for change
6. **Replication** – adopting and adapting approaches that have been found to be effective in one context, so that they will similarly work when implemented in another context/place.

But in order to *apply* successfully these six principles to practice locally, the agencies engaging with the problem-solving approach to crime reduction need to have essential *skills and resources*. A cursory look at the checklist of the skills required by these agencies and partnerships reveals a number of resource problems they face, including: suitably qualified staff; ease of access to up-to-date research (including on-line access); opportunities for staff to update their knowledge base; the ability to think critically and laterally about crime and crime reduction policies; the ability to suggest creative alternative interventions; and finally and crucially, the effective collection storage and retrieval of crime and disorder data in ways which facilitate their analysis from a problem-solving perspective (Tilley and Laycock, 2002). This suggests that what works cannot work without the appropriate infrastructure and skills base to support it.

The dynamics and 'disconnections' of what works

However, at this point we need to take a step back in order to critically address some of the assumptions underlying the list of principles for EBP reproduced above. Firstly, the construction of the list in itself can be seen to present a *technicist view* of the processes of policy-making, implementation and evaluation that echoes the 'high modernist' perspective alluded to by McLaughlin earlier. Similarly, a plethora of Home Office what works 'toolkits' offer simple 'off the shelf' (and more often, 'off the web') guides to practice, which drive a naïve and uncritical approach to crime reduction policies (Hughes, 2004b). While sharing ideas on effective practice can be valuable, it is also important to recognise the uniqueness of 'place' and localities in the development of community safety strategy. If toolkits and good practice guidelines are seen as a short cut to policy-making and are adopted uncritically and wholesale, they may undermine the 'down-up', community empowerment, partnership model which lies at the heart of community safety principles. Imaginative and locally driven responses are therefore likely to be stifled by top-down prescriptions of what works elsewhere – nationally and internationally. This brings us to a second set of problematic EBP issues, around *context and replication*.

There is a tendency inherent within what works to assume that there is 'out there' an objective reality to be studied and a full grasp of the context (historical, social, economic, cultural and spatial) in which policy interventions are to be applied. But these *contexts are dynamic and contested*: for example, in relation to community safety priorities and policy aims, there will inevitably be competing views held by the police, local councillors and community safety 'professionals', and local residents. The task of adapting and implementing crime reduction policy (or any other kind of policy) according to local contexts is far from a static or a politically neutral process. It also raises the question of the extent to which we can ever replicate what works in one place in another place or time. It also raises some fundamental questions about the construction of 'the' knowledge base for what works – whose knowledge is it, where does it come from, where does it apply, and to what end was it generated?

If we look at the empirical case studies drawn upon in the Home Office commissioned report *Reducing Offending* (itself the centrepiece of New Labour's £250 million Crime Reduction Programme, launched in 1999), we find that many are based on US 'experiments' (Goldblatt and Lewis, 1998). The same may be said of more recent systematic reviews on other issues (for instance on the effectiveness of interventions designed to reduce criminal behaviour among drug users) where authors note the dominance of US studies and a 'gap' in relation to evaluations of interventions in the UK (Holloway et al., 2005). The extent to which US studies are robust, reliable and relevant in the UK context is open to debate (Fraser, 1998). But, even if generated in the UK, 'what works' evaluations may (possibly with good intentions) serve alternative interests or agendas. For example, the extensive Home Office Guidelines produced when implementing the Crime and Disorder Act (1998) are largely made up of 'what works' case studies from a range of UK pilots and locally based community safety programmes. Such pilots and programmes are geared to demonstrating 'success' or 'progress', not least because this is often the only way to ensure continued funding. Therefore there is an enthusiasm for *demonstrating 'wins'* – and 'quick wins' at that – to ensure programme survival and the jobs of those involved (Raynor, 2004). At the same time, the what works approach (based on 'scientific' analyses) raises expectations of success and so, when programmes fail to deliver that success, the failure is often blamed on the subject – the offender (Boone, 2004).

'What works' studies in the field of crime reduction may also suffer from the same criticisms that Jamie Peck made of workfare experiments and exemplars in the US – that they are *disembedded* and lead to the tendency to construct policy on the basis of 'facts from nowhere', or at least from somewhere else (Peck, 1998:141). Peck's criticisms are equally relevant for both the criminal justice and social policy spheres: he persuasively argues that in the US poverty and welfare dependency have been conceptualised as largely inner city problems, but the 'local solutions' posed, especially the workfare solution, have come from very different places, notably 'rural' areas of Wisconsin and Riverside in California. Policy solutions transposed to the UK may therefore suffer from a ***double disconnection*** – at both inter- and intranational levels: clearly what is seen to work in Wisconsin may not work in entirely different social, economic and cultural contexts of Glasgow and the Scottish Highlands, Cardiff and West Wales, or Birmingham and rural Shropshire. According to Peck this 'profound spatial disconnect is largely buried under the decontextualised pseudo-science of workfare advocacy' (ibid:141). The 'science' or ideology of the intervention itself thus displaces issues relating to the socio-cultural, economic and spatial contexts in which it is implemented. It is significant then that 'exemplar' US workfare experiments have had such a powerful influence on UK policy, despite the profound historical, cultural and spatial disconnects between the two countries and settings (Deacon, 1997; Cook, 2001; Daguerre, 2004). In a similar way the UK Home Office off-the-web toolkits present facts 'from somewhere else' and so may, too, be regarded as the spatially disconnected products of crime (pseudo)science. In the realm of crime reduction, as in that of workfare, 'Sub-national experiences leaving a strong imprint on national debates' in the sense that we may feel we know 'what' works, but are unsure if or where else it will work. In relation to both crime reduction and workfare then, effectiveness is 'contingent on local conditions', not least local economic and ('flexible') labour market conditions (Peck, 1998).

'What works' as governance? The Case of the Crime Reduction Programme 1999–2002

As we have seen, many of the initiatives constituting the ambitious Crime Reduction Programme (CRP) were inspired or justified with reference to US research studies and, therefore, may suffer from the problem of 'disconnection'. Nevertheless, the launch of the £250 million CRP in 1999 was greeted with much enthusiasm: it encompassed a wide range of initiatives, accorded unprecedented importance (and 10% of its budget) to evaluation and offered, for the first time, the prospect of long-term, sustainable multi-agency approaches to crime reduction (Maguire, 2004). But although the CRP promised much, it largely failed to deliver the promised understanding of 'what works'. Reasons for this are complex and numerous but include:

- Its over-ambitious scale, with unrealistic expectations of outcomes
- Implementation failure, which itself involved: the nature and (unrealistically tight) timetables of programmes; slow, bureaucratic procedures; capacity of programme managers; and the priorities of local managers in the police and Crime and Disorder Reduction Partnerships (CDRPs)
- Poorer than expected police data
- Lower than expected commitment to evaluation by project staff
- Where implementation was successful, difficulty in attributing cause and effect (partly because projects comprised several strands of preventive action running simultaneously).

(*Sources*: Hough, 2004:240; Maguire, 2004:213)

Consequently, the evaluations that came out of the CRP could 'say a great deal about ways of improving implementation, but very much less about *what* to implement' (Hough, 2004:240, emphasis added). As a result, politicians began to lose faith in the programme (and, to some extent, in the researchers conducting evaluations) and the CRP ran for three years rather than the ten years originally envisaged (ibid). Some academics, too, lost faith in evidence-based policy-making arguing it had in practice given rise to **networks of governance** within which the boundaries between political, administrative and scientific interests and expertise became excessively blurred (Hope, 2004). Such networks accomplish a central task of governance as a 'tool to help govern a complex society, whose complexity is continuously expanding as a result of the application of science to social problems' (ibid:302). Crucial to these networks, and vying for policy influence, are what Hope terms **the new crime sciences** which are seen to operate 'symbiotically in the construction of political programmes' (ibid:302). In this way the scientific rationalism inherent in the CRP was subverted into a kind of 'scientific reductionism' in which the complexities of the worlds of local managers and partners were either not appreciated fully (or were ignored) in the interests of governance (Hough, 2004). Nevertheless, many academics are still reluctant to jettison the notion of EBP either seeing it as a necessary antidote to the political conservatism inherent in the impossibilism of 'nothing works' (Maguire, 2004), or as important to enabling local actors/partners, in particular, to make informed policy choices (Hough, 2004).

What works and empowerment

Despite a welcome and renewed emphasis on the importance of the 'rootedness' of research evidence (Shaxson, 2005), the what works paradigm is still seen by many as fundamentally at odds with the principles of *'down-up' empowering research* in which the perspectives of users and practitioners are valued and voiced. While realistic evaluation does offer the potential to listen and learn lessons from policy experiences, it is often mistakenly assumed to be merely about 'hard' quantitative data. But valuable qualitative, 'soft' evidence can and does come from engagement with users and practitioners too (as the CEBSS rightly stated, above). There are powerful arguments from this alternative perspective that may counter the govermentality that is seen to underlie EBP and what works: many of these arguments emanate from those promoting user-led and user-controlled research (Beresford, 2002; Bennett and Roberts, 2004; Lister, 2004). The process of critiquing and unpackaging research and policy within the what works paradigm therefore opens up the space for social researchers to ask alternative and important questions such as: What's the problem, and who says so? What might be done about it? By whom? Who should be asked and about what? Who is the evaluation for? The final two questions are vital as they require and enable researchers to engage with (and for), users and potential users of the service or intervention being studied. In this sense, evaluation research can be rendered more democratic and empowering (Fetterman, 2001). As we will see later, this approach is increasingly being taken forward in community-based research around safety, poverty and social inclusion. The challenge for policy research is to find ways to reconcile the best reflective and generative elements from realistic evaluation with innovative, user focused elements of democratic research and evaluation.

3. The Use, and Misuse, of 'What Works'

As we have seen, some of the key principles underlying the 'what works' paradigm are positive ones: firstly, whether in the fields of health, social care or criminal justice, citizens and service users should be able to benefit from policies based on the most sound, up-to-date and appropriate research evidence. Secondly, that policy should be evidence-*led* rather than wholly evidence-*based*, as the perspectives of citizens, service users and practitioners should also shape the policy process. But the importance of national politics (and political perspectives on public opinion) should not be underestimated: drawing on the example of the CRP, there is a powerful view that 'future policies may be *informed* by research, but they will be *shaped* by politics and by a political perception of public sentiment' (Raynor, 2003:86, original emphasis).

Nonetheless, it is crucial not to descend into the impossibilism of the nothing works mentality. There are examples of **what does work**, and not all of the initiatives that *do* work are centrally driven or derived from replications of programmes from the what works mould. For example, if we take the issue of domestic violence, many important initiatives geared to addressing domestic violence have emanated from the innovative work of the voluntary and community sectors and others engaged with supporting victims and their families (such as the Leeds Inter Agency Project, the Help, Advice and the Law Team (HALT) in Leeds, the Cardiff Women's Safety Unit, Women's Aid and, of course, the Refuge movement). If, for instance, we take the introduction of Specialist Domestic Violence Courts (SDVCs) into the UK as one such positive initiative, this was not mainly or solely driven by the agencies of the CJS. Led by the example of the Leeds 'cluster court' launched in 1999, Magistrates' Courts in Cardiff, West London and Wolverhampton had all worked in **partnership** with local domestic violence fora (and their constituent voluntary and community groups) to develop SDVC arrangements locally. The evaluation of five such court schemes, also including an additional CPS-led scheme in Derby, evidenced that SDVCs and fast track arrangements *did* work to provide enhanced services for victims and survivors (Cook et al., 2004). This evidence, in turn, provided the basis for wider roll-out nationally (Home Office Press Release, 31 March 2005). It is encouraging, then, that national policy innovation in the sphere of domestic violence, as elsewhere, *can* be driven by local actors, practitioners, and voluntary and community sector groups.

Conversely, it should be noted that not all of the evidence from research projects, and the recommendations flowing from them, are heeded by government, particularly where costs are involved: for example, in the SDVC project, one key recommendation proposing a national funding programme for voluntary and community sector advocacy groups working with victims and survivors was not taken forward, despite the research finding that the success of SDVCs would depend on accessible and sustainable advocacy and support services. (In addition, the funding allocated to 'roll out' SDVCs nationally provided only £1 million to 'set up' 25 courts, but no funds are allocated to ensure their sustainability – Home Office Press Release, 31 March 2005). Nevertheless, this and subsequent research (Vallely et al., 2005) have indeed shown that SDVCs can 'work'. Perhaps less clear is exactly *why* they work: this cannot be simply attributed to CJS processes or to the remit and operation of support services at court. Rather, complex issues around the politics of local partnership and, crucially, the driving role of key individuals can make the difference between overwhelming success and relative failure.

The what works paradigm, based on the model of the natural sciences, is far from equipped to deal with the complex and dynamic effects of organisational culture and personal agency on 'programme' success. A further issue is therefore that *programme fetishism* itself focuses on implementing 'programmes or interventions' rather than providing an experience of case work, case management, outreach work, support and/or supervision (HM Inspectorate of Probation, 2002). In this sense, a focus on 'what works' alone produces a 'one dimensional' approach to measuring outcomes that concentrates on one variable (the programme) at the expense of many other independent variables. Once again, the scientific/medical model inherent in the what works paradigm fails to come to grips with the messy and complex relations, and contested realities, of social life and social 'problems'.

Changes in research philosophy and practice are, however, proving fruitful. The development of more generative and 'rooted' approaches to research and the use and enhancement of multiple methodologies are beginning to establish that, in relation to criminal justice and social policy interventions, some approaches do indeed work better than others. In this sense, the 'nothing works' era is at an end and research is providing some 'useful leads' (Bottoms, 2005). Nonetheless, there is a temptation to over-egg positive results and rush to quick fixes. However, if, as Tony Bottoms argues, 'we are serious about an evidence-based approach, the evidence has to be allowed to accumulate incrementally, with policy and practice built slowly alongside the evaluations' (Bottoms, 2005:12). The difficulty remains that the exigencies of politics and governance frequently demand a quick fix rather than a considered development of policy and its evaluation over the longer term. This, and other problems with 'what works' discussed thus far, are summarised in Figure 4.1 opposite.

Bearing in mind these concerns, and the issues around what works discussed so far, we will move on, finally, to explore some of the issues and problems for policy-making associated with the use, and misuse, of 'what works'. This will be accomplished by examining three selected, and necessarily brief, case studies:

1. 'On the spot' punishment – the Penalty Notice for Disorder
2. Identity cards
3. ICT and the technological fix

1. ***Knee-jerk definitions*** of those 'problems' that are seen to be in need of research and policy solution (for example, penalty notices for disorder and 'street crime')
2. ***'Initiativitis'*** from central government with, as one political commentator noted, 'more pilots than British Airways', and a parallel failure of co-ordination at local and national levels and subsequently...
3. A veritable ***flood of evaluation research***, in which it becomes more difficult to explore what is working, where, for whom, why and under what circumstances
4. ***Pitfalls of meta-evaluations*** which in part attempt to deal with the problem of proliferation of (local) findings, but can be highly selective and gloss over much important detail
5. ***Accentuating the positive***, with pressure deriving from research funders and some academic conventions to produce positive results rather than to report programme failure or 'bad news'
6. ***Short-termism*** – the timescales (and budgets) for much important policy evaluation work are limited, for instance, to fit in with political policy cycles (such as the Comprehensive Spending Review and Budget cycles) and of course general elections. This is also linked with the desire for...
7. ***Quick fixes***, particularly to perceived crime and disorder issues, to demonstrate 'success' and to enhance media and electoral support (see Tonry, 2004)
8. ***Shooting (or rubbishing) the messenger*** – where research indicates to funders that favoured policy options will *not* work, it is likely to be dismissed (as we will see in the discussion of ID cards)
9. ***Gathering dust*** – on the other hand, if researchers say what does work and the policy interventions they recommend are seen as 'off message' (or too costly) the research may be shelved, to gather dust (see Chapter 5 for a discussion of SEU recommendations in relation to ex-prisoners)
10. ***Policy-based evidence-making*** – given all of the above, politicians and policy-makers may take decisions to (a) implement policies which they know will probably *not* work but 'fit' with wider political priorities; and/or (b) fail to implement policies which *are* likely to work because they don't fit or are too expensive. In this way they may entirely reverse the principles of EBP.

Figure 4.1   Pitfalls of Policy Research Within the 'What Works' Paradigm

'On the spot' punishment – Penalty Notices for Disorder (PND)

A thug may think twice about kicking your gate, throwing traffic cones around your street, hurling abuse into the night sky if he thought he might get picked up by the police, taken to a cash point and asked to pay an on-the-spot fine of, for example, £100. (Tony Blair, speech to the Global Ethics Foundation, June 2000)

Tony Blair has long been a passionate advocate of 'what works', so can we presume that this proposal, made in a speech to the Global Ethics Foundation in Germany, emanated from extensive, robust research within this paradigm? Apparently not, and yet this vision of 'summary justice' was brought into law the following year (in the 2001 Criminal Justice and Police Act) despite the fact that 12 month pilot projects evaluating PNDs in four police force areas only started in August 2002. The policy was, therefore, launched in advance of any research evidence to support it: by the time the results of pilot evaluations were published (in September 2004) the PND scheme had already been rolled out nationally. Although the evaluation did conclude that 'on the whole the PND project has been a success' this success was judged in terms of *police* attitudes, and it seemed that the police had 'warmed to this disposal as a way of dealing with anti-social behaviour in a swift, decisive manner', hence the initiative was judged a success (Home Office, 2005f:6). The PND is therefore a good example of *policy-based-evidence-making* and a sobering example of the abrogation of what works in favour of a political 'quick win'.

According to critics, the PND also demonstrates a further blurring of the boundaries between the civil and the criminal law: notices can be issued by police officers, some community support officers and '"accredited" persons such as neighbourhood wardens and security staff' for a range of 'disorderly behaviour' (Roberts and Garside, 2005). Examples of such behaviour range from throwing fireworks in a thoroughfare, throwing stones and depositing litter to 'behaviour likely to cause harassment, alarm or distress'.

Of the total of 63,639 PNDs issued in England and Wales in 2004:

- The vast majority (78%) were issued for the two offences of 'causing harassment, alarm and distress' and being 'drunk and disorderly'
- 94% were issued to adults and 6% to juveniles (aged 16–17 years)
- Only 38% of PNDs issued were paid in full by the statutory 21 day deadline[1]
- After the initial 21 day period, just over half (52%) of PNDs were eventually paid without recourse to court action
- Fines were registered for 44% of PNDs for adults and 45% for juveniles.

(*Sources*: Home Office, 2004; Home Office, 2005f).

If we take *compliance* with notices as a measure of success, the data presented by the Home Office for the first full year in operation hardly justifies the initial evaluation that PNDs were successful. The PND was a policy also designed to make justice quicker, hence Blair's notion of 'marching' offenders to a cash point. But if an offender is drunk (as there are in a majority of PND cases), they cannot *receive* a PND on the street, and so invariably the notion of swift summary justice begins to dissipate. Where swift *payment* is concerned, the data on payment rates within the 21 day notice period indicate that only 38% pay. The notion of 'justice' (summary or otherwise) is also questionable given the potential for differential impacts of an £80 or £50 fine (depending on the offence) on relatively wealthy and on poorer offenders. This inequity may be compounded by the imposition of a further fine and a 'quasi-criminal record' for those who cannot pay (Roberts and Garside, 2005). There is also evidence that much of the PDN 'new business' is for those offences which may have previously resulted in an informal warning: this raises the issue of the *net-widening* effects of the order. Taken together, this brief case study shows that this particular

---

[1] By contrast, the payment rate for penalty notices for motoring offences is 59% (Home Office, 2005a).

policy initiative was *not* grounded in evidence of what works, was stimulated by knee-jerk politics and may well prove counter-productive for justice – both criminal and social.

Identity cards

> Instead of wasting hundreds of millions of pounds on compulsory ID cards as the Tory Right demand, let that money provide thousands more police officers on the beat in our local communities. (Tony Blair, Leader of the Opposition, Labour Party Conference, Brighton, 1995)

Of course, as discussed in Chapters 2 and 3, there have been profound national and global changes since 1995 when Tony Blair made this speech, in opposition to the then Conservative government's proposals. What a difference a decade makes, as the now Prime Minister argues precisely the reverse:

> 'People recognise the benefits of a scheme that will allow us to tackle identity fraud more effectively, bear down on illegal working, illegal immigration, abuse of our public services and help the fight against organised crime and terrorism, and these are all strong arguments for moving forward with identity cards. (Tony Blair, Prime Minister, House of Commons debate on second reading of the Identity Cards Bill, 28 June 2005)

The claims made here in relation to the aims, benefits and support for identity (ID) cards appear strong, but to what extent are they based upon robust evidence of what will and what will not work? What research evidence there is indicates that ID systems work best when they are established for clear and focused purposes, but critics have expressed concerns about complexity and *function creep* in the current proposals outlined in the 2005 Identity Cards Bill (Liberty, 2005). Government ministers have, at different times, stressed differing aspects of the ID card's benefits in terms of tackling the following: identity theft (allegedly costing £1.3 billion per year); illegal immigration and working in the hidden economy; misuse of public services; and organised crime and terrorism. A six month research project conducted by academics from the Enterprise Privacy Group at the London School of Economics (LSE) examined the government's proposals and likelihood of meeting all, or any, of these aims in a (cost) effective way. They concluded that 'The proposals are too complex, technically unsafe, overly prescriptive and lack a foundation in public trust and confidence' and proposed an alternative model which, they argued, was more appropriate and could be delivered at one tenth of the cost (LSE, 2005). To summarise very briefly, the concerns of the LSE Identity Project Group, Liberty, The Register and others, they argue that there is *no evidence* that the government's proposed ID Scheme will:

- **Combat international terrorism** – as a compulsory ID scheme in Spain did not prevent the bombings in Madrid in 2004, and 9/11 and 7/7 terrorists did not conceal their identity

- **Reduce crime and increase detection rates** – the Police Service argues that the ID scheme will not itself lead to this because identity itself is rarely an issue, though police resources are
- **Reduce benefit fraud** – the vast majority of benefit fraud cases relate to misrepresented circumstances, with only an estimated 5% relating to false identities
- **Tackle illegal immigration and illegal working** – those seeking asylum have been required to carry identity cards since 2000; and the location of many illegal immigrants and their workplaces is already well known to the authorities (as is evident, for instance, in the tragic case of those working in Morecambe Bay)
- **Reduce the £1.3 billion a year lost through identity theft** – the LSE report states that 'many of the claims about the prevalence of identity theft are without foundation' and many regard the estimate of £1.3 billion as 'a fraud' in itself: the figure merely adds together a range of disparate estimates of the costs of, for example, overall plastic card crime, false insurance claims and the costs of dealing with immigrants to the UK who arrive with false documents.

The LSE Project also questioned government figures of the costs of the (initially voluntary[2]) scheme put at £5.8 billion by government and instead put the costs of implementation at between £12 billion and £18 billion. Crucially, it also concluded that the technology envisioned for the scheme was 'untried, untested and unreliable'.

For the purposes of this chapter, what is notable in this case study is the abandonment of the 'what works' principle (in favour of policy-based evidence-making) and, in addition, the *rubbishing of academic research* which counters official policy. In relation to the latter point, the Home Secretary Charles Clarke, variously described the LSE findings (which followed on from interviews with over 100 academic and business experts in the field and a comprehensive analysis of the implications of the scheme – technical, legal, political and financial) as 'total nonsense', 'simply mad' and part of a media scare campaign (*TimesOnline*, 16 June 2005). The final case study will look at policies which, like the ID card Bill, seek to deploy technical fixes for criminal justice and social policy problems.

ICTs and the technological fix

> Not only does... [the government]... believe that ICTs have the ability to improve public services and make them more relevant to individual needs, it believes that services will be improved irrespective of context, be they run by the public, private or voluntary sector, the remit of the NHS, the Department

---

[2]The Scheme is envisaged as initially voluntary, although the programme to introduce biometric data on passports by the end of the decade will mean that the ID scheme will in effect become compulsory for all those wishing to travel beyond the UK. However, until then it is difficult to see how the rationale of tackling international terrorism could be applied to this proposed voluntary scheme and slow, progressive roll-out.

for Trade and Industry (DTI) or York City Council, funded by charging, by advertising or general taxation, it does not matter: services will be improved by
greater use of ICTs. (Hudson, J., 2003:274, original emphasis)

Belief in ICT and the technological fix has become the holy grail of New Labour.
Their strategy for modernisation is not rooted in the what works paradigm, but
rather represents an act of faith in ICT. As discussed in Chapter 3, ICT is not always
(or even mostly) the efficient, empowering and democratising tool it was envisaged:
on the contrary, it may be inefficient, controlling and excluding. The brief examples
that follow indicate some of the issues for 'what works', and for criminal and social
justice, which are raised by recourses to 'the technological fix'.

Welfare – Jobcentre Plus

The status quo, so far as the welfare state is concerned, has not worked. (Tony
Blair, quoted in the *Observer*, 14 December 1997:2)

New Labour set out to make welfare (and welfare claimants) 'work'. The welfare to
work project launched in 1997 focused on the perceived problems of welfare dependency and inefficient welfare systems. In this context ICT was also seen to offer technical solutions in the sphere of policy management and delivery too (for instance in
streamlining benefit claiming and assessment, countering benefit fraud and enabling
direct payments to claimants). One means of addressing problems of welfare dependency and management using ICT as an engine for change was the notion of a 'One
Stop Shop' and policies geared to this end – the 'ONE' initiative, followed by
Jobcentre Plus and electronic service delivery (ESD) – were seen by New Labour as key
elements in the modernisation of welfare.

The remit of Jobcentre Plus is central to the welfare to work project in providing
'integrated and efficient labour market and benefit services to people of working age'
(DWP, 2005b) Although this has led to significant political fallout: the national
roll-out of Jobcentre Plus (to be completed in 2006) has involved the closure of over
200 former Benefit Agency local offices, leading to vocal protests that these closures
marked a reduction rather than an enhancement of services, particularly in rural
areas (Citizens Advice, 2004). The staff involved, too, have protested at the lack of
consultation in a process which, in their view, will change their roles from offering
responsive 'face to face' advice on benefit entitlement, to a 'call centre worker' conducting initial telephone interviews according to a prepared script. In such ways
modernisation can create barriers which reduce front-line contact, particularly 'for
those with limited English or keyboard skills' (Finn, 2003:722).

Such criticisms and problems are not unique to the UK: recent research on the
computerisation of social security systems in 13 OECD countries has concluded that
'information technologies have generally increased the control of staff and claimants
by management rather than empowered them' (Henman and Adler, 2003:139).
In Ontario, Canada, the process of 'screening' claims through call centres (similar to
that used by Jobcentre Plus) has also proved problematic:

While social assistance recipients were promised a streamlined, efficient and user-friendly application process, the reality is a convoluted, unreliable and extraordinarily complex one. (Herd et al., 2005:69)

This project concluded that the Canadian welfare to work regime subjected welfare recipients to administrative processes that they described as 'dehumanizing, degrading and demoralizing' (ibid:73). Crucial to this process was the increase in 'social distance' between customer and welfare provider, which also characterises the UK model. While Jobcentre Plus office environments are bright, well furnished and usually in 'high street' settings, the interactions of staff and customer are tightly controlled and choreographed. These practices constitute new forms of governance through which both welfare claimant and staff are managed and controlled. In such contexts:

technology is not simply a tool with which to implement welfare state policies, but is a productive partner alongside discourses and practices in constituting and transforming governmental relations. (Henman and Adler, 2003:159)

Do the principles and practices of the modernised Jobcentre Plus 'work' to enhance services to working age benefit claimants? Recently published evaluation research (authored by internal DWP researchers, with external social research input) concluded modestly that 'satisfaction levels of Jobcentre Plus customers are comparable with satisfaction levels for respondents from legacy offices' (DWP, 2005:157), which hardly signals a dramatically enhanced service from the customers perspective. Moreover, the evaluation found that if customers' needs were 'straightforward' (for example, where benefits are paid direct into a bank account) they had *less* contact with the service and were *more* satisfied, and conversely, those with more complex 'non-standard' needs tended to have more frequent contact and their levels of satisfaction were lower (ibid: 159). In assessing whether this or any other initiative is 'working' we also need to bear in mind that 'definitions and measures of service improvement are not technical and universal but politically constructed and contingent on a variety of circumstances' (Boyne, 2003:224), and hence the bulk of this evaluation refers to DWP measures of effectiveness in terms of returns to work. Jobcentre Plus is seen as a positive model in France and Germany (Clegg, 2005), although if the primary rationale for Jobcentre Plus was an enhanced, modernised service for citizens, based on best use of ICT, then in my view the jury is still out.

Welfare – tax credits

As already indicated in Chapter 2, tax credits have proved costly and difficult for the Inland Revenue (now HM Revenue and Customs – HMRC) to administer. At the time of writing the issue has come to a head with the publication of a Citizens Advice Report documenting Citizens' Advice Bureau (CAB) clients' experiences of tax credits. The report used the catchphrase of the tax credit take up campaign – *Money with Your Name on it?* – with much irony and with a question mark added (CAB, 2005b).

Its findings were based on analysis of the number and nature of tax credit problems which bureaux had advised on – these numbered 150,000 in the year to March 2005. In relation to the role of the IT system in generating these problems the report was damning:

> The lack of sophistication of the computer system has led to huge overpayments as calculations have been made based on incompatible data, and there have been random and undue payments. (CAB, 2005b:9)

It repeated HMRC data for 2003/4 showing that: 46% of all tax credit families had been either over or underpaid; overpaid tax credit amounted to £1.9 billion; a third of all families had been overpaid; and a third of these overpayments exceeded £1000. The fiasco has had a disproportionate effect on the poorest families who suffered considerable hardship when payments were reduced, and in 82% of the cases reported to CABs, this reduction happened without warning (ibid:38). Despite all this (and, rarely, an apology from the Prime Minister), the Minister responsible, the Paymaster General, Dawn Primarolo, denied that the system was near collapse (*BBC News*, 22 June 2005).

Policing

Returning to the sphere of criminal justice, some of the principle problems relating to ICT have been outlined in Chapter 3, notably the disaster of the courts' Libra system. There clearly was, and still is, a need for harmonisation of ICT systems to enable transfer of files and data between agencies in order to improve both CJS efficiency and victim satisfaction. In relation to policing, the Police Information Technology Organisation (Pito) was established in 1998 largely to assist in this harmonisation by delivering a national IT system to cover all 43 forces in England and Wales. Reporting on the release of the independent McFarland review (written before the May 2005 election but not published until late June) *Computer Weekly* reports that it:

> depicted the Police IT Organisation (Pito) as largely dysfunctional and set up on the basis of offering national systems that some police forces perceive as delayed, expensive and technically backward. (*Computer Weekly*, 28 June 2005)

But relations had clearly broken down on both sides as:

> Pito management 'regard the governance systems under which they operate as unnecessarily bureaucratic, wasteful and demoralising.' These views are shared by all stakeholders, including police IT directors. (ibid)

The report indicates the damaging effects of the conflict between accepting *delays*, which may well lead to better relations with forces and better functionality of the system, and the imperative of meeting *Home Office targets* for delivery of a national system. The system designed to deliver the modernisation of ICT in the

NHS – Connecting Health – is at an earlier stage of development, but may suffer a similar fate and consequently be shunned by clinicians (Collins, 2005). Taken together, these examples seem to support the view of computer experts that ministers[3] have little grasp of the task of delivering IT projects on such a massive scale. At the same time, they also demonstrate the inter-relationship between IT, governance and EBP which, in theory at least, should be 'an approach to decision-making which is transparent, accountable and based on careful consideration of the most compelling evidence' (MacDonald, 2001).

CCTV

CCTV is a national obsession: 10% of the world's total CCTV cameras are located in Britain; it is the most heavily funded non-criminal justice crime prevention measure in England and Wales, with £170 million of government money spent between 1999–2001; and in 1996–8 CCTV accounted for over three quarters of Home Office expenditure on crime prevention (Welsh and Farrington, 2002:44). There were so many software-based surveillance and IT systems embedded in British cities in 1999 that the UK Audit Commission had difficulty finding them to ensure they would function in the year 2000 (Graham and Wood, 2003:233). Given this faith, and this level of investment, it is of serious concern that evidence that CCTV 'works' as a crime prevention measure remains limited.

The systematic review conducted for the Home Office by Welsh and Farrington (2004) concluded there was 'some support, albeit with the advantage of hindsight, for government expenditure on CCTV initiatives'. This retrospective 'support' was gleaned from just 22 evaluations from different spatial contexts (car parks, city centres and public transport), which met the stated criteria for systematic review. Of these 22 studies, only half found 'desirable effects' on crime, five found undesirable effects, five found null effects, with the final one 'uncertain'. This is hardly a ringing endorsement of such massive expenditure. More recently a more comprehensive national evaluation of 14 CCTV systems in England and Wales reported only small-scale impacts, and found only two areas where it was possible that CCTV was a significant factor in reducing recorded crime (Gill et al., 2005:34). The example of CCTV therefore presents us, once again, with an example of an important policy being funded and implemented with an unswerving faith in technology, but no evidence that it would work for the stated purpose.

In addition, CCTV poses challenges for 'justice' and transparency in contemporary societies: it is frequently difficult to establish who operates CCTV systems and for what purpose, yet according to some this 'opacity and ubiquity' functions as 'digital surveillance' and the 'electronic disciplining of subjects against redefined norms' (Graham and Wood, 2003:233). The linked issues of ICT, surveillance, discipline and

---

[3]For instance, during the second reading debate on the ID Card Bill the Home Secretary attempted to defend the governments record in running large scale IT projects by citing the positive example of Chip and Pin – which is not a government project at all.

the redefinition of norms have implications for both criminal and social justice, particularly in relation to behaviour which is 'seen' to constitute anti-social behaviour (see Chapter 6). CCTV, and its capacity for surveillance, was positively lauded following the attacks on the London transport system on 7 July 2005 (and the failed attempts on 14 July), when public and private systems were seen to contribute to the identification of the perpetrators and assisted with the timeline of the investigations. But here CCTV served a (retrospective) surveillance and identification function, rather than a (preventative) crime reduction role.

---

4. 'What Works' – Policy Implementation and Governance

Returning to the Southwark speech which opened this chapter, Tony Blair was determined to signal that his New Labour government was going to 'hit the ground running' in 1997 in terms of researching what works and implementing policies accordingly. In relation to criminal and social justice, government departments drove forward a wide range of policies geared to tackling 'crime and the causes of crime'. The parallel commitments to modernisation and joined-up government lay at the heart of both the crime reduction and social inclusion strategies launched by the newly elected government. In the Southwark speech both sets of strategies were sold to the public as being predicated on 'what works', coupled with a firm belief in the role of ICT, public sector modernisation and performance management to ensure the effective *implementation* of those interventions that were adjudged to 'work'. However, as we will have seen, it was not as simple as that. The unwavering faith and optimism of New Labour in 'what works' often proved to be misplaced (or misused) and *failure in implementation* has bedevilled many policies aimed at enhancing criminal and social justice.

Many implementation failures derived from deeper problems surrounding *national and local governance*. The term 'governance' is not used consistently but, according to Tom Ling, 'it gestures towards: new types of public-private partnerships, 'flatter' relationships between organisations; a blurring of the boundaries between previously distinct functions; and new ways of managing consequential relationships' (2000:624). These new ways of working are predicated on *NPSM techniques* which include, for instance, setting clear aims and objectives, identifying targets and measurable outcomes designed to meet those objectives, with 'performance indicators for all parties, and a plan of action (and milestones towards completion) detailing who is responsible for what and by when. This may sound very laudable and, in theory, many aspects of NPSM *should* assist effective policy implementation. However, the underlying principle of NPSM – that 'what is measurable can be managed' – may lead to over-bureaucratic (and not enabling or flexible) management and delivery structures.

The consequences of managerialism, on the ground, are vividly described by John Braithwaite (2002) in his account of nursing home regulation in the US. These consequences are equally applicable to UK settings where NPSM may encourage local managers to be 'creative' in the ways in which they meet their targets: for example,

> When rewards were put in place for the number of residents participating in activity programmes, we noted sleeping residents in wheelchairs being wheeled into the room where an activity such as a craft or game was going on so that they could be recorded on the head count. (Braithwaite, 2002:15)

Similarly, the 'empowerment' of residents was to be 'measured' in by the use of personal items and other ways of de-institutionalising space: and so, for instance, this standard was operationalised by counting the number of pictures on the wall. Here, creative compliance to this standard meant 'slapping up' pictures of film stars and also hiring pot plants. In summary, Braithwaite concluded that 'the bigger the incentive, the more complex the phenomenon regulated, the worse creative compliance gets' (ibid).

Social and public policy has also been permeated by mechanisms for compliance through 'contractual governance'. Where the regulation of criminal, or anti-social behaviour, is concerned, anti-social behaviour orders, curfew orders and acceptable behaviour contracts all seek to generate conformity and order by means of 'regulated self-regulation' (Crawford, 2003:488). But if the contract is broken, it is the individual who is seen to have failed to meet their part of the bargain. Contractual governance – whether in crime control, housing policy or other spheres – thus constitutes 'market based' forms of governance through contracts, which 'recast social obligations in forms of parochial control' (ibid:479).

More generally, new modes of governance also serve to **displace professional autonomy with managerial control**, and this can be deeply de-motivating for professionals engaged in the criminal justice and social policy spheres. For example, where lawyers are concerned, Hilary Sommerlad (2001) argues that changes in the delivery of legal services in the UK which form part of the NPSM agenda are producing 'high output, low morale' legal practitioners. The NPSM logic is, according to Sommerlad, producing a market *in* and not *for* clients within which delivery of services is both standardised and set at a low level, with worrying implications for the rights of the Legal Aid client and for the 'degradation' of the legal aid professional. But, she argues, this logic is flawed, not least because it is impossible to deliver a purely 'technical service' where the complexities of advocacy, values and justice are concerned.

But there are those who see issues of justice and confidence in the systems through which it (allegedly) flows as both simple and 'technical'. For example, Sir Robin Auld in his *Review of the Criminal Courts of England and Wales* articulated this view:

> Public confidence is not an end in itself; it is or should be an outcome of a fair and efficient system. The proper approach is to make the system fair and efficient and, if public ignorance stands in the way of public confidence, take steps adequately to demonstrate to the public that it is so. (Auld, quoted in Morgan, 2002:312)

The complex issue of how to secure, maintain and measure 'public confidence in the criminal justice system' in the context of an unequal society has been reduced to a PSI target for all constituent CJS agencies, but this did not pose a problem for Auld: merely 'make the system fair', tell the public that it is fair, and the job is done!

Despite the New Labour rhetoric of modernisation and joined-up working, there remain significant problems of communication (including ICTs), partnership working and 'silo' mentalities. Bureaucratic structures, inefficiency, delay and (inter-organisational) competition have therefore bedevilled the implementation of many 'joined-up policies'. The tight proscription of policies – their objectives, targets, performance indicator and modes of delivery – often undercut attempts to gain a genuine sense of *local ownership* of policy. For example, in relation to the work of YOTs, teams were initially meant to develop their own youth justice plan, but 'were heavily constrained by the prescriptive nature of legislation and by detailed specification templates, and performance indicators' (Burnett and Appleton, 2004:48). In this context, the success of many YOTs and their contribution to innovations in youth justice policy is therefore remarkable: this success stems from the professionalism and commitment of team members and is achieved *despite* the frameworks of governance within which they operate (as we will discuss further in Chapter 7).

Organisational and delivery structures over-determined by NPSM are ill-equipped to deal with the complexities arising from 'modernised' frameworks of governance – most notably *multi-agency and partnership working*. Under reformed and modernised structures, large, bureaucratic 'silos' were to be a thing of the past as power would be located in partnerships and flatter (horizontal) relations. However, Ling argues that part of the reason for local failures is a failure to engage in genuine JUG at the top: the *conflicting and competing priorities* of government's two leading departments (the Treasury and the Cabinet Office) have undermined joined up working at the centre, with negative impacts on national, regional and local implementation. It is to issues of policy engagement and impact – nationally and locally – that we now turn.

○ *five* ○ The 'Upside Down Duck': Participation and Engagement for Criminal and Social Justice

──────────────────────────────── **Introduction** ────────────────────────────────

Moving on from issues of 'what works' *and* criminal and social justice, this chapter will look at the effect *of* criminal justice and social policies on people's lives on the ground. It also addresses the extent to which individuals and communities are engaged with the processes of policy formation, evaluation and development. Given this focus on **policy engagement and impact**, the chapter's title may seem puzzling at first.

To explain: the image of an 'upside down duck' emerged from discussions with colleagues[1] in the late 1990s when we were all attempting to make sense of the bewildering array of social policy interventions launched by New Labour after 1997 and the effects they were – or were not – having on the lives of people on the ground (both in communities and in the local agencies serving them). If we were to see society as a pond, we could envisage the policy process (policy-makers and implementers) operating like ducks, smoothly moving through sometimes troubled waters, their calm vision and direction steering social policies, which are implemented through the firm direction of the paddling webbed-feet, working rhythmically and powerfully below the surface, translating policy into action and direction. If we 'run with' this analogy, I would argue that, since 1997, the duck's channel through social waters has been far from smooth. In fact, the duck has been turned upside down by a plethora of government papers, policies and initiatives which have literally swamped those agencies (most notably LAs, health authorities and criminal justice agencies) charged with their implementation. The duck is turned upside-down, its

---

[1]Particularly Martin Roberts (Spatial Research) who helped me to develop this rather curious analogy.

rapidly paddling feet now flay energetically in mid-air without firm strategic direction but, at the same time, little is actually happening in the waters below. Moreover, before long the duck is likely to drown!

The purpose of this analogy is to use it to try to visualise the impact of a vast array of criminal justice and social policies on those charged with implementation and those at the receiving end of policy. This chapter will examine the view that both are drowning – the former because of the impossibly heavy demands of successive rafts of policies and the latter because, for many, very little has changed in terms of their experience of inequality, poverty and social exclusion. As we have seen, New Labour came to power in 1997 committed to criminal justice and social policies driven by the principles of modernisation, effective governance and social inclusion. Key policy mantras underpinning these overarching themes were, and still are:

- **Participation** and engagement of individuals and groups, especially at local level
- **Partnership**, both as a new mode of governance and a means to achieve participation and engagement
- **Community**, both as the pathway for policy interventions and site for development of capacity and 'social capital' (with a key role for voluntary and community sector organisations).

Central to the 'joining up' of the New Labour project in relation to these three core issues was the requirement to engage in consultation with communities. The planners and deliverers of policies ranging from New Deal for Communities, Neighbourhood Renewal, Health, Education and Employment Action Zones, Surestart, Local Authority Best Value reviews, National Service Frameworks (NSFs) and Crime Reduction and Community Safety strategies, *all* have obligations to consult service users, carers, local communities, and voluntary and community sector groups in the planning, evaluation and review of services. The acid test of 'New Labour's' second term commitment to 'delivery, delivery, delivery' in public services could largely be measured in terms of its success (or otherwise) in listening and responding to lessons learned from the consultation process. Its new third term mantra of 'respect' (discussed in more depth in Chapter 7) will similarly depend on listening to and responding to the concerns and priorities of individuals, groups and communities. The concepts of *participation, partnership* and *community* are therefore crucial to the successful delivery of criminal and social justice and *consultation* and *engagement* are the channels through which all of these elements will (or will not) be realised in the course of New Labour's historic third term in office.

This chapter will, firstly, address the issue of *engagement* for criminal and social justice. It will draw on a range of recent community-based research projects undertaken in the West Midlands region and beyond,[2] and analyse the practices and the

---

[2]The original research which is referred to and discussed here represents a number of applied social research and evaluation projects undertaken over the last four years by staff from the Policy Research Institute (formerly the 'Regional Research Institute'), at the University of Wolverhampton. Research reports released in the public domain are available at: http://www.wlv.ac.uk/pri

consequences of what passes for 'consultation' at local levels. As we will see, these practices may range from tick-box tokenism to innovative and empowering work. At the same time, it is important to recognise that the political discourse of consultation and engagement itself conceals complex processes of 'governance'. The analysis will therefore also look at the ways in which the managerial imperative to consult (and be seen to consult) itself constitutes an important aspect of govenmentality.

Secondly, the chapter will at the same time be examining the vexed issue of policy *impact*, seeking to explore some of the 'on the ground' outcomes of post-1997 criminal justice and social policies, particularly for vulnerable and socially excluded groups. Within the context of a vast array of local initiatives, policy impact is very difficult to assess, although clearly the outcomes of criminal justice and social policies are often diverse, contradictory and unintended. In attempting to shed light on some of the problems and paradoxes of policies 'on the ground' the chapter will try to test whether or not the imaginary duck of the title is in fact drowning, and the extent to which pond life (particularly in the muddier waters) has experienced the breath of change or remains stagnant.

1. Responsibilisation, Inclusion and Consultation

As we have seen in Chapters 3 and 4, transformations within (and the 'hollowing out' of) the modern state have given rise to new forms of governance that are complex, multi-layered and grounded in partnership and cross sector working (Newman et al., 2004). As a result, public, private, voluntary and community sector agencies, and actors are all charged with engaging with communities through multi-agency partnership working and through the requirement to consult with service users and communities. Multi-agency working and consultation can be seen as tools and channels for governance, but can also be regarded as an extension of wider social *responsibilisation strategies*. It is through the activities and relations of responsibilisation that the linkages between the modernisation, democratisation and communitarian projects are forged.

According to Garland (2001) responsibilisation strategies involve the devolution of certain social controls to communities which are then called upon to take an active role in resolving the problems in their own midst. Local problems, most notably of crime and social (dis)order, are thus constituted as a problem of and for individuals and communities, who are then responsible for their solution: for instance, anti-social behaviour then becomes a problem not just (or even principally) for politicians or the police, but for individuals themselves, for parents, communities and 'community leaders', teachers and so on.

But these communities, and the individuals who comprise them, have to be seen to act responsibly and dutifully in order to be eligible for fully *social inclusion*. Yet those behaviours which characterise social inclusion are defined in restricted and very specific ways (as we will see in Chapter 6). For instance, when governments set out definitions of what constitutes unacceptable or anti-social behaviour, it effectively defines out the 'others' who are outwith the limits of acceptability and they remain by definition socially excluded (Colley and Hodgkinson, 2001; Young and Matthews, 2003). It is through these discursive practices – and the professional and managerial practices that accompany them – that the consequences of 'responsibilisation' are made real for those who do *not* engage in, for example, education, paid work, training or effective parenting. Not only are they 'blamed' for their own situation, but:

> Deep seated structural inequalities are rendered invisible, as social exclusion is addressed through a strongly individualistic strategy based on personal agency. (Colley and Hodgkinson, 2001)

Community consultation is an important component of the responsibilisation project: as a tool of governance, consultation processes put the obligation on communities themselves to become engaged and 'have their say'. If they 'fail' to do so, they can hardly complain. In these respects consultation is, at the same time, a managerial practice, a tool of governance and a means of obtaining policy legitimation. The government acknowledges that 'by enabling communities to help shape decisions on policies and services, we will support civil renewal and strengthen the legitimacy of government' (ODPM, 2005b:7). After eight years in power it remains vital for the success and legitimacy of New Labour's modernisation and democratisation projects that new, flexible and appropriate approaches to consultation are developed and effectively used.

2. Community Consultation – In Theory and Practice

According to the Audit Commission (1999), consultation is 'a process of dialogue that leads to a decision'. This implies an ongoing process in which different parties listen to and take account of each other's views. At the same time, consultation is related closely to decision-making. Overall, the literature on community consultation falls broadly into two types: firstly, 'how to do' guidance and manuals and, secondly, more reflective work, which addresses pitfalls and problems with the process in addition to raising issues around the aims, purposes and outcomes of the process itself. There is no shortage of official advice on 'how to do' public or community consultation; most government departments offer an array of guidance notes, 'toolkits', exemplars of best practice and lists of the essential 'dos and don'ts' (for instance: the Cabinet Office, ODPM, DOH, Home Office and Audit Commission all produce such guidance). Before examining consultation in practice, it is useful to look at the second type of literature, which examines the contexts in which consultation can take place and, in particular, at how the scope and parameters of the exercise are defined by those obliged to do the consulting.

Scope and parameters

More than a decade ago the Joseph Rowntree Foundation (JRF) published *The Guide to Effective Participation* (1994). This was more than a 'how to do' piece and within it

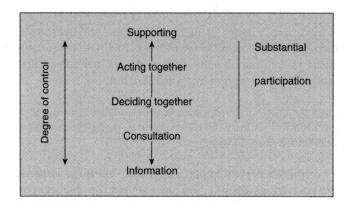

Figure 5.1   Levels of Participation
(*Source*: JRF, 1994 Reproduced with kind permission of the JRF.)

a 'five-rung ladder' of participation was proposed to reflect the differing stances an organisation promoting participation may take. This framework (indicated in Figure 5.1) remains useful as it acts as a litmus test for the aims, scope and the degree of control exerted over any consultation exercise, as indicated in more detail in the level descriptors which follow.

- **Level 1 – Information**: consultation at this level involves merely telling people what is planned
- **Level 2 – Consultation**: offering some options, li stening to feedback, but not allowing new ideas
- **Level 3 – Deciding together**: encouraging additional options and ideas, and providing opportunities for joint decision-making
- **Level 4 – Acting together**: not only do different interests decide together on what is best, they form a partnership to carry it out
- **Level 5 – Supporting independent community interests**: local groups or organisations are offered funds, advice or other support to develop their own agendas within guidelines.

Despite the current political rhetoric of democratisation, social capital, social inclusion and empowerment, my view is that government shrinks from the implications – in terms of funding and devolution of control – of community participation at 'Level 5'. (Outside of the housing sector, and the devolution of control to certain tenants, there are few examples.) Rather, my own research has found that agencies often decide upon the scope and limits of their policy options and *reverse engineer the consultation processes* to suit. In other words, their use of relatively tokenistic approaches to consultation reflects not only managerial imperatives (consultation *has to* take place), but also the taking of strategic decisions on what *can* and what *cannot* be done in terms of policy outcomes. This would not be so bad if local policy actors debated or discussed (or even articulated) the parameters they operated within with the communities they serve, but for the most part they do not. The tactical use of market research-type consultation frequently masks a patronising and complacent attitude to service users whom, it is believed, 'cannot be bothered to' respond to (often 'paper-based') surveys and so are not regarded as eligible to take their place as sovereign consumers in shaping the services they should receive.

Active citizens who participate in (for example) LA Citizens' Panels or Citizens' Juries and those who respond to traditional paper/text based consultations and surveys are relatively *easy to reach*. They may also be older, better off and 'articulate complainers'. There is, however, a pressing need to focus efforts on positive attempts to identify and engage those individuals and groups who are *not* currently or usually participating in consultation. Techniques for so doing vary depending upon the scope of the consultation exercise and the service provided, but may most usefully involve a range of *bottom-up* approaches which are most effectively undertaken by users and communities themselves. These may involve: using community-based networks to gain initial access; thereafter snowballing contacts within communities; using 'face to face' contacts; attending drop-ins and informal events; conducting focus groups and interviews in community-based or home settings; and training and capacity building, which are essential for such participation. (Such activities may be undertaken *in addition* to any paper-based consultations that are regarded as appropriate for users, carers and advocates.) Crucially, all of this should involve the active engagement of members of the community in shaping and conducting policy research; not merely as passive research subjects (Commission on Poverty, Participation and Power, 2000: Beresford, 2001; Bennett and Roberts, 2004; Butt and O'Neill, 2004; Lister, 2004; Hanley, 2005). As part of a longer-term project, The Commission on Poverty, Participation and Power (2000) looked particularly at the role and voice of people in poverty in shaping social policies and quite rightly asserted that participation in the policy process by people in poverty 'is a basic human right'. Moreover they argued that such participation would: improve decision-making; empower individuals and communities; and promote healthier democracy. The Commission found that 'phoney' consultation was all too common and disillusioning, messages were not being heard or 'getting through' to action, and that professional attitudes undermined the process.

It is also vital to recognise that users do want to (and they deserve to) receive something from their participation in the consultation and policy process: put simply, having given of their time and energy, consultees are entitled to receive not only respect as research partners, but at the very least adequate feedback (in a suitable form) on:

• The findings and results of the consultation exercise
• The action that was taken as a result
• If the action they recommended was not taken, the reasons why not.

In this way, *closing the feedback loop* is essential to assure the ethical conduct, validity and sustainability of any consultation process. A further problem for those involved with consultation is that past failures to ensure appropriate feedback and action has often led both to deep frustration and to disengagement from future exercises. For instance, JRF sponsored research (Butt and O'Neill, 2004) with older people from black and minority ethnic communities revealed that they felt that: they had been 'researched to death' for the past 15 years, and yet their views had not been acted upon; there was little acknowledgement of the positive aspects on their lives and culture; and they were seen as 'problems' rather than as possessing strengths to be valued. As a result, black and minority ethnic older people did not want *more* research or consultation, but **action and change** in response to issues that were already well documented. Black and minority ethnic groups are, in general, often termed 'hard to reach' and yet such findings indicate that when they are reached, and their voices heard in consultation and research, policy-makers still fail to listen to or to understand them.

Consultation, 'hard to reach groups' and governance

One of the key challenges facing those seeking to consult users on policy issues is how to access the views of those who are not proportionally, currently or usually engaged in consultation processes.

This broad challenge is, in turn, filtered into the more specific and contentious problem of accessing what are often termed **hard to reach groups**. This loose and ambiguous term is both misleading and counter-productive when used in a pejorative way. For example, the research brief for one study of anxiety about crime in a rural (and fairly prosperous) area of south England explicitly aimed to explore 'fear of crime amongst hard to reach groups'. The definition of this term by the local authority commissioning the work included (for example) travellers and the gay community. However, in discussion with people within these communities, their response to our research team was a very firm **'Who says we are hard to reach?'** This kind of disjunction between official and users'/subject's views of this term is echoed in other research, most notably in the field of policing.

The police, like other service providers, are required to consult with users in formulating, implementing and evaluating their policies. But there are significant concerns over the representativeness of those individuals and groups who *are* regularly consulted by them. For instance, where black and minority ethnic groups are concerned, those consulted are often older, male and established 'community leaders' and may enjoy good relations with the police, whereas younger and disadvantaged members of the community may be more hostile. From this critical perspective, consultation with **the usual suspects** is tokenistic and unrepresentative in terms of the community as a whole. Conversely, some police officers feel that consultative meetings can often be hostile and critical of the police – features that do not support the claims about passivity of consultees or 'capture' of the consultation process (Jones and Newburn, 2001). More generally, though, it is the view of many sceptics that the consultation equation can be summarised as 'Usual methods + usual suspects = old answers' (Commission on Poverty, Participation and Power, 2000).

Moving beyond the usual suspects, how is 'hard to reach' officially defined? Early guidance for Community Safety Partnerships established under the Crime and Disorder Act (1998) offered a comprehensive list of 'hard to reach groups' which included:

> young men, the homeless, drug users, the gay community, members of minority ethnic communities, children, those who suffer domestic abuse, and the elderly. (ibid)

Taken together, this list included a very significant proportion of the population of England and Wales! Even leaving aside the deep-rooted problem of treating such groups in a crassly homogeneous way, what is implicit in such guidance is that, despite their diversities, such groups are lumped together in sharing their shared 'hard to reach' label because they have something in common – *they* are seen (for different reasons) to have problems relating to the police. Many would contend it is the other way around – that the police have problems engaging with many of the communities and populations they serve.

The term 'hard to reach' is both stigmatising and falsely assumes homogeneity among the individuals within the groups so labelled. In an effort to come to terms with some of these difficulties, more recent Home Office research (Home Office, 2003a, 2003b) on consultation by Police Authorities (PAs) uses the term **hard to hear**. This may be a slight improvement, but we should be asking why it is that policy-makers and deliverers are unable to hear *some* voices while they are acutely attuned to those of *others* (most notably the tabloid press – see Tonry, 2004).

Nonetheless, usage of the notion of 'hard to reach' persists, with differing definitions emerging from a range of other policy areas, for example, the *On Track* programme which was established in 2000 to provide multiple interventions for 'at risk' children aged 4–12 years and their families through 24 local *On Track* partnerships. Based on the perspectives of practitioners within these partnerships, Doherty et al. produced a typology of 'the hard to reach' as follows:

- **Minority groups** – the marginalised, disadvantaged and socially excluded (including minority ethnic groups, travellers and asylum seekers)
- **Slipping through the net** – the invisible or those unable to articulate their needs (including those with mental health problems, people who fall just outside the remit of a service provider)
- **The service resistant** – those unwilling to engage with service providers, the suspicious, the over targeted or disaffected (including those 'known' to agencies such as social services and those hostile to providers, possibly due to alcohol or drug use).

(*Source*: Doherty et al., 2004)

These categories of 'the hard to reach' are not only overlapping, but also problematic because they are defined by agency practitioners in terms of their own roles and remits – that is, they are determined from the top down. Once again, *the problem* of effective consultation becomes constituted as emanating from *individuals* who are marginalised, invisible or hostile, or a mixture of all three. But professionals' perceptions and concerns about the 'barriers' to effective consultation noted in this study serve to reveal an alternative picture with professional concerns expressed around: agencies' genuine commitment to consult and the skills and capacities available to do so; the rejection of plans to consult with hard to reach groups because the effort required would divert resources from elsewhere; and the dangers of raising service users' expectations (which also features prominently). Yet these issues do not derive from the difficulties of consulting 'problem' individuals or groups, but from the concerns and constraints of the agencies who are meant to provide services for them. Here consultation is revealed as a component and a tool of governance: the role of such agencies in multi-agency partnerships can be recast as attempting to 're-socialise' (Hill and Wright, 2003) and manage difficult groups (and their expectations), rather than including and empowering them through consultation and participation in the policy process.

The aims of consultation

As we have seen, the context and 'level' at which community consultation is pitched serves to delimit the scope and parameters of the exercise itself. In addition, agencies may have a range of different *aims* in mind when designing and conducting community consultation and so we need to ask 'What is consultation for?' To return to the example of policing, there are important concerns about the differing *purposes and expectations* of the consultation process on the part of the police and of the communities they serve: the gap in their relative perceptions of the 'Aims and Objectives of the Service' are summarised in Figure 5.2 below. The vision of consultation which is implicit in the *police perspective* is essentially a reactive one, which is located within the terms and operational priorities set by the police themselves. By contrast, the *community perspective* seeks a proactive role for consultation, which derives from an active engagement with an agenda not of the police's making: for example, encouraging awareness of culture and diversity and encouraging police

Police perspective	Community perspective
• To identify local issues and problems • To inform the delivery of policing services and the development of policing methods • To inform communities of forthcoming operations • To inform and educate the public about policing • To promote support for and co-operation with the police	• To influence local policing policy and/or style • Encourage action on specific problems • To elicit police recognition of community dynamics and cultural differences • Accountability and conflict resolution • To obtain access to police resources and facilities

Figure 5.2   The Aims and Objectives of Consultation – Policing
(*Source*: Jones and Newburn, 2001)

action on community-defined problems. Consultation is thus rendered a problematic and contested process which may display both tokenism and instrumentalism on the part of the police. Within this contested framework, the 'tick-box' approach to police consultation (purely for managerial accountability) and the 'cascade down' approach (for operational accountability, that is 'We will tell you what we are going to do') are both rendered redundant exercises. Instead, a more flexible response and two-way dialogue is essential if genuine consultation is to take place, and this consultation would need to be part of an on-going *process* and not a one-off *event*.

It is important, however, to recognise there are very welcome indications that some police forces are increasingly aware of the pitfalls of current approaches to consultation. For example, the West Midlands Police, in its *Best Value Review of Public Consultations and Expectations* (2004), was candid about its previous performance in stating that: although a wide range of activities were undertaken, much consultation was unco-ordinated and inefficient; there was duplication of effort between the force and the PA; and there was no corporate strategy outlining the aims of and principles for undertaking consultation activities which were 'appropriate, informed, balanced, relevant, transparent and honest and result in informed reflection of all views' (West Midlands Police, 2004:3). The performance review concluded that the force's consultation processes did not currently represent 'best value' and exposed the force to many risks, including wasting resources in duplicated efforts and failing to meet community expectations. These problems are common to other forces and many other agencies too, and emanate in part from a situation of consultation overload at local level.

Consultation overload

As we have seen, the New Labour government's early emphasis on 'joined-up' policies required an equally 'joined-up' approach to engaging with users and communities in shaping policy and turning policy into effective practice. But the sheer number and scope of centrally driven initiatives has proved confusing in practice locally. For example, initiatives including the latter stages of the Single Regeneration Budget (SRB), New Deal for Communities (NDCs), Neighbourhood Renewal, Education Action Zones (EAZs), Health Action Zones (HAZs), Drug Action Teams (DATs), Private Finance Initiatives (PFI), the genesis of Primary Care Trusts (PCTs) to deliver and manage health care, Crime and Disorder Reduction Programmes (CDRPs), Communities that Care (CTCs), Community Fund projects, Surestart programmes, the Children's Fund and so on, have all meant that 'at local level, the array of nationally driven programmes is bewildering' (JRF, 2000).

On the ground, the cumulative effects of consultation *overload* arising from this vast array of programmes, have swamped LAs and other statutory bodies engaged in consultation and also their service users. Members of black and minority ethnic communities, in particular, express *consultation fatigue* and yet (as we have seen) dismay that the messages they have relayed in a series of consultations have not been listened to or responded to. In addition to the problems of overload, the timescales set by central government for obtaining, analysing and responding to community and service user consultation are often impossibly tight. This, coupled with the exponential growth of government demands for consultation across the range of policy areas already cited, meant that there was (and still is), insufficient 'time out' for LAs and partner agencies to think strategically about how best to manage and maximise the potential of the process. This means consultation may become an end in itself to be 'ticked off' the organisation's 'to do' list in order to meet government targets. Consultation and engagement with communities thus becomes a tool of governance, a token device to justify local policies that are principally determined centrally. At the same time, there is a lack of government recognition that answers to multi-layered (often structural) problems cannot be provided at local level alone, and certainly not overnight.

Local solutions to local problems?

'Local solutions to local problems' and partnership working have been key policy mantras underpinning the consultation process under New Labour but, eight years on, they are still proving elusive to achieve on the ground. Firstly, although initially envisaged and sold in terms of *equal partnership*, many of the important multi-agency forums designed to identify priorities, discuss and deliver policy at local level are very far from equal in practice. Key partners who are mandated to provide local solutions frequently vie with one another for power and influence. For example, community safety research has consistently demonstrated the dominance of the police and local authority community safety 'experts' over both the voluntary and community sector and local voices when it comes to strategy and priority setting (Hughes, 2004b). At the same time, the role of local elected members – from Parish to local Borough Councillors – may also prove influential in gate-keeping what issues will, and will not, be deemed a 'local problem' for which a solution is required.[3] For many, this raises additional concerns around the 'representativeness', leadership skills and calibre of elected members who have key roles in partnership working (McManus, 2004).

Secondly, recent research also highlights that what local partnerships need most to work more effectively is *time and money* – notably to resource networking, training and support. As one local government officer commented, nobody complained about a lack of information, just 'the time to access it and the available systems to make this process as straightforward as possible' (MacDonald, 2003:9). But while local groups may be formally included in discussions over local issues, where regeneration is concerned, determining priorities and resource allocation lie outside the

---

[3]For example, one recent study quoted a councillor – speaking on behalf of 'the public' – stating that the public was not worried about domestic violence (Follett, 2004).

immediate regeneration areas themselves (Perrons and Sykers, 2003). Community consultation and engagement clearly involves listening and voicing, but giving *real* voice 'means making claims on others' (Forester, 1998, quoted in Perrons and Sykes, 2003:266). However, these claims cannot be effectively made or met within the rules of governance and finance which are pre-determined by central government. Nevertheless, the importance of the local is continually stressed by New Labour as, for instance, in a speech to the DEMOS foundation entitled *Localism: the need for a new settlement*. In this speech Alan Milburn re-iterated that 'local problems require local solutions' and focused on the central role of 'local communities' in regeneration. It is also significant that here the criminal and the social are explicitly linked, because:

> it is at this level that crime and grime issues – anti-social behaviour and street cleaning – are probably best dealt with. (Milburn, 2004)

While crime reduction and community safety policy remains a cornerstone of both anti-exclusion and anti-crime policies, the political commitment to localism is tightly limited in practice, not least because the resources to deliver such solutions are not adequately provided by central government. Nonetheless the discourse of a 'new localism' stubbornly persists as was evident in yet another action plan – *Together we can* – launched in June 2005. It reinvented the concept of joined-up government, involving 12 government departments in, once again, setting out government commitment to 'communities and public bodies working together to set and achieve common goals' (Home Office Press Release, 28 June 2005). Despite the rhetoric of the launch on 'passing power to local people, and empowering communities to tackle problems together', there is little change or substance here. Moreover, the ODPM acknowledged there had, to date, been

> little assessment of the extent to which participation and consultation exercises actually influences [sic] decision-making processes. (2005a)

Under such circumstances it is not surprising that there is scepticism about seeking 'local solutions to local problems' to be solved, if the genesis of those problems, or the funding of their solution, lies beyond the scope of the locality itself and if consultation itself is not seen to be effecting change. Despite numerous 'case studies' presented in this recent ODPM report, few (with the exception of Tenant Management Organisations) would pass muster as genuinely engaging with communities in an empowering and participatory way.

Happily, there are some more positive examples, where working relationships within partnerships geared to social inclusion are productive and characterised by mutual respect, as for example, in the case of key initiatives in rural Northern Ireland which have successfully bridged barriers of religion, identity and politics (Williamson et al., 2004). It is from such genuine examples of successful and innovative partnership working, participation and empowerment that lessons may usefully be learned.

3. From Consultation to Empowerment?

There is a widespread acknowledgment among those involved in social policy (whether academics, practitioners or policy-makers) that consultation is a crucial yet deeply problematic process. As we have seen, some of the main challenges facing any consultation or feedback mechanism include: reaching and hearing a diverse range of service users and/or client groups; understanding and responding appropriately to the needs and views they express in consultation; building the outcomes of con-sultation into collaborative planning and service delivery within complex (and sometimes competitive) partnership-based agendas; and feeding back these out-comes to those who participated in the consultation process.

Despite these challenges there is a long-held optimistic view that holds that an 'old' model of consultation – often tokenistic, unrepresentative and not engaging – is being replaced with a 'new' one. This progressive perspective was exemplified not only in the ODPM report on 'New Localism' discussed above, but by others including the Joint Review Team (JRT) which evaluates the performance of all councils with social services responsibilities. In their Annual Report for 2000/1 the JRT summarised problems around working with users and carers in the up-beat terms of *'familiar problems, new solutions'* (Joint Review Team, 2001). 'Old' solutions were seen to be limited to formal consultation at (policy) planning stages and nominal representation on planning groups. But the 'new solutions' were identified in terms of:

- User-led services
- Direct payments
- Involvement in Best Value
- Involvement in commissioning decisions.

Under New Labour **Best Value** replaced CCT (compulsory competitive tendering) as the key means of ensuring quality and value for money in public services. Its key ingredients are *the four 'C's*: challenge, compare, consult and compete, with 'consulting' vital to agencies in accessing user needs and their views on local policy and service delivery. In terms of the JRT vision of the 'policy wheel' (reproduced in Figure 5.3 opposite) the 'new solutions', which included Best Value, would signal a change of gear from (often tokenistic) consultation, through the phase of partici-pation (in monitoring and developing services), towards empowerment, which enables users and carers to set priorities and manage services.

Based on research I have conducted in a range of fields[4] there are several problems with this optimistic vision. Firstly, it assumes that all service users and carers (across ages, genders, ethnic groups, abilities and sexualities) will have equal motivation and

---

[4]For example: on the delivery of health and social care services to older people; Surestart; Community Safety; Crime and Disorder Reduction Partnerships; Domestic Violence prevention; Substance Misuse; and Homelessness (see http://www.wlv.ac.uk/pri).

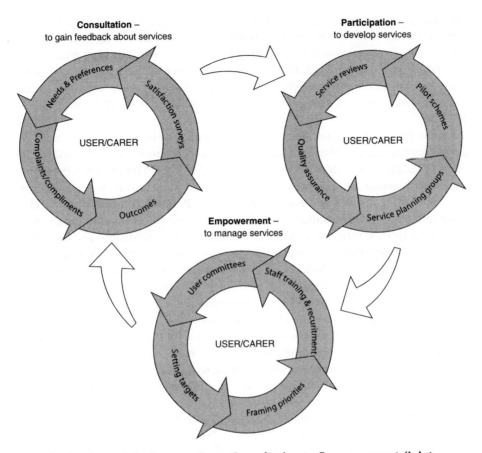

Figure 5.3   Aims of the Process: From Consultation to Empowerment (Joint Review Team, 2001)

capacity to contribute to and participate in the development and management of the services they do, or potentially should, receive (for a discussion of 'the public' in public participation see Barnes et al., 2003). Secondly, it assumes that service providers will have the resources – financial and human – to deliver the services and priorities which these diverse users have determined.

The first problem would in part be addressed by capacity building and the development of networks and social capital which may equip and empower individuals in diverse communities to become engaged in the policy process. However, in relation to social *capital*, Roche (2004a) observed that although a great deal of *political* capital has been invested in the concept, there is little evidence that **social capital** has brought anything new to the policy process. Secondly, as I have argued elsewhere (Cook, 2002), engaging communities in the policy process is capital and labour intensive and demands a long-term commitment. But the desire for **quick wins** is a strong driver of consultation policy, practice and outcomes and so it is rare that LAs and other partners are willing or able to commit to critical, reflective and participatory research and evaluation. The constraints of costs and the need to demonstrate quick wins (and meet government targets) therefore tends to win out over genuine and long-term community engagement.[5] As one SRB scheme officer commented in the context of a discussion of research 'benchmarking' community participation, 'it pays dividends over time – it's a long-term investment, not a quick fix' (Wilson and Wilde, 2003:19).

A short digression here on agency discourse: firstly, the managerial lexis, including the use of terms such as 'benchmarking', may seem incongruous when discussing community participation, as does the usage of the notion of 'road testing' initiatives (ibid). But the terminology and practices of managerialism and the private sector are increasingly permeating research and evaluation discourse. Research consultancy firms, charitable trusts and other organisations with a background in community development are playing an increasing role in local and national policy evaluations and some have an important contribution to make (for instance, Groundwork[6]). Nonetheless, it is important to recognise the influence of the (business, organisational and managerial) conceptual frameworks that often underpin their methods, analyses and recommendations of studies in the field of community consultation.

Secondly, the costs of funding effective consultation is a crucial issue: across the policy spectrum there are serious doubts about the extent to which the community engagement, and the deeper longer-term capacity building which is vital to its success, are being *adequately recognised and resourced*. As the JRF noted five years ago when commenting on the National Strategy for Neighbourhood Renewal:

> [it] will place a heavy emphasis on involving communities in the planning, implementation and management process. But this won't happen unless it is properly resourced. It needs: support from central government down to individuals community development workers; co-ordinated action at national regional and local level; new, inclusive and holistic forms of local management; significant shifts in institutional cultures; and targeted funding. (Joseph Rowntree Foundation, 2000)

But, five years on, these levels of support have often proved elusive or absent and the processes and outcomes of participation and empowerment remain bounded by fiscal and political constraints. Genuine and sustainable consultation is costly, and acting responsively to the issues and needs it identifies is even more so: even if client's views and needs are voiced and heard; it is quite another thing to develop and fund effective policy responses. Consequently, for example in the case of older people:

---

[5]There are welcome exceptions to this tendency: for example, Wolverhampton Crime and Disorder Reduction Partnership who have funded a three year longitudinal evaluation of their strategy, incorporating elements of participatory appraisal within one identified neighbourhood.

[6]See Groundwork website: http://www.groundwork.org.uk

> The voice of older people may ultimately be a demanding one. The challenge is whether the government and local authorities can meet this demand. (Fenge, 2001)

Finally, we should not forget the *costs of consultation for voluntary and community sector groups* who are increasingly being called upon to deliver more community-based services which are not provided by statutory bodies (as, for instance, in the case of refuge and outreach support for victims of domestic violence, where the role of the voluntary and community sector is vital – see Cook, 2003; Robinson, 2003). But to survive (and this usually means securing 'soft' funding, year on year) such groups must demonstrate partnership working and influence which, in turn, places additional stress upon them. As Marilyn Taylor noted:

> A key player in the local voluntary (non-profit) sector told us she was participating in 48 partnership bodies, while a respondent in another case study site counted 83 partnerships in the locality overall. (2003:135)

Similarly, in my own research experience, those involved in supporting domestic violence survivors have extremely heavy workloads and some have expressed the concern that the demands of 'attending meetings' threaten to pull them away from their core work in supporting women and families. Once again, the problem of inadequate resources lies beneath many of the fundamental problems faced by those attempting to work in communities, in partnership.

4. Participatory Approaches to Consultation and Engagement

> Researchers attended a 'community forum' in a community centre on the estate... Thirty-two people were seated around a table discussing crime prevention projects, yet all represented local service delivery agencies. Only two of the people in the room actually lived on the estate, and they were only present by virtue of their roles as part-time youth workers. (Squires and Measor, 2001:239)

This scene is typical in some ways and not in others: 32 people is an unusually high turnout for a community forum, but the 'rounding up of the usual suspects' is indeed typical of many of the activities that pass for consultation. The scene described here shows all too clearly that there is a real need for more genuine community engagement for criminal and social justice: one way of accomplishing this is through the use of participatory approaches to consultation and research. As Bennett and Roberts (2004) cogently argue, participatory research and practice does not so much consist of an identifiable set of methodologies as offer a very different 'interactive', as opposed to 'extractive', way of working. In this context research is seen as part of a more inclusive project where people are recognised as having *authority, control and influence* over the research process, its findings and the ways in which they may be developed in policy. There is vast expertise in such work, often emanating from international work in so-called 'developing countries' or the southern hemisphere (see overview in Bennett and Roberts, 2004). The challenge that all researchers now face is learning lessons 'from south to north' and incorporating innovative, interactive and participatory approaches into mainstream applied social research in the UK (RRI/CIDT, 2003). This poses several challenges, not least because of (in my experience) the demands and priorities of those commissioning research who:

1. Often want *quick and dirty* evaluations as opposed to investing both time and money in participatory research. Planning timescales allow too little time for community empowerment before decisions are reached.
2. Usually want *numbers:* while quantitative data may be generated by such work, it is usually not its primary focus. (At the same time, qualitative research and participatory approaches are both seen as subjective, 'less valid' and difficult to compare over place and time – Bennett and Roche, 2000.)
3. Are reluctant to devolve *control* over the research process to service users and/or communities.
4. Are unfamiliar with the research *tools and outputs* from participatory approaches, which may include spider diagrams, hand drawn street maps, photographs, video etc. UK policy-makers and deliverers are more used to dealing with formal reports and statistics (the written rather than the visual or oral).
5. There are, therefore, difficulties for many UK policy-makers in the *negotiation and translation* of participatory research into policy recommendations. This can only be addressed through training, and more joint working and exposure to alternative participatory methods and outputs.
6. It *costs* more to engage in participatory research and practices, not only because of longer research schedules but because the costs of people's participation needs to be recognised and adequately rewarded.
7. *Recognition* needs to be accorded to participants in other ways too, such as the formal accreditation or certification of research training or workshop attendance.

Despite the problems and reservations that research commissioners may have, the advantages of participatory approaches are many and varied: academics can climb down from their ivory towers and engage with people and communities, sharing and exchanging their differing knowledges; genuine empowerment and sustainable community engagement becomes a possibility; and research findings and the policy recommendations which flow from them will be more informed and stand a better chance of working. At the same time social justice can be enhanced in, and through, the relations and processes of participation itself.

What of the potential impact of participatory research and enquiry? Where the issue of poverty is concerned, Bennett and Roberts argue that:

> Participatory research on poverty cannot achieve social change on its own; but it can provide opportunities for people living in poverty to have an influence. (2004:ix)

The title of the report from which this quote is taken – *From Input to Influence* – aptly describes the shift which needs to take place in relation to the contribution of people in poverty to policy research and enquiry. It also signals the need for a change in the overall mindset of those funding (and those undertaking) much current research around poverty and social exclusion.

More broadly still, there is a pressing need for those engaged in policy evaluation and research to attend much more to *'the people pieces'* (Foster, 2002). If we are to avoid policy being driven by managerial imperatives and by government preoccupation with 'middle England' and the tabloids, it is crucial to voice and to value all the 'people' perspectives. Also vital is *genuine* localism, acknowledging and attending in research design and practice to the role of local actors and activists (often from the voluntary, community and charitable sectors) who are working 'on the ground'. As Gordon Hughes persuasively states:

> ... the debate on what might be meant by such notions of 'community' and lately the seemingly ever-present magic pill of 'social capital' is not just an academic exercise for ivory tower dwellers. Rather they are necessarily part of the everyday dilemmas – if not explicit conversations – for local activists and 'community builders' when they are sent out (or 'parachuted') into communities and neighbourhoods to foster partnership work and 'community capacity building'. (2004a:9)

It is clearly essential to engage with these issues together with those for whom they constitute everyday challenges. And so while academics may be fascinated with (and may build impressive careers upon) high level theorising, we should take care not to descend into 'an elitist theoreticism' (Carlen, 2002). If academics, in addition to, or working with, researchers, practitioners, local activists and campaigners genuinely seek to have an impact on social and criminal justice policies, they need to participate too (as we will see in the final chapter of this book in discussions on moving 'upstream' – Sinfield, 2004).

5. The Social Inclusion Agenda

Having addressed issues of community participation and engagement for criminal and social justice, what follows will look (albeit necessarily briefly) at the complex issue of policy impact for vulnerable and socially excluded groups and those living in the most deprived neighbourhoods. To set these policies in context it is useful to recall the context in which New Labour social inclusion policies were developed and the key driving role of the SEU. In its first report (*Bringing Britain Together: a National Strategy for Neighbourhood Renewal*) the SEU distanced itself from previous area-based programmes addressing deprivation and exclusion and committed itself to not making the mistakes of the past. The problems that it argued had beset previous area-based programmes were:

> Absence of effective national policies to deal with the structural causes of decline; a tendency to parachute solutions in from the outside, rather than

engaging local communities, and too much emphasis on physical renewal instead of better opportunities for local people. Above all, a joined up problem has never been addressed in a joined up way. (1998:9)

Eight years on, we can usefully ask to what extent policies geared to social inclusion have had positive effects in addressing the issues identified by the SEU – neighbourhood decline, engaging local communities, providing local opportunities and 'joining up' policy solutions in local contexts? Given the constraints of space, this question will be answered here by referring to some of the key elements of post-1997 social inclusion strategy which affect issues of criminal and social justice, namely: ICT; 'partnership'; young people, justice and inclusion; tackling crime and disorder; and the prevention of re-offending.

ICT and social inclusion?

As Chapters 3 and 4 have shown, an unshakeable belief in ICT as a policy end (in terms of education, work and opportunity) and a means (for participation, modernisation and enhanced service management and delivery) has characterised successive New Labour governments. Its ambitious *e-government* strategy aimed to bridge the digital divide between the information haves and have-nots. ICT thus constituted an important element of the social inclusion agenda, and since 1999 the government has invested £400 million in supporting ICT centres in over 6000 deprived inner city and rural locations in England. These *community informatics* initiatives have aimed to offer tools for individuals, socially excluded groups and communities to 'reconnect' them in social relationships (Loader, 2004). However, a recent review of research indicates that such initiatives have not yet made 'significant challenges' to the social inequalities associated with the adoption of ICT. At the same time, one crucial *e*-government target – that all citizens would have electronic access to government departments through home computers with Internet access, or through community access points by 2005 – has not been reached. In short, the digital divide remains. The relative failure of policies seeking to reconnect socially excluded groups and communities through ICT inevitably holds profound implications for participation and for social justice.

New Labour also envisaged that ICT could overcome critical time and space barriers to learning and enhance local opportunities through further education. But a recent report on the *Adult Learning @ Home* project indicated that *e*-learning was most often concerned with the technology itself, rather than as a means to learn something else and so, as the researchers observed, they had 'met pensioners who had learned to turn spreadsheets into pie charts then never used them' (ESRC Press Release, 30 September 2004). This, and other research, indicates that, in terms of contributing to social inclusion (whether through community informatics or lifelong leaning), the positive impact of ICT policy initiatives with socially excluded groups and communities remains limited.

Policy impact – 'partnership' revisited

In assessing the impact of policies geared to fostering social inclusion, *partnership and 'joined-up' working* was acknowledged by the SEU to be a key element. 'Partnership' is itself now central to contemporary political discourse – it is significant that the term was used in parliament 6197 times in 1999 compared with just 38 times a decade earlier (Jupp, 2000). Partnership is, however, more than just a way of working. It potentially offers additional benefits in terms of the cost and quality of public services. As Tom Ling summarises, partnership:

> focuses on the mechanisms used by two or more organisations to work together on a shared agenda while keeping their own identity and purpose. It offers the prospect of securing greater value for money through the co-ordination activities and promises better public services. (2000:625)

Despite the political currency and the promises of partnership, there are those who remain deeply pessimistic about the prospects it holds out for enhancing empowerment and social inclusion. For instance, Byrne argues that relations of power prevent individuals and communities genuinely engaging through partnership because their efforts are:

> that at best attempts to reconcile irreconcilables and at worst, which means usually in practice, offers the objects of policy, at the very most, some role in influencing the implementation of strategies which have already been decided on. This is incorporation, not partnership. (2001:256)

From this perspective, the results of social inclusion polices, as currently constituted, will be tokenistic at best.

As discussed earlier in this chapter, the proliferation of partnerships has led to considerable 'overload' for local agencies – overload in consultation requirements and overload in terms of the time and resources devoted (by statutory, voluntary and community sector agencies) to maintaining presence and influence within partnerships. Beyond these 'local' difficulties there are additional issues in joining up differing *levels* of partnership working. In addition to *thematic* anti-exclusion measures targeting vulnerable individuals and groups (wherever they live), New Labour developed a hybrid approach to exclusion which also incorporated *area-based* initiatives (notably Action Zones – for Employment, Health and Education). As we have seen, the SEU clearly wished to avoid the pitfalls of earlier area-based programmes; to what extent has it succeeded? Recent research has addressed the ways in which wider (thematic or people-based) initiatives and area-based (regeneration) schemes have been able to integrate and to offer a genuinely joined up approach to addressing social exclusion (McGregor et al., 2003). The authors found that those implementing area-based and other social inclusion interventions faced many barriers which prevented them from maximising the benefits of co-ordination and integration of services: these barriers are summarised in Figure 5.4.

The table summarises some of the key barriers to the more effective integration of area regeneration and welfare to work initiatives, based on the views of the staff involved.

	Area generation initiatives	Welfare to work programmes
1. No one told us to work together	✓	✓
2. Not sure out superiors want us to work together		✓
3. Detracts from meeting our targets		✓
4. Don't have the time or resources to integrate	✓	✓
5. We don't know how to work together:		
• limited knowledge of each other's programmes	✓	✓
• tack of skills in development work		✓
• limited skills in partnership working		✓
6. We don't see it as a priority	✓	✓
7. We don't know with whom to work		✓
8. They're different from us	✓	✓
9. They don't understand us	✓	✓
10. They don't like us		✓
11. We don't like there	✓	
12. We don't have any autonomy at a local level		✓
13. There is limited incentive to work jointly	✓	✓

Figure 5.4   Barriers to Integration

(*Source*: JRF 2003, Reproduced with kind permission of the JRF)

In summary, the research indicated that many programmes were 'top-down' and emanated from central government departments which were over-centralised, inflexible and not responsive to local needs. Different government departments were not themselves 'joined up', often having differing targets, priorities, administrative and monitoring systems. Proliferation and duplication meant some programmes were competing with others for local clients to meet their centrally defined targets. The problems associated with operational and spatial boundaries (discussed earlier) also hampered effective partnership and joint working, which was also in need of *incentivisation*, *integration* and much *development* to make anti-exclusion policies 'work'.

Young people, justice and inclusion

Some of the issues raised in relation to the integration of national and local levels of anti-exclusion interventions similarly apply to 'thematic' initiatives – for example, joined up working for youth inclusion and youth justice. The Chief Executive of a county council commenting on a YOT felt that while, from the perspective of the Home Office or YJB 'the patchwork quilt of distant operations' looks perfectly rational:

you also have to live in the real world of these institutions, be they schools, primary care groups, social services managers, and realise that they are actually having a set of agendas imposed on them from a whole range of 'silos' where this particular issue is actually a long way down the hierarchy... (Chief executive, quoted in Burnett and Appleton, 2004:45)

Crucially, these 'silos' may work on the basis of differing boundaries, remits and ICT systems, and institutions may have competing priorities and targets (Cook and Roberts, 2001: Cook and Vallely, 2003; Cook et al., 2004). These issues are also raised in Marian Fitzgerald's research on the experiences and patterns of street crime among young people in London (Fitzgerald et al., 2003). This study went on to argue that the governance and practices of multi-agency 'partnership' working may actually present *barriers* to tackling street crime by young people because of:

The different priorities of the potential partners and the imperative of each to meet individual targets which are not necessarily compatible with each other and which militate against achieving the co-ordination strategy which [is] needed. (2003:8)

Frustratingly, many of the answers to questions around effective youth justice interventions are already 'known', but they raise doubts about the privileging of individual (as opposed to social) models as the basis for policy responses. Authors of this research conducted for Youth Justice Board (YJB) in the year 2001/2 confirmed that interaction between social, economic, environmental and individual factors all affected patterns of offending among young people in London, notably in relation to street crime (Fitzgerald et al., 2003). The authors found that four recent developments had particularly influenced the extent and patterns of youth offending. These were, and are:

- *Technological advance* (as symbolised by the mobile phone)
- *Patterns of consumption* (with increasing and ever changing numbers of items seen as essential by young people, in large measure driven by fashion)
- *Social fragmentation* (seen especially in neighbourhoods where social ties are weak and in the increasing numbers of families experiencing various forms of disruption in relationships); and
- *Economic polarisation* (in contexts where the proximity of others heightens a sense of relative deprivation among those who have least).

(Source: Fitgerald et al., 2003:69)

It is therefore counter-productive to eschew technological, economic and social factors when addressing youth crime and promoting youth inclusion. The interplay between these wider dimensions of exclusion with individual and peer group factors, and the ways in which these are played out in deprived communities, are well described in the following extract:

The criminogenic factors in their environment add to the individual risks for young people in these [deprived] areas – not least because of the peer group norms they produce; and the problems may further be exacerbated in areas where social cohesion is weakest. In these areas the need for support from the statutory sector is therefore likely to be most acute, for example in terms of social services support, health care and educational opportunities. Yet it is here also that the relevant agencies may themselves be at their weakest, with high vacancy and turnover rates reflecting the stress of work in these types of area and adding in turn to the stresses of staff in post. All of this may have a knock on effect to lowering the quality of services available to young people in areas where disproportionate numbers are in need of them. (Fitzgerald et al., 2003:5)

Positioning anti-exclusion interventions in thematic and area-based 'silos' will fail to address the multi-faceted and the economic factors which contribute to youth exclusion (see also Webster et al., 2004). Significantly, the period of Marian Fitzgerald's YJB-sponsored study overlapped with the launch of the national Street Crime Initiative (SCI) in 2002 which sought to address many of the same issues: indeed the authors ended their report with the fervent hope that the SCI would sustain and underpin those collaborative strategies essential to address youth crime (Fitzgerald et al., 2003:84).

The Street Crime Initiative (SCI)

The SCI itself offers a revealing insight into the politics of crime control and the governance of crime, which is worthy of lengthier discussion than is possible here. The phenomenon of 'street crime' brings together political and popular concerns around crime and disorder which predominantly focus on young people as the root of the problem, and sees multi-agency partnership working as the focus for solutions. In the spring of 2002, Tony Blair declared that street crime was 'a national emergency' and went on to invest significant time and resources working at high and cross-departmental levels with the aim of tackling the problem in just six months.

Unsurprisingly, six months later the SCI Joint Inspection Report enabled the government to claim that the problem was indeed 'under control' at the end of September 2002, with a 25% reduction in street robbery and a 16% reduction in 'snatch thefts' as a result of the SCI. However, the joint inspectors assessment, taken in its entirety, is rather more circumspect. Reflecting on the initiative in its report – *Streets Ahead* – they noted that although it had 're-invigorated' some dormant partnerships, it had not achieved its full potential, 'in particular as a partnership initiative' (Home Office, 2003g:10). Moreover:

the quality of communication, both within and between organisations, was often poor. Clear rationale rarely reached the practitioner levels whilst progress reports fed back up through the command chain put an over-optimistic slant on achievements, in some areas. (ibid:11)

They did find examples of good practice – 'in isolated pockets' – but highlighted the persistence of problems including flagging and tracking certain (SC) cases, lack of shared ownership and accountability of partners, failure to learn lessons from relevant previous initiatives (notably the Persistent Young Offenders scheme) and a feeling, even among the police, that street crime was not a high priority or a suitable vehicle for partners to 'own'. The SCI can be seen as a clear example of knee-jerk politics, and although it clearly had enormous *political* impact, its ability to shape policy and multi-agency practice 'on the ground' appears to have been very limited.

Social inclusion and ex-prisoners

The final example of policies geared to social inclusion is ex-prisoners. Tony Blair defined this as a priority area for the SEU in New Labour's second term and in July 2002 the SEU published its weighty final report *Reducing Reoffending by Ex-prisoners*. It included a comprehensive analysis of the profile and multiple needs of people released from prison together with 60 action points designed to address them and, in so doing, reduce reoffending. Figure 5.5 below, based on the SEU report, together with additional Prison Reform Trust data, summarises some of the main issues raised by comparing the social characteristics of ex-prisoners with those of the general population. It is worth bearing in mind that these analyses now apply to a dramatically increased prison population, which currently stands at 76,297. This figure marks an increase of 1400 on the previous year and, overall, a 20% increase since 1997 (*Prison Population and Accommodation Briefing*, 8 July 2005; Home Office, 1998). The latest Home Office projections envisage the 'high' scenario of a potential prison population of 91,500 in 2010 (Home Office, 2005c)

As Figure 5.5 demonstrates, the SEU report confirmed that 'many prisoners have experienced a lifetime of social exclusion'. Moreover the report argued that: these experiences of exclusion have a profound effect on the risk of reoffending; despite high levels of need they have been denied access to services to meet these needs; and a prison sentence might make matters even worse. Based on a comprehensive analysis of social and criminological research on patterns of reoffending the report concluded that nine key 'risk' factors were at work:

1. Education
2. Employment
3. Drug and alcohol misuse
4. Mental and physical health
5. Attitudes and self-control
6. Institionalisation and life-skills
7. Housing
8. Financial support and debt
9. Family networks.

(*Source*: SEU, 2002:2)

It went on to suggest ways of addressing these risks through a wide-ranging and long-term strategy for rehabilitation and the reduction of reoffending. Despite the SEUs

Characteristic	General population*	Prison population*	Additional information**
Ran away from home as a child	11%	47% male sentenced prisoners, 50% of female sentenced prisoners	
Taken into care as a child	2%	27%	Over half of prisoners aged 5–17 years old have been in local authority care
Regularly truanted from school	3%	30%	
Excluded from school	2%	49% male, 33% of female sentenced prisoners	Almost three quarters of young people in prison (18–20 year olds) had been excluded from school
No qualifications	15%	52% of male, 71% female prisoners	Half of all prisoners do not have the skills for 96% of jobs
Numeracy at or below Level 1 (level expected of an 11 year old)	23%	65%	
Reading ability at or below Level 1	21–23%	48%	Only 1 in 5 prisoners can complete a job application form
Unemployed (before imprisonment)	5%	67%	Remand prisoners are even more likely to be unemployed before entering custody
Homeless	0.9%	32%	Around 1 in 20 prisoners was sleeping rough before they went to prison 30% of all prisoners (and 49% of prisoners with mental health problems) have no fixed address on leaving prison
Suffer from two or more mental disorders	5% of men and 2% of women	72% of male, 70% of female sentenced prisoners	
Psychotic disorder	0.5% of men and 0.6% of women	7% of male, 14% of female sentenced prisoners	

Figure 5.5 (Continued)

Characteristic	General population*	Prison population*	Additional information**
Drug use in the previous year	13% of men and 8% of women	66% of male, 55% of female sentenced prisoners	In 2004 there were 95 suicides in prisons in England and Wales. Of these, nearly two-thirds had a history of drug misuse. 55% of prisoners reported their offending as drug related
Hazardous drinking	38% of men and 15% of women	63% of male, 39% of female sentenced prisoners	The Prison Services' Alcohol Strategy for Prisoners (2004) has not been supported by any additional resources

Figure 5.5 Social Characteristics of Prisoners
(*Sources*: *SEU, 2002; **Prison Reform Trust, 2005)

strategy, a 60 point action plan, and the admission that a more effective cross-government strategy was 'urgently' needed, two years on very little action had been taken as the recommendations were gradually 'killed off' (*Guardian*, 22 June 2005). One of the SEU report authors – Julian Corner – resigned, dismayed at the 'failure of strategy and joined up working' that this represented (Corner, 2004). Key recommendations in the following areas were not implemented: housing entitlement for prisoners (to be deemed a vulnerable person); access to housing benefit; faster benefit payments; increases in the prisoner discharge grant; access to GPs on release; funds for detoxification and treatment programmes in prisons; Sure Start targeting prisoners' children; and social services to target reuniting prisoners' families. However, a recommendation on employment advice in prison has been acted on, with Jobcentre Plus services now available in prisons, signalling the government's stress on paid work. For Corner, the policy response to this plank of the government's social inclusion strategy represents 'a catalogue of indifference' which begs the question 'Are prisoners really so unpopular and stigmatised that we have to resist acting humanely and rationally on their behalf?' Sadly the answer appears to be 'yes' (Corner, 2004).

To summarise this section on the impact of social inclusion policies on vulnerable groups and those living in deprived communities, it is worth returning to the quote from the first SEU Report which opened this section. The SEU had seen the errors of its predecessors in the following terms:

> Absence of effective national policies to deal with the structural causes of decline; a tendency to parachute solutions in from the outside, rather than engaging local communities, and too much emphasis on physical renewal instead of better opportunities for local people. Above all, a joined up problem has never been addressed in a joined up way. (1998:9)

Although there have been pockets of success and exemplars of good practice at local levels, I would argue that the fundamental problems identified here by the SEU at its inception – and which it was committed to address – have yet to be resolved on the ground. The establishment of the SEU was a very welcome response to an awareness that 'wicked' problems demanded innovative and integrated solutions. There have been successes in some policy areas (for instance, rough sleeping) but in others (for instance, *Reoffending and Ex-prisoners*) the SEU has offered ways forward towards integrated solutions but New Labour's realpolitik,[7] together with the power of the treasury, has prevented their full adoption. Taken together, the arguments presented here suggest that the impact of anti-exclusion policies 'on the ground' has been patchy at best. To return to the original analogy in the title of this chapter (the upside-down duck), this analysis would suggest that, in terms of the social inclusion agenda, there was evidence of the frantic activity of flaying webbed feet (at all levels of policy making and implementation), but relatively little change in the muddy waters of the local pond beneath.

6. Summarising Policy Impact – 'For Better or Worse'?

The final section of this chapter will briefly outline the available evidence on the effects of post-1997 social policies across a range of areas. Space does not permit detailed analyses and critical comment on specific policies here and, in any event, this is a task which has been performed admirably by others, notably the LSE's Centre for the Analysis of Social Exclusion (CASE) (Hills and Stewart, 2005) and Polly Toynbee and David Walker in their book *Better or Worse? Has Labour Delivered?* (2005). The aim here is to offer the current 'headlines' in terms of the achievements of, and gaps in, policy, in order to better understand to what extent social and criminal justice have been enhanced (or not) over the past eight years and thereafter (in Chapter 7) to position the possibilities for change.

Figure 5.6 reproduces the main findings of JRF-sponsored research conducted by members of CASE which surveyed evidence of the impact of policies geared to addressing poverty, inequality and social inclusion (Hills and Stewart, 2005). Clearly there have been some successes, although they need to be both qualified and contextualised. Firstly, the improvements which have taken place have done so against a background of economic growth which has inevitably made the achievement of some targets easier. Secondly, and at the same time, the extent and depth of poverty and inequality facing New Labour in 1997 meant that the 'bar' for success was inevitably set low and it would have been difficult *not* to succeed to some extent. Thirdly, positive changes need to be assessed in relation to expectations of change which were raised in 1997, and this issue will be discussed further in Chapter 7.

---

[7]'Realpolitik' refers to the belief that the pragmatic pursuit of self-interest and power, backed up by force when convenient, is the only realistic option for a great state. The term was coined in 1859 to describe the policies of the German chancellor Bismark.

Issue	Recognition, targets and policies	Impacts	Problems and gaps
Child poverty	Prominent reduction target. Major tax benefit reforms benefiting low income families with children	Fall in relative child poverty 1996/7 to 2002/3. On or close to 2004/5 target. Falls in deprivation, and higher child-related spending by parents.	Still above EU average. Long way to be 'best in Europe'. Adult elements of family benefits linked to prices.
Working-age poverty	Policy focus on worklessness not poverty in itself. Policies aimed at employment and income at work.	Fell against absolute line, but only slight fall in relative poverty, which has increased for those with no children.	Despite fall in registered unemployment, many remain without income from work and dependant on price-linked benefits.
Pensioner poverty	Green Papers and 'Opportunity for All' indicators. General aim of ending pensioner poverty. More focus on extending means-tested benefits.	Relative poverty down by 2002/3 after allowing for housing costs, but not before them. Further falls likely by 2004/5.	Lack of take-up of means-tested minimum.
Income inequality	Reduction in overall income inequality is not an aim. Focus on relative poverty for selected groups and on life chances. Income inequality monitored at EU level.	Inequality has neither risen nor fallen significantly since 1997.Gap between income at the very bottom and very top has increased a little, but the gap between those near the bottom and those near the top has fallen a little.	Incomes and earnings at the very top continue to increase fastest. Some at the bottom left behind through price-linked benefits or lack of take-up.
Employment	Clearest initial priority. Action through New Deals and 'active' policy towards unemployed.	Lowest unemployment for 30 years, but economic activity falling only slowly. Jobless households still high.	Initial impact of New Deals has slowed. High unemployment remains for 16–17 year olds.
Education	Blair declared top three priorities in 1997 were 'education, education and education.' Targets for school attainment. Higher spending since low-point of 1999.	Positive impacts on primary level with poor-est schools improving fastest. More mixed picture at secondary level.	Large social class differences remain. Tensions between improvements for all and closing gaps.

(Continued)

Figure 5.6 (Continued)

Issue	Recognition, targets and policies	Impacts	Problems and gaps
Health inequalities	Unprecedented focus of analysis: Acheson Report and follow-up. However, main thrust of policy is overall health and NHS spending.	Too early to judge, but few attributable impacts yet visible. Time trends show little evidence of narrowing gaps.	Gap between analysis and implementation.
Political participation	Some aspects of constitutional reform and SEU agenda for neighbourhood renewal. Participation requirements embedded in nearly all policy areas. Targets for volunteering and confidence in institutions.	Formal political participation continues to decline. Better responsiveness of providers to participation. Positive evidence on quality of involvement, and on better targeting excluded groups.	Many low-income families feel they 'have no influence at all'. Achievements have not led to excitement about participation and involvement.
Poor neighbourhoods	Major focus of SEU, with ambitious overall target. Policies both area-based and for mainstream services.	At aggregate level, progress being made, but not fast enough to meet targets. Substantial differences between low income neighbourhoods.	Not all poor neighbourhoods improving. Some improvements perceived as slow.
Children and early years	Has moved up the agenda with reviews in 1998 and 2004. Large increase in resources.	Participation of 3 and 4 year olds in education increased. More childcare places, but short of target. SureStart is popular but evaluation shows mixed results.	Despite increases, spending and childcare provision remain low in European terms. Quality of childcare remains an issue.
Older people – services and long-term incomes	Royal Commission on Long-term Care, but divided report and responses in England and Scotland. State Second Pension and Pension Credit reforms.	Shift in care towards higher intensity and private provision. Falling value of private pensions for new employees. Increase in working after 50.	Impacts of means-testing of a wider range of services and potentially of future private pensions.
Ethnic inequalities	Response to MacPherson Report and 'institutional racism'. Ethnicity generally a sub-focus within disadvantage, rather than focus of specific policies.	Diverse experience between minority ethnic groups. Narrowing of gaps in GCSE attainment, but not in labour market.	Ethnic inequalities remain large in many dimensions. Area segregation remains a major issue.

Figure 5.6 (Continued)

Issue	Recognition, targets and policies	Impacts	Problems and gaps
Vulnerable groups	Focus of SEU on certain groups, especially vulnerable young people, with subsequent policy change. Asylum policy involves reduction in rights.	Mixed outcomes for targeted groups – most success on rough sleeping, less on truancy and teenage conception.	Some action less strong than warranted by analysis. Some vulnerable groups lower down the agenda, and asylum seekers expressly excluded from the inclusion agenda.

Figure 5.6   Policies Towards Poverty, Inequality and Exclusion Since 1997: Recognition, Targets, Policies Impacts and Gaps

(*Source*: Joseph Rowntree Foundation. Reproduced with kind permission of the JRF, 2005)

Hills and Stewart emphasise some of the gaps and problems associated with post-1997 social policies, some of which centre on 'the conflict between raising standards for all and reducing differences between disadvantaged groups and others' (Hills and Stewart, 2005). For the purposes of this book, some of the critical issues and gaps identified in, and arising from, the CASE research are as follows:

- Absence of any policy priority accorded to the reduction of income inequality
- The persistence of class-based inequalities (notably in income, education and in health)
- Lack of delivery on participation and democratisation
- Inattention to the problem of working age poverty
- Persistence of 'old' problems, for example:
  - Economic inactivity (worklessness)
  - Means-testing (especially for older people)
  - Benefit take-up
  - The (ab)use of differing poverty measurements (BHC and AHC)
- The UK's relative position in Europe remains low in relation to key policy indicators (such as child poverty and childcare expenditure, provision and access)
- A gap between policy analysis and implementation (health and some area-based policies)
- Lack of a clear focus on the inequalities suffered by minority ethnic groups
- The exclusion of asylum seekers from the government's social inclusion agenda.

All of these issues have profound consequences for the lived experiences of criminal and social justice for the poorest and most vulnerable people in contemporary Britain (and will be discussed in more depth in the final two chapters of this book). Conversely, it would be disingenuous and inaccurate to suggest that some positive changes (for instance steps towards the elimination of child and pensioner poverty) had *not* taken place since 1997 – the economic wind was favourable and, as the CASE authors suggest, we can certainly say 'the tide has turned'. Nevertheless, Britain has not *yet* become a more equal society and certain groups remain untouched by the tranche of policies surveyed here.

Returning, finally, to the image of the upside-down duck, it certainly needs to be re-balanced and given a firmer steer and sense of direction. This could be accomplished by, for example: more effective joined-up working by sometimes-competing government departments; a loosening of tight managerial and fiscal reigns to enable the development of genuine localism; genuine individual and community participation in policy-making, shaping and assessment; in turn, partnership working that is less a tool and mode of governance and more a dialogue towards shared aims; and above all, for all of the above to work, a firm statement and understanding of what precisely those aims are – pragmatism and electoral success are not enough. It is to this issue – the lack of a 'big idea' – that we will return in Chapter 7.

○ *six* ○ Locating Middle England: 'Otherness' and Criminal and Social Justice

Introduction

Much has been said, in recent years, about 'middle England'. What was once a term used literally in a geographical context became one loaded with different meanings – economic, social, political and cultural. The notion of a 'middle' constituency borrows from Richard Nixon's appeal to 'middle America' which helped him to win the US Presidency in 1968 (Stober and Strober, 1994; Cowie, 2002). In this context, 'middle America' was not so much a place as a state of mind comprising elements of aspiration, morality, fear and prejudice: many would argue that the notion of a 'middle England' demographic deployed by New Labour since 1997 comprises some of those same elements. As in the US context, the notion of middle England embodies an explicit appeal to a forgotten or 'silent majority' which seeks to engage them in politics: the archetypal middle Englander is supposedly neither rich nor poor and expresses no firm political or religious belief. The primary purpose for mobilising the term – and the constituency to which it refers, whether in a US or UK context – is to engage in politics those who are seen as apolitical, and so ensure electoral success. This politics therefore seeks to identify and reflect the key values and interests of a potentially influential, although allegedly 'forgotten', section of the population.

In the UK, the emphasis on middle England coincided with the rise of Third Way (New Labour) politics and similarly attempted to position itself between 'Old Labour' and new right conservatism in an effort to appeal to those individuals and notions of Englishness (to be discussed below), the concept of middle England sought both to build and to capture a market for the political 'brand' that was New Labour. The residents of middle England were typified as 'Mondeo Man' and 'Worcester Woman':

the former term was coined by Tony Blair (when he observed such a man polishing his car), to convey a stereotypical thirty-something, middle income earning houseowner whom Labour needed to win over from the Conservatives in 1997. Worcester Woman was similarly a demographic, an electoral construct of the pollsters who defined her as middle class, aged 35–44 with two children, earning around £18,000pa (part-time), a Conservative voter in 1992, and fond of holidays in Florida (Hilton, 2001).

But visions of middle England also draw on an element of nostalgia for a long-lost England: journalist John Pilger, reflecting on the discourse of New Labour as a kind of 'ideological scrabble', commented on words like 'stakeholder', 'civic society', 'governance' and then came:

> 'Middle England', a middle class idyll similar to that described by John Major when he yearned for cycling spinsters, cricket and warm beer. That one in four Britons lived in poverty was unmentionable. (Pilger, 2003)

The dichotomy between the idyll of 'middle England' and harsh reality of 'poverty' is a telling one, which also mirrors the political concerns and constituencies of New and Old Labour respectively: the former regarded the British working class as dead, and instead saw 'mass politics' as 'middle-class' politics (Gould, 1998:396).

The purposes of this chapter are to explore these and other dichotomies and to 'locate' the meanings and the significance of 'middle England' for criminal and social justice policies in contemporary Britain. In so doing, it will address issues of identity, place, economy and culture as well as morality, fear and prejudice. All of these complex issues frequently coalesce around the topic of crime. For example, in *Crime and Social Change in Middle England* the authors explore the ways in which residents of a 'middle England' town (Macclesfield) imagine and talk about crime, control and order, and found that:

> ... in speaking of crime people routinely register its entanglement with other aspects of economic, moral and social life; attribute responsibility and blame; demand accountability and justice, and draw lines of affiliation and distance between 'us' and various categories of 'them'. (Girling et al., 2000:170)

It is the drawing of the line between 'us' and 'them' that marks the boundaries of middle England and, while these boundaries are strongly influenced by local sensibilities and place, they are not fixed to – or determined by – places alone. Central to this chapter are the dynamic and complex ways in which these categories – 'us' and 'them' – are produced and reproduced, and their consequences for criminal and social justice. These constructions and consequences will be examined through the following themes:

1. Area
2. Asylum and immigration
3. Anti-social behaviour.

The thematic framework of these three 'A's will enable a critical engagement with the complex social, cultural, economic and political dimensions of middle England through which national and local identities are re-imagined and re-constructed. In so doing, the chapter will aim to draw together three sets of concerns: firstly, how, where and why certain individuals and social groups have been cast as outsiders, problems, or 'others'; secondly, how this 'otherness' is manifested in twenty-first-century Britain; and thirdly, the implications that these processes of 'othering' hold for our hopes of reconciling criminal and social justice in Britain.

1. Area

It has already been established that local sensibilities are important in shaping our understanding of a range of issues, including crime (Girling et al., 2000). The importance of place also makes it difficult to transfer policies from one area to another without some level of disconnection (Peck, 1998). Place is also an important (though by no means the primary) factor in the process of constructing identity – whether this identity is manifested at local, regional, national levels or based upon cross-cutting communities of faith or interest. In the case of the latter, certain places (of worship, of meeting, leisure or living) become, for those outside of them, almost synonymous with the people who inhabit them. This short section cannot deal with all of complex ways in which place and identity relate to one another, but will instead focus on the ways in which places acquire meanings or *reputations* which have impacts on the relations of power and constructions of 'otherness' within their (often-flexible) boundaries.

Centre and court

In terms of Britain's geographies of power, discussion almost inevitably starts at the 'centre'. The centre – of power, wealth and influence – is London and the south of England, with other regions often suffering deep and persistent inequalities. Those arguing for a 'decentred' approach to identity and policy have observed that 'British political life has a distinctive spatial grammar which lies at the heart of its unequal distribution of power' (Amin et al., 2003). Centralised modes of policy, fiscal control, governance and an almost 'courtly' structure all contribute to ossifying a geographical configuration in which the south-eastern part of England is the 'home' for national policy.

The primacy of the south as the seat of government and power is also reflected in its economic and social advantages over the diminishing towns and cities of the north and west. A study based on an analysis of 2001 Census data (Dorning and Thomas, 2004) concluded that outside of the south and London was 'the "archipelago of the provinces" – city islands that appear to be slowly sinking demographically, socially and economically'. This 'sinking' gave rise to inequalities which were manifested in a number of ways, including the health and well-being of a region's populations: for instance, in 2004 there were more doctors per person in the south of England than in the north and Wales, although rates of long-term disability were over 11% in the population in Merthyr Tydfil (Wales) and Easington (north) compared with 1.5% in Wokingham (south) (ibid). No wonder Britain's population is moving slowly south. We cannot, therefore, ignore the importance of space in patterning inequality and power, with the latter residing at the 'centre court'. But, at the same time 'middle England' is not just or mainly spatially bounded: the imagined middle England is exclusive, in differing ways, of those 'others' who are poor, vulnerable or in some way defined as a 'problem' (as we have seen in Chapter 2).

Location, location, location?

The spatial dimension is itself more than a map – it represents the outcomes of a complex interplay of social factors which include class, race, gender, age and so on (Powell and Boyne, 2001). And so, for example, the 'postcode lottery' which often determines the quality of, and access to, a range of public services, is not literally because of an individual's postcode, but because their choices about where to live are conditional upon a range of economic and social factors. The postcode argument implicitly argues for greater consistency and equity across locations, regions and the country. But there is an inevitable tension between *spatial equality* and *local autonomy* and the latter may be extremely beneficial in terms of taking account of local contexts in the planning and delivery of services (ibid). Working through the tensions between the two, it becomes clear that 'equity' is not 'sameness' and so localism will not (and should not) result in precisely the *same* outcomes in all places, but those perhaps differing outcomes should be equally *just*, wherever they are. However, for me, problems arise when local economies, social policies and resource allocation (national and local) combine to produce *unjust consequences*. However, these 'unjust consequences' may not be seen as problems by everyone – they may prove positive for middle Englanders who are best placed to maximise the benefits of public and private sector services and opportunities, particularly in relation to housing and education. In relation to the former, middle Englanders who made vast profits following the boom in house prices (particularly in the south of England) have a range of choices: buy-to-let; escape to the country (and own two homes in the process); or buy a holiday home in Europe.

Where education was concerned, middle Englanders had by the 1990s become politically vital to electoral success and their concerns were astutely tapped into as 'education, education, education' was *the* key priority for New Labour after the 1997 election. Sally Tomlinson persuasively argues that their policies in this sphere 'can be understood as a way of serving the anxious middle classes in an insecure world'. Highly selective polices which streamed, setted and excluded less able and 'troublesome' pupils all served to *advantage* these 'aspirant groups' (2001:270). At the same time, middle Englanders were, and still are, able to circumvent any perceived place-based disadvantages by moving house or having the capacity – in terms of knowledge, skill and money – to exercise their parental 'choice' in other ways (including opting for the public, grammar, 'specialist' schools and technology colleges which were now open to them).

Middle England is also located in incomes and in aspirations: the former are spatially patterned (Dorning and Thomas, 2004) although differences *within* and *between* locales and communities may be wide and significant. In short, location does matter and shapes the contexts and the ways in which middle Englanders aspire to, and are able to, distance themselves from the 'others'. In defining these others, mythologies about place are pivotal.

Mythologies of place

The postcode has much more to answer for than the lottery of service provision: it has also come to indicate and signify a range of desirable and undesirable economic and social features. For instance, at the touch of a mouse, middle Englanders (who are more likely to have the required ICT skills and Internet access) have access to information on crime rates, schools' test results and other *'quality of life' indicators* against which they can judge an area. These indicators and informal notions of *'reputation'* can reinforce and compound existing disadvantages. Research on urban inclusion in four deprived neighbourhoods (Teeside, London, Liverpool and Nottingham) found that these locales were characterised by strong local bonds of 'reciprocity and mutual aid', but despite these positive aspects, the residents suffered a range of disadvantages which they felt were generated by stigma:

> In the two Teeside estates, residents felt that they were excluded compared with the wider population in that: there had been a weakening of their right to be protected by the police; they were being denied equal participation in the labour market; they had unequal access to educational opportunity; and they were being denied access to credit and services. In general, young people particularly resented the sharp, persistent but often unwarranted labelling that they experienced. In many cases external people had no idea that positive changes had taken place on estates. (Forest and Kearns, 1999)

These findings resonate with research conducted in the late 1990s on a deprived Black Country estate which had received substantial regeneration funding. Here residents felt that the stigma associated with the name of the estate cast 'a shadow over new initiatives and people's daily lives' (Cook et al., 1998). Although regeneration initiatives may have many environmentally beneficial effects, they can also have perverse and unintended consequences which are yet more excluding for the poorer groups who live there. For instance, research on local crime prevention work in London (Hallsworth, 2002) shows the merits and demerits of 'inner city' regeneration. On the one hand it made 'a once notorious inner city area attractive both to business and to new professionals'. On the other hand, in making the area a desirable place to live, regeneration (coupled with the property-owning ambitions of middle Englanders) pushed up house prices. As a result, poorer populations had no option but to live in the pockets of serious disadvantage which remained, leading to spatial segregation and a more 'criminogenic environment' than before (ibid:211).

It is also important to recognise the uniqueness of place and, in particular, that not all 'inner cities' are the same: in her research on two high crime urban areas around Salford, Greater Manchester, Sandra Walklate observed that these areas were 'less than two miles apart, yet displayed very different ways of managing their relationships with crime' (ibid:58). These were 'predominantly white areas where the traditional working class historically co-existed with the "social scum" and those who were endeavouring to better themselves as market forces permitted' (ibid:60). Her research supported the contention that for those who do 'better themselves', the spatial proximity to the 'scum' engenders dislike and disdain and reinforces the *social segregation of 'us and them'* (Walklate, 2000; Hallsworth, 2002).

'Otherness' is also produced where issues of place and 'race' intersect and here, too, proximity can breed tension and contempt. Lemos's recent research on young people's attitudes towards 'race' and identity found that ethnically diverse towns and cities (such as Rochdale and Peterborough) had a greater proportion of young people with intolerant attitudes compared with smaller 'monochrome' towns such as Stafford. It is of serious concern that proximity is more likely to lead to social segregation rather than tolerance of minority ethnic groups (Lemos, 2005:56). It is to the issues of 'race', space, segregation and exclusion that we now turn.

Parallel lives

On the 1st June the house of the Asian Deputy Mayor of Oldham was fire-bombed, he and his family only narrowly escaping. A week later the town was again in the news as the British National Party scored its biggest success ever in a UK election, taking over 6,500 votes in Oldham West and Ryton, 16% of the vote, and over 5,000 votes in Oldham East and Saddleworth, or 11%. This confirmed the view of many that something was seriously wrong in Oldham, that there was a community more polarised on racial lines than anything seen in the UK... (David Ritchie, Chairman, Oldham Independent Review, 2001)

Later that month 'violent community disorders' involving an estimated 500 people took place in Oldham, causing damage estimated at £1.4 million (Ministerial Group on Public Order and Community Cohesion, 2002:7). In June, 400 people took part in similar disorders in Burnley. Bradford had experienced disturbances at Easter and later, in July, up to 500 people were involved in the most serious disorders of the summer in which over 300 people were injured and an estimated £7.5–10 million damage cased (ibid). In addition to a Ministerial Group, the government set up an independent Review Team under Ted Cantle to bring together the views of local residents on these events and to make recommendations geared to enhancing 'community cohesion' (Cantle, 2001). The opening paragraph of the Cantle Report speaks of a lack of surprise at the physical segregation of housing in the areas, but goes on to note the surprise of the Review Team at the *depth* of the polarisation they found, and the ways in which this impacted on other aspects of daily life:

> Separate educational arrangements, community and voluntary bodies, employ- ment, places of worship, language, social and cultural networks, means that communities operate on the basis of a series of parallel lives. These lives do not touch at any point, let alone overlap and promote meaningful interchanges. (2001:9)

These parallel lives can be understood only in relation to the particular historical, social and economic contexts in which they are lived: for instance where Oldham was concerned, the dire economic consequences of the decline of the textile industries, traditions of owner-occupation and living within particular neighbourhoods along- side friends and family, availability of only low-skilled, low-paid work, working the 'night shift' and so not coming into contact with white society, and the shared expe- rience of racism all played a part (Oldham Independent Review, 2001:8). At the same time key commonalities did emerge across those northern towns experiencing dis- turbance, and the Ministerial Group's *Denham Report* concluded that the most impor- tant common issues included: lack of a strong civic identity; weak political and community leadership; segregation; inadequate provision of youth services and facil- ities; youth disengagement; high unemployment; weakness and disparity of police responses to community issues; activities of extremist groups; and irresponsible local media coverage (Ministerial Group on Public Order and Community Cohension, 2002:7).

But, in addition to official responses, additional perspectives are available that stress that the events signified the 'violence of hopelessness' among young men who, in Oldham, suffer 50% unemployment and felt disconnected from their community leaders or 'patriarchs' who, since the 1980s, were seen to have glossed over commu- nity disquiet and resistance (Kundnani, 2001; Amin, 2003). It is also important to recognise the damaging consequences of regeneration policies so strongly criticised by Cantle:

> The plethora of initiatives and programmes, with their baffling array of local out- comes, boundaries, timescales and other conditions, seemed to ensure divisive- ness and a perception of unfairness in almost every section of the communities we visited. (2001:10)

In this way the bureaucratic, managerial and essentially competitive regimes of gov- ernance which characterise urban regeneration initiatives were seen as partly to blame for community discontent.

What has happened since Cantle, in terms of implementing policies geared to com- munity cohesion and racial equality? The government's strategy published in 2005 was entitled *Improving Opportunity, Strengthening Society* and appears to envisage that cohesion and racial equality will automatically emerge from existing opportunity-based strategies across government departments: in terms of employment it speaks of 'tailored support for jobseekers' from disadvantaged communities; in health, greater 'patient choice'; in education, Surestart and Aiming High programmes; in housing, 'mainstreaming' cohesion (ODPM, 2004b); and in terms of integration and citizenship, opportunities for volunteering and citizenship ceremonies (Home Office, 2005c). The fundamental problems surrounding skills and the (demand-side) issue of sustainable, well-paid work have not been addressed, nor do lessons on the problems of governance in highly deprived and ethnically mixed communities appear to have been learned.

Finally, it remains to be seen whether the government's community cohesion and racial equality strategy offers anything like an appropriate and sufficient response to the challenges of community cohesion posed by the events of 7 July 2005 in London: the terrorist bombings on the London transport system, apparently undertaken by young British Muslim men from towns in the north of England, will inevitably strain community relations still further. By defining the events of 7 July as 'a perversion of Islam', Tony Blair seemed to narrow down and simplify the complex conditions leading to such events but, as Salma Yaqoob observed, in blaming 'shoddy theology', he dislocated the violence from deep seated political and foreign policy issues. Moreover:

> No number of sniffer dogs or sermons denouncing the use of violence against innocents can remove the pain and anger that drives extremists to their terrible acts. The truth is that shoddy theology does not exist without dodgy foreign policy. (2005)

At the same time, the events of what is becoming known as '7/7' are leading to fissures *within* Muslim communities too, with a younger generation refusing to ignore issues of injustice and castigating some of their elders for not wishing to 'rock the boat' (Aslam, 2005). Taken together, the legacy of (and missed opportunities following) Bradford, Burnley and Oldham in 2001, coupled with the first suicide bombings in Britain in 2005, make it more difficult to prevent 'us' and 'them' living parallel lives, though that is no reason to stop trying.

2. Asylum and Immigration

When considering the complex constructions of 'us' and 'them', one of the most obvious examples of 'them' – where popular discourse and politics are concerned – is asylum seekers. They perhaps signify the ultimate 'other' for middle England: whether selling the *Big Issue* or begging on *our* streets, speaking *their* strange languages and buying food in *our* shops, locked away in detention centres or resettled in *our* cities and countryside, they are certainly *not* one of '*us*'. But the word asylum has not always conjured up such vile imagery as this. The UK is signatory to the 1951

Refugee Convention under which those people fleeing persecution may seek refuge – asylum – in the UK. Under this Convention the word *'asylum'* connotes a place of sanctuary and safety, in sharp contrast to contemporary popular discourse which conveys almost entirely negative meanings implying questionable status (if not outright fraud) and, consequently, invoking the need to control and exclude rather than to welcome and protect.

The politics of asylum

The *politics of asylum* has in the past decade been permeated by many of the distasteful features associated with immigration policies and discourses in the last half of the twentieth century. These features include: the racialisation of the issue itself; playing 'the numbers game' to call for controls and reductions; the language of fear and 'swamping', which defines asylum seekers (like immigrants) as 'a problem' for 'our' culture and social order; and the mantra of 'no recourse to public funds' in response to the charge that asylum seekers (like immigrants) are drawn to the 'honeypot' of the generous British welfare state (Cook, 1993). The perceived problems of immigration, asylum and social security fraud are often homogenised in the registers used by politicians and media alike, through the usage of the pejorative term 'bogus' to refer to asylum seekers and the implication of benefit fraud and abuse. This has led to a blurring of the boundaries between civil and criminal jurisdictions and serves to rationalise the control through forcible detention of many asylum seekers; an estimated 30% of whom will be detained by the end of 2005 (Joint Council for the Welfare of Immigrants, 2005). As already noted in Chapter 5, the work of New Labour's flagship Social Inclusion Unit specifically *excluded* asylum seekers from its remit (perhaps in order to appeal to the perceived sensibilities of middle Englanders). But to fully grasp the politics of asylum, it is necessary to explore its connections with the (perceived) concerns of middle England and, underpinning these, notions of Britishness and Englishness.

Asylum and imagined identities

There have been lengthy and sometimes vitriolic debates over what it is to be 'English': similar debates have surrounded the notion of 'Britishness' although the two terms convey altogether different meanings. Post-devolution 'Britain' could be seen as an umbrella under which the identities of Welsh, Scottish and English can shelter, although each assiduously protects its own sense of national identity. Interestingly, the 1998 devolution of powers to the Scottish Parliament and Welsh Assembly has raised serious issues for 'English' national identity, including: the lack of an assembly for England; rejection or apathy towards regional assemblies in England; and charges that the only parliament representing the English people – Westminster – is dominated by what Jeremy Paxman termed 'the Scottish raj' (*Sunday Herald*, 20 March, 2005). Despite attempts by some, notably the Chancellor Gordon

Brown, a Scot,[1] to celebrate the values of 'Britishness' (and others celebrating its constituent identities – see Blunkett, 2005), the term fails to convey the required positive sense of identity because 'Britain' is too closely associated with the racist and oppressive connotations of 'Empire' (Zephaniah, 2003).

Some may argue that relating to an idea of 'Britishness' is both difficult and uninspiring because notions of national identity are not based upon political boundaries but, rather, are 'rooted' in a sense of place and of heritage:

> As Scotland is the land of William Wallace or Robert the Bruce; so England continues to be imagined as King Arthur's Isle or William Blake's 'green and pleasant land': a metaphorical, if not a genealogical link to those 'true' inhabitants is established. (Lynn and Lea, 2003:426)

By implication, then, 'true' inhabitants of England, Scotland and Wales would not have parents who were born in other countries, non-white complexions or faiths other than Christian. This clearly flies in the face of the reality of a contemporary, vibrant, multi-cultural British society, and one in which Christianity is on the decline: any 're-awakened' sense of national identity is, therefore, predicated on the notion of a common heritage which is not real at all, but *imagined*. Lynn and Lea argue that this imagined common heritage, and the relative 'fuzziness' of national identity, will persist so long as visible differences are minimal and people share geographies and space. But this '"fuzziness" is soon pulled into sharper focus when it relates to those from "with-out"; be they Muslim or Hindu; Arab or Asian; immigrant or asylum seeker.' (Lynn and Lea, 2003:427). Political events such as the terrorist attacks of 11 September 2001 in the US and 7 July 2005 in London are bound to make this focus on those seen as 'with-out' sharper still, as distinctions are rarely made, in the popular imagination, between British Asians, 'terrorists' and asylum seekers (Lemos, 2005).

In their research on the social construction of asylum seekers, Lynn and Lea examined the discourses employed by British national newspapers (and their readers who fill the letters pages) and identified three overlapping discursive strategies at work:

- **The differentiation of the 'other'** – distinctions are made between *genuine* or *bogus* asylum seekers (or 'economic refugees')
- **The differentiation of the 'self'** – differentiating British people, particularly with reference to the plight of vulnerable and marginalised groups who allegedly 'play second fiddle' to asylum seekers who are seen to enjoy privileged access to welfare services (and to jobs)
- **The enemy in our midst** – the enemies here may be twofold. Firstly, asylum seekers may pose a threat to law, order and national security. Secondly, the State and 'white liberals' are also to blame for 'forcing' these refugees and asylum seekers on the British public.

---

[1]See for example Gordon Brown's 'Britishness' speeches to the British Council, 7 July 2004 and to the London Business School, 27 April 2005 (HM Treasury, 2004, 2005).

Lynn and Lea conclude that 'the phantom menace may be just that, but that 'the "New Apartheid" is tangible enough' through the pages of our newspapers (2003:448) and, one could add, in the detention centres and residual housing where many asylum seekers are forced to live. At the same time, one seedbed for national identity and attitudes – sport – continues to offer little hope of enhanced tolerance. For instance, despite the Football Association's efforts, racism still permeates 'the beautiful game' and, as a result, there were many who expressed disquiet after the 2002 World Cup and Euro 2004 competitions at the ubiquitous sight of the flag of Saint George, use of military metaphors, xenophobic media coverage and the jingoistic sentiments that may lie behind the fans' chants of 'In-ger-land' (Garland, 2004).

For middle England, the asylum seeker offers a doubly excluded vision of the 'Other'. While those living in poverty in the UK are invariably constituted as 'other' (Lister, 2004:101), the asylum seeker represents someone who is entirely out of bounds for inclusion in British society. It becomes a label (or 'master status') which is almost impossible to lose: even when a claim to asylum is successful, the negative connotations for the individual and his or her family is likely to persist. At the same time, the asylum seeker offers, to those who are in (or on the edge of) poverty, the prospect of sharing in the values of middle England peddled by the tabloid media: the asylum seeker potentially offers an 'other' from which even the poorest UK citizen can distinguish themselves. In this way, the asylum seeker as 'other' helps to sustain the social divisions and paradoxes which are inherent in the mythology of middle England.

Asylum and immigration policy

> There is no doubt that the asylum system is being abused by those seeking to migrate for other reasons. Many claims are simply a tissue of lies. (Home Office, 1998, quoted in Burchardt, 2005:223)

The discursive strategy through which the 'other' is differentiated (as bogus) is clearly evident in this statement from the Home office: this statement also demonstrates that, as Tania Burchardt noted with some irony, asylum is an area of policy which is clearly not evidence based. As we have already seen, asylum policy is not an example of 'joined-up' government either: while other New Labour policies seek, for instance, to reduce rough sleeping, encourage paid work and productivity and create an inclusive society, the Home Office subverts all of these aims through the social exclusion of a particularly vulnerable group – those fleeing persecution and seeking asylum in the UK (ibid). Asylum and immigration policy therefore runs counter to government objectives in a range of areas including: social cohesion and diversity, equality of opportunity, multiculturalism, pluralism, human rights, co-operative foreign policy and international development (Joint Council for the Welfare of Immigrants, 2005:7). It is also worrying (but indicative of the policy marginalistion and 'exclusion' of the asylum issue), that in the government's latest strategy to increase race equality and community cohesion the word 'asylum' is mentioned only three times: once referring, in passing, to it as a 'distinct but related issue' and a future publication; once referring to a reduction in the number of asylum applications; and one mention in the context of the need for local partnership discussion on 'difficult issues such as asylum, economic migration and crime' (Home Office, 2005d).

Looking back to 1997 when New Labour came to power, no manifesto commitment was made to repeal the Conservative's controversial Asylum and Immigration Act (1996). This Act was regarded by many as draconian in excluding asylum seekers from local authority housing waiting lists and curtailing their rights to work (being unable to work for the first six months in the UK), and to claim welfare benefits (to 90% of Income Support levels, and even then this reduced rate was only payable to those who claimed asylum 'at port of entry'). Now, in 2005, there have been three further Acts passed under New Labour (the 1999 Immigration and Asylum Act; 2002 Nationality, Asylum and Immigration Act; 2004 Asylum and Immigration Act), which have led to a further 'tightening of the screws' on asylum seekers (Burchardt, 2005). Worryingly for human rights and campaigning groups, the provisions of the latest Asylum and Immigration Act (2004) include:

- **A new offence of entering the UK without valid passport/immigration documentation:** punishable by a prison sentence of up to two years, and applying to all aged 10 years or over. There are concerns that this law applies to children; that those fleeing oppressive regimes are unlikely to have sought to obtain a passport from those regimes; and that it may also penalise victims of human trafficking (often women and children).
- **Withdrawal of basic support for families:** a failed asylum seeker with dependent children is not eligible for any support (from local authorities, social services, etc). In the event of a child's welfare being compromised, support under the Children Act (1989) may be provided to under 18s and, if necessary, they will be separated from their families. Critics argue this undermines the principles both of the Children Act and Human Rights.
- **Electronic monitoring:** those over 18 who have restrictions (to report or reside, or where immigration bail is granted) may be subject to monitoring either through electronic tagging (only used so far in criminal cases) or voice recognition reporting (by phone).

(Refugee Council, 2004, 2005a; Amnesty International, 2005).

These provisions in themselves create asylum seekers as 'others' who are not entitled to the same rights (to welfare, jobs and homes) as 'us'. They also enable physical exclusion (through detention). Critics argue that the 'blanket' provisions of the Act (particularly in relation to risk and detention) prevent cases being dealt with on an individual case basis, thereby opening up spaces for injustice. For example, Amnesty expressed concern that the government was using the risk of absconding to justify detention 'without a detailed and meaningful assessment of the risk posed by each individual, if any' and, moreover, they found particularly unacceptable the detention of families, including mothers with very young children and victims of torture. In summary, an Amnesty report on the plight of those seeking asylum in the

UK – *United Kingdom: Seeking Asylum Is Not a Crime* – concluded that 'detention is not being carried out according to international standards, is arbitrary and serves little purpose in the majority of cases where measures short of detention would suffice' (Amnesty International, 2005).

Asylum postscript: the 'five year plan' and the 2005 general election

The government's strategy for immigration and asylum for the next five years – *Controlling Our Borders: Making Migration Work for Britain* – was published in February 2005 (Cm 6472 (2005)). The Joint Council for the Welfare of Immigrants (JWCI) commented that the strategy was designed to persuade the British public that immigration is 'heavily controlled' and to reassure them with statistics on refusals, refused entries and deportations (2005:7). But despite such 'reassurances', the May 2005 general election witnessed an uneasy Dutch auction between New Labour and the Conservatives on asylum and immigration, with the opposition leader, Michael Howard, accusing Blair of 'pussyfooting' on immigration which, he stated, was 'out of control' (*BBC News*, 10 April 2005). While Howard denied that it was racist to broach the subject during an election campaign, his party's slogan – 'Are you thinking what we're thinking' – clearly opened up an unspoken political space within which racist attitudes could flourish. Perhaps more worrying still was what the electorate *was* thinking about immigration and asylum. The British Social Attitudes Survey (2004) had indicated a hardening of attitudes towards 'immigrants' under New Labour which became even more apparent in the 2005 election. Firstly, in terms of popular priorities, a MORI poll held during the campaign found that those interviewed placed 'asylum' in sixth place as 'the most important' election issue, ahead of managing the economy, unemployment, Iraq, transport and the environment. Secondly, when asked which party had 'the best' policy on asylum, 52% felt the (hard-line, quota-based) Conservative policies were 'best' and only 11% supported the policies of the eventual election winners – New Labour (MORI, 2005). Although church and refugee organisations and the UNHCR had all urged politicians to act responsibly and not perpetuate asylum myths, only the Liberal Democrats demonstrably refused to get into a 'bidding war' on these issues (*BBC News*, 9 April 2005; Churches Commission for Racial Justice, 2005; Refugee Council, 2005b; UNHCR, 2005).

After the general election (and, inevitably, also following on from the continuing impact of 9/11 and subsequent shock of 7/7), popular attitudes towards 'race' religion and asylum are all hardening. Recent research shows that children and young people all too readily stereotype asylum seekers as potential hijackers or terrorists (Lemos, 2005). The full social and personal consequences of 'bidding up' ever tougher and more 'controlling' asylum and immigration policies are beginning to emerge. For failed asylum seekers, who have been deported to states from which they fled, these consequences can be dire. There has, for instance, been evidence of violence by the oppressive Mugabe regime against those forcibly returned by the UK to Zimbabwe (*The Times*, 4 July 2005). At the time of writing (July 2005) more than 50 Zimbabweans in British detention who had been on hunger strike have called off their protest, and the deportation of failed asylum seekers to Zimbabwe is suspended pending a hearing of evidence from the Refugee Council in August. In the meantime, the implementation of the 2004 Immigration and Asylum Act, and the five year plan which accompanies it, raises serious concerns not just for social justice but for the UK's human rights record and the future of race relations (ECRI, 2005).

3. Anti-social Behaviour

As noted in Chapter 3, the definition of what constitutes anti-social behaviour (ASB) is broad and inclusive, with the 1998 CDA defining it in terms of behaviour that 'caused, or was likely to cause harassment, alarm or distress to one or more persons not of the same household as the perpetrator.' Although tackling ASB is a major focus of government policy (and now forms a Home Office Public Service Agreement , PSA, target), the definitions of ASB in use on the ground are shifting and 'pragmatic', with wide variations between geographical areas and between social groups (Wood, 2004; Millie et al., 2005). Evidence from the British Crime Survey suggests falling levels of concern over many of the aspects of ASB previously highlighted by government (notably drugs, burned out cars, vandalism and graffiti), and increased concern over public drunkenness and rowdiness (Wood, 2004). But despite an apparent cooling off of public anxieties about ASB, it remains a powerful element in the construction of threats of the 'other' and remains a crucial element in the government's third term 'Respect' agenda.

The genesis of the ASBO

As a tool of crime and disorder reduction, anti-social behaviour orders (ASBOs) were slow to take off: many local authorities and some police forces preferred to use alternative methods of regulation and dispute resolution, and some felt that issuing ASBO indicated a failure to use productive alternatives. In the two years and nine months to the end of 2001, only 518 orders were issued, much to the dismay of the then Home Secretary Jack Straw. The perceived under-use of the orders reflected what Elizabeth Burney described as a 'talking tough, acting coy' approach to ASB, although clearly there has, since then, been a dramatic uptake to almost 5000 orders which was the number anticipated at the time of legislation (Burney, 2002). Unsurprisingly, then, in 2004 a total of 4649 ASBOs were issued. The self-fulfilling prophecy which surrounds the use of ASBOs is also evident in terms of their target group: original Home Office guidelines envisaged them as applying 'normally' to adults, but this was unpopular with local authorities (ibid:473). Consequently, 44% of the 4649 ASBOs issued in 2004 were for those aged 10–17 (Home Office, 2005e). For Burney, the ASBO 'saga' represented, in 2002, the 'political processes at work in the contemporary governance of crime and disorder' and given local reluctance to impose orders and curfews which the law enabled, she foresaw the development of local strategies which diverged from the central vision (Burney, 2002:482). However, there has, in fact,

been a convergence, as those police and local authorities who initially saw the imposition of ASBOs for young people as a failure came to heel and played along with the
politicians and the Home Office. The result has been a dramatic increase in the use
of ASBO and curfew orders.

ASB and policy paradoxes

The fight against ASB is a core theme of New Labour's third-term agenda. However,
the policy importance accorded to ASB is largely at odds with the priorities of most
(though not all) people in the UK. Research has demonstrated that *anxiety* about
crime and ASB is not as prevalent as politicians would have us believe: while they can
be acute concerns for a *minority* of people in some areas (mostly urban and deprived
areas) it is *not* a big problem for the majority of people in England and Wales (Farrell
and Gadd, 2004; Millie et al., 2005).

At the same time, the strong emphasis on ASB is at odds with goals in other policy
domains, including *social inclusion* and *child protection*. Where the former is concerned, discourses around community safety rest upon the rhetoric of participation
and social inclusion. But within the ASB discourse young people are as objects for
policing and regulatory intervention rather than for positive engagement for safety
(Hill and Wright, 2003). 'Community' has come to mean a community of adults
only, as the day-to-day behaviours of many young people are marginalised and crim-
inalised. For example, a West Midlands study asked young people (aged 13–19) to
identify what behaviour they considered was 'OK when out with friends' and their
responses included: 'sitting talking and having a laugh'; 'having a laugh, playing
football'; 'playing football in the park, hanging outside the shop'; 'sitting down and
chilling'; 'walking the streets'; and 'drinking, but only if you can handle it' (Holmes,
2003). For many older onlookers these activities, seen by young people as 'OK' and
part and parcel of 'hanging out with friends', constitute ASB. In the British Crime
Survey (and in other research), the consistent message is that the very presence of
young people in public spaces is seen as a threat: 'teenagers hanging around' is most
commonly cited as the top ASB problem (Millie et al., 2005). There is a strong sense
in which community safety becomes 'a notion to be secured by blaming, isolating
and silencing youth' (Hill and Wright, 2003:291). Consequently:

> Local child curfew orders, child safety orders and anti-social behaviour orders,
> supported by increased custodial provisions available to youth courts, indicate
> an identification of young people as the true threat to community safety. (Hill
> and Wright, 2003:294)

(Although in some locales, prostitution may be regarded as the key problem as we
will see below.)

Where issues of child safety are concerned, campaigning groups point to the contradictions inherent in upholding the principles of the Children Act and tackling
crime and anti-social behaviour:

A child affected by poverty, neglect or abuse is seen as a child in need under The Children Act, yet that same child, once he or she crosses a boundary into offending behaviour becomes an object of retribution. (Pam Hibbert, Barnardo's Press Release,18 November 2003)

The Youth Justice Coalition report *Children in Trouble* (which Pam Hibbert co-authored) went on to express concerns at: the blurring of the boundaries of the CJS, particularly where ASB was concerned; the tendency to criminalise children at younger ages; and the dangers of centralised and prescriptive responses to children in trouble (Monaghan et al., 2003).

Revisiting 'criminalising the social'

As we saw in Chapter 2, the ways in which certain behaviours are defined as ASB is widening the net of criminalisation to include more and more young people. But it is not only troublesome *behaviour* which is labelled as anti-social, but also informal codes of conduct and dress. For example, a recent ban on youths wearing baseball caps or hooded tops from the Bluewater shopping centre in Kent, and similar ban at the Trafford Centre in Manchester, illustrate these processes of exclusion at work: both initiatives were lauded by the Prime Minister who expressed 'total sympathy' and agreement, going on to state that 'people are rightly fed up with street corner and shopping centre thugs' (*Manchester Evening News*, 13 May 2005). But here it was not thuggish or yobbish **behaviour** itself which generated such condemnation and exclusionary rhetoric, but the type of **clothing** (stereo)typically worn by many children, young men and women. As Richard Garside of the Crime and Society Foundation wryly commented, the Prime Minister's comments were:

> more in keeping with an episode of 'What not to wear', rather than a Downing Street press conference ... It is a strange state of affairs when the sartorial choices of today's teenagers provides a focus for the Prime Minister's proscription for promoting a sense of community. (Crime and Society Press Release, 12 May 2005)

More seriously, it is important to identify the underlying discourses within which it becomes possible to cast young people as 'other' and to identify this otherness so readily. Recent research has identified and explored three narratives which residents in differing localities used to understand the causes of ASB in their area:

1. social and moral decline
2. disengaged youth and families
3. 'kids will be kids'.

(*Source*: Millie et al., 2005:27–33)

These three narratives are not mutually exclusive, although they do invoke very different policy responses: the first seems to call for enforcement, but the views expressed by residents conveyed a deeper cynicism over the effectiveness of enforcement (primarily, policing) to address ASB. The second narrative stresses the need for longer-term, one-to-one youth work and effective community partnership-based interventions to engage young people in constructive ways. The third focuses on the relativity of ASB and so the need for better dialogue with older people, and also suggests the need to offer affordable 'diversionary' activities for young people to engage in (ibid). Taken together, a coherent approach to ASB would involve some elements of all three – enforcement, but balanced with a range of inclusionary measures. In this sense, the authors conclude, the government needs to tone down the anxious rhetoric around ASB and be 'tougher' on its causes – these causes are social and economic as well as individual.

Postscript: curfew orders

Like ASBOs, curfew orders are seen as an essential tool to combat ASB. These orders enable police or community support officers (CSOs) to forcibly remove anyone under the age of 16 from designated curfew areas. Despite evidence that they fail entirely as a deterrent (recent Home Office figures indicate that 75% of the 777 offenders aged 10–17 years, placed under curfew orders, were reconvicted within one year), they remain popular with politicians, the media and middle Englanders who have 'clout' to demand a police presence in *their* spaces, whether they need one or not (*Guardian*, 20 July 2005). At the time of writing the government has experienced a severe setback to its ASB policy with the success of a legal challenge to police powers under curfew orders by a 15 year old boy (who had not been in trouble with the police and was described as 'a model student'). Lord Justice Brook ruled in favour of the young man arguing that:

> If parliament were to be taken to have regarded all children found in such areas between the relevant hours as potential sources of anti-social behaviour, a coercive power to remove them might be a natural corollary. However, to attribute such an intention to parliament would be to assume that it ignored this country's international obligations to treat each child as an autonomous human being. (Lord Justice Brook's judgement, quoted in Liberty, 2005)

In short, young people cannot be subjected to coercive state powers, in breach of their human rights, simply because they are young and in the wrong place at the wrong time. This judgement cuts away the core assumptions of the government's ASB policy and opens up spaces for future resistance and challenge.

ASB and discourses around prostitution and the 'others'

Although ASB is overwhelmingly associated with male youth, it is worth stressing that there are additional vulnerable and socially excluded groups who fall within its remit and are subject to the processes of 'othering' which the term 'anti-social' connotes. Stenson (2000) relates these processes to *zero tolerance policing* (ZTP) which itself is a policy born of the sensibilities of middle England, although based on the example of New York. For middle Englanders (and New Yorkers before them) ZTP is grounded in the fears that 'others' in their midst – 'beggars, muggers, drug dealers, pimps and prostitutes' (ibid:222) – are contributing to crime, decline and pessimism. If we take the example of prostitution, the unequal consequences of ZTP become clear.

The two parties in the sex trade – the kerb crawler and prostitute – are constituted very differently in popular discourse: the former may be associated with notions of 'nuisance', but the sex worker herself is seen as a moral and physical threat, for whom there should be either very limited[2] or zero tolerance. The ZT approach was taken by some residents in the district of Balsall Heath in Birmingham. Here the prostitutes were described in the local media as 'human scavengers polluting our streets' while members of the male 'Street Watch' campaign who patrolled the area were reported as 'the men who cleared Birmingham of 12 street scum' (*Birmingham Evening Mail*, quoted in Kantola and Squires, 2004:81). More worrying still was the way in which the Balsall Heath Forum and its Street Watch campaign was cited by the Home Secretary, David Blunkett, as an example of 'how far a good mix of innovation and nous can go' (Blunkett, 2003:42). This assessment flew in the face of Home Office sponsored research indicating the pressing need to treat prostitution as a welfare not a policing issue, in need of holistic not penal solutions (Hester and Westmorland, 2004). As a final observation, the advocates of ZTP in New York have come to regret the eagerness with which this policy was pursued, at the expense of other social measures. Michael Jacobson, the former New York Commissioner for Corrections under Major Giuliani, regarded the mass imprisonment arising from such 'tough' penal policies as 'public policy gone mad' and went on to state:

> Public safety is not the sole province of the criminal justice system. Accessible health care, community-based mental health and child care, reasonable school class sizes and well-trained teachers, well-funded environmental and transport agencies all protect public safety. Money spent on spiralling corrections cost has come at the expense of other crucial governmental services. (Jacobson, quoted in Crime and Society Press Release, 13 June 2005)

It is to arguments such as this – and the need to *reverse* the process of criminalising the social – that we return in the final chapter.

---

4. Summary: Middle England and the 'Others'

This chapter has attempted to locate and to explore the notion of 'middle England' as a lens though which to focus on the complex ways in which certain individuals

---

[2]Or 'zones of tolerance' (Gwinnett, 1997).

and social groups have been cast as outsiders, problems or 'other'. In twenty-first-century Britain this *otherness* is manifested in both spatial and imaginary ways: spatially, through inequalities of power, income, employment, health and education that may be patterned between and within regions, boroughs and neighbourhoods. In imagined terms, through the construction of 'others' who are seen to threaten or undermine middle England's social order and interests, including: young people, unemployed people, lone mothers, minority ethnic groups, asylum seekers and residents of poor neighbourhoods. But, as Janet Foster notes:

> All too frequently high crime communities are perceived to be full of 'problem people', not people who may have problems. (2002:168 original emphasis)

Central to theoretical understandings of how and why only *some* groups are constituted as problems (and not as people who may have problems) is, as we have seen, the concept of *otherness*. The risk and 'ontological insecurities' that characterise postmodern societies have given rise to a pressing need to re-establish a sense of personal security and identity (Garland, 2001). Central to this sense of self and security is the casting of somebody else as 'the other', the opposite of oneself, whose 'vices... are the inverse of our virtues' (Young, 2002:552).[3] When it comes to defining the 'others', Jock Young aptly summarises who the usual suspects are likely to be:

> Who, by definition, could be a better candidate for such negative 'othering' than the criminal and the culture that he or she is seen to live in? Thus the criminal underclass replete with single mothers and living in slum estates or ghettos, drug addicts committing crime to maintain their habits and the immigrants who commit crime to deceitfully enter the country and continue their lives of crime, in order to maintain themselves become the three main foci of emerging discourses around law and order – that is the welfare 'scrounger', the 'junkie' and the 'immigrant.' (2002:265)

The processes of *negative othering* described in this chapter (in relation to young people, asylum seekers, minority ethnic groups and residents of deprived neighbourhoods) affect both criminal and social justice. As we have seen, middle England constructions of 'others' imply policy responses which seek to individualise (not socialise) problems, and to deter, discipline, regulate and control problem and 'other' groups.

Figure 6.1 below attempts to summarise some of the issues raised here and, at the same time, to visually represent the ways in which social constructions of welfare claimants, minority ethnic groups, the young, the undeserving poor, crime (including drugs, prostitution and human trafficking), problem places and problem people are interrelated. The list of people and problems within this diagram is far from

---

[3]It is important, too, to consider who does *not* count as 'other' – for example, tax evaders or supporters of illegal fox hunting.

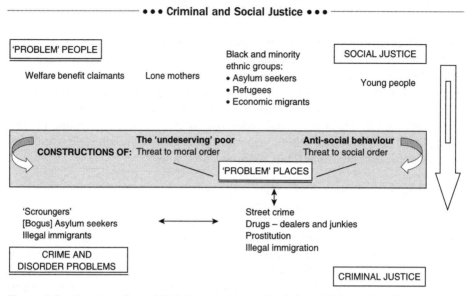

Figure 6.1   Construction of Relations between Social and Criminal Justice for 'Other' and 'Problem' Groups

exhaustive, not least because these processes are fluid and dynamic. For instance, contemporary constructions of the 'war on terror' cut across many of the places, social groups and themes represented in Figure 6.1 (notably those of immigration, asylum, problem places, young people, ethnicity and religion). But drawing on what we know of historical continuities, shifts in discourses and the processes of 'negative othering', it attempts to sketch out some of the overarching themes and the complexities involved in understanding the relationships between the criminal and the social for contemporary middle England. It is the task of the final chapter to seek ways forward in addressing the inequities and injustices of these relations, and to work towards reconciling criminal and social justice.

○ *seven* ○ **Reconciling Criminal and Social Justice**

The key concern of this book has been to illustrate the ways in which criminal justice and social justice are interconnected and interdependent concepts, in theory and in the day-to-day realities of our lives. At the same time, it has attempted to examine and critique the ways in which, over the past eight years, policy initiatives within and across these two spheres have often led to contradictory and mutually defeating outcomes. The task of this final chapter is to draw together the preceding analyses to offer positive ways forward to achieving greater justice – criminal and social – in contemporary Britain.

The chapter will be divided into three parts: the first will offer some personal reflections on the May 2005 election and the momentous events of July 2005 which are, at the time of writing, highlighting a range of tensions – global, national and local – around issues of poverty, human rights, violence and justice. It would be counter-productive not to acknowledge the importance of these issues as they mould the socio-economic, political and cultural contexts within which any progressive change must take place. The second part of the chapter will, in this dynamic context, build upon the analysis of previous chapters and summarise some of the key issues and challenges facing us in our attempts to reconcile and advance criminal and social justice: it will also begin to signal ways in which these challenges could be addressed. The third part will outline some 'good enough' (Williams, 2000) principles upon which the future reconciliation of criminal and social justice may be based, thereby offering possibilities for positive challenge and for change.

1. Reflections in 2005

Firstly, a flashback to 2001:

> Emblazoned on the hustings and battle buses during the 2001 election were
> More Schools, More Hospitals, More Police. These were middle England's
> issues, so Labour calculated. The posters and the party political broadcasts did
> not say More Social Justice, Fewer Poor People or, heaven forbid, More Equality.
> (Toynbee and Walker, 2005:47, emphasis added)

By the *general election of May 2005* little had changed except that, four years on
from this observation, the Conservative Party had sought to claw back these same
middle England issues from New Labour. As if reading the floating voters' minds they
asked, and then answered, the question:

> ARE YOU THINKING WHAT WE'RE THINKING?
> More police; cleaner hospitals; lower taxes; school discipline; controlled immi-
> gration; accountability. (Conservative Party Manifesto, 2005)

To their credit, the Liberal Democrat Manifesto differed somewhat by including a
strong 'green' theme and by stressing 'fairness' in its proposal to raise the top rate of
income tax to 50% for earnings above £100,000 a year. New Labour once again did
its homework and then unashamedly appealed to middle England's concerns, with
its policy pledges reading:

> Your family better off; your child achieving more; your children with the best
> start; your family treated better and faster; your community safer; your borders
> protected. (Labour Party Manifesto Pledge Card, 2005)

It worked. But if in 1997 the champagne flowed freely for the celebrations of the New
Labour party faithful, had been limited to 'a quarter of a bottle of champagne each'
in 2001,[1] it seemed that by 2005 their victory probably merited no more than a tepid
glass of Labrusco. Despite the political priority accorded to democratisation and participation the electorate seemed disengaged: election turnout in 2001 had been the
lowest ever at 59.17% and in 2005 this inched up to just 61.5%, though this was
probably due more to the novelty of postal voting than enthusiasm for politics.
Rather than a ringing endorsement of New Labour and high hopes for the policies of
a historic third term, there seemed to be two more plausible – but negative – reasons
for voting in a third Blair government: the first was the feeling that Blair was probably the lesser of two evils; the second, that opposition leader Michael Howard was
the evil of two lessers. Either way, positive engagement, trust, belief and idealism
were absent from the polling booths.

---

[1]According to Toynbee and Walker (2005) this was the Mill Bank HQ allocation, per person,
in 2001.

Humbly confessing that he had 'listened' to the people during the election cam-paign, Tony Blair went on to announce the defining issues of his third term as *'reform and respect'* – but in that order. The 45 new Bills announced in the Queen's Speech were seen by most as 'quintessentially New Labour', and included measures on: ID cards, 'market-oriented' reforms in health, education and family welfare and 'tough' measures to combat crime, anti-social behaviour and illegal immigration (White, 2005). Both during and after the May 2005 general election the issues of social justice, equality and the reduction of poverty were conspicuous by their absence – at least until the build-up to the G8 summit in Gleneagles in July, when this agenda was seized upon by the Live 8 and the *Make Poverty History* campaigns to tackle poverty in Africa. Their three aims – 'trade justice, drop the debt, more and better aid' – were only partially addressed in the final announcement of the leaders of the G8 nations: some debt was cancelled for the poorest nations, aid to Africa was doubled (from $25 million to $50 million) but the calls for trade justice went unheeded. The campaign leaders noted that while the people of the world were 'already on the road to justice... the G8 need to run much faster to catch up' (*Make Poverty History Team,* 8 July 2005).

Less prominent had been an earlier briefing issued by the Tax Justice Network enti-tled *The Price of Offshore* (Tax Justice Network, 2005). It noted that in 1998 the Merrill Lynch/Cap Gemini *'World Wealth Report'* estimated that one third of the wealth of the world's high net worth individuals (HNWIs[2]) was held 'off shore' and so not laible to tax. The Network went on to report conservative estimates that – in 2003 – the value of these offshore assetts was between $11–12 trillion, and that the **tax lost** on interest accruing on these assets is in the region of $255 billion a year (ibid). The staggering scale of these figures is put into perspective if we consider that the leaders of the G8 nations at the 2005 summit *doubled* the aid pledged to relieve poverty in Africa *to* $50 billion (and, incidentially, promised a $3 billion financial package for the Palestinian Authority 'over the next few years' – *Financial Times*, 8 July 2005). In other words, the richest individuals in the world, just by moving their financial assets off shore in 2003, could avoid tax which is worth more than five times the total G8 aid budget for the continent of Africa, two years later. This gross inequity is reminis-cent of Tawney's observation that 'What thoughtful rich people call the problem of poverty, thoughtful poor people call, with equal justice, the problem of riches' (Tawney, 1931, quoted in Sinfield, 2004). This is rarely acknowledged as a 'problem' at all, though John Christensen, co-ordinator of the Tax Justice Network, argues that the problem of tax evasion and avoidance, and the norms which underpin it, mark:

> ... one of the defining crises of our times. One of the most fundamental changes in our society in recent years is how money and the rich have become more mobile. This has resulted in the wealthy becoming less inclined to associ-ate with normal society and feeling no obligation to pay taxes. (*Accountancy Age*, 2005)

---

[2]HNWIs have liquid financial assets of $1 million or more and number around 7.7 million people worldwide (http://www.taxjustice.net).

The lack of attention to this crisis of the 'overclass', the justice agenda or, indeed, any clear 'flight path' for New Labour has long been an issue of concern for political commentators: some felt the tension (or 'internal combustion') between Tony Blair and Gordon Brown explained this absence in the second term (Toynbee and Walker, 2005). If this is an accurate assessment, there may be some hope for genuine engagement with issues of inequality and social justice under any future Brown leadership in New Labour's third term of office. But, at the time of writing, politics is dominated by issues of *'terror' rather than justice* and, moreover, the Prime Minister and Foreign Secretary have explicitly rejected any connection between the two – nationally or globally.[3] However, there are concerns (expressed by Muslim community leaders and by the Prime Minister's wife, Cherie Booth[4]) that civil liberties may be a casualty of the war on terror in the UK.

Things do not look good. Where the economy is concerned, business is no longer booming and *Industry Watch* reports a 3% increase in business failures in the past year, and predicts this will rise by a further 4% in 2006. Analysts conclude that the UK consumer boom is over, as falling house prices have undermined consumer confidence (BDO Stoy Hayward, 2005). On the one hand, this time may seem by some as an inappropriate one to call for radical policy shifts in the criminal justice and social spheres. On the other hand, it could be argued that the time is right for such progressive change.

2. Issues and Challenges

Taking the elements of the economic, social and political context just described, this part of the chapter will, using the analyses outlined in the previous chapters of the book, attempt to accomplish two things: firstly, to summarise the challenges ahead in reconciling criminal and social justice in contemporary Britain; and secondly, to begin to suggest ways of responding positively to these challenges.

2.1. The trust deficit

As we saw in Chapter 3, the vexed issue of trust cannot be addressed merely by politicians and their acolytes 'getting the message over' in more effective ways or through other 'technical' means. In other words, we cannot expect trust to just reappear by doing things better, technically, than we did before. Rather, there is a need to develop

---

[3]While Tony Blair and Jack Straw are correct in arguing that there are 'no *excuses*' for acts of terror, the automatic de-coupling of the issue of justice is unhelpful. As Tony Benn observed on the day following the 9/11 attacks, there is a need to be 'tough on terror and tough on the causes of terror'.

[4]See http://edition.cnn.com/2005/WORLD/europe/07/27/cherie.bombings/

alternative organisational structures and ways of working based on notions of *'grown-up trust'* (Skidmore and Harkin, 2003). Implicitly this also involves the challenge of *culture change* in an especially low-trust British society, a problem which is not new: Perri 6 argued a decade ago that the new mission for government was to *'re-imagine the state so that it can facilitate the society that organises itself in a milieu of trust'*. But, hampered by the short-termism and election timetabled nature of British politics, this remains, ten years on, an incomplete 'mission' for a progressive government to take up (Perri 6, 1995).

Trust is also a 'two-way street': if politicians wish to secure the trust of the electorate; they need to trust the electorate in return. Government therefore needs to respect and trust local policy actors and communities to engage positively in shared reform and inclusion agendas, and to trust professionals (whether, for instance, in the fields of health and social care or criminal justice) to implement policy and deliver services in the most appropriate and effective ways, taking into account their clients' needs. Unfortunately, the discussions of governance in Chapters 4 and 6 and accounts of processes of consultation in Chapter 5 have demonstrated that there is little trust flowing in this direction – from government at the centre to communities and practitioners at the local level. The rhetoric of a new localism is currently subverted by the bureaucratic realities of planning and reporting schedules, targets, performance indicators and the centralised control which these forms of governance exert (as we will see in section 2.3 below). For a *genuine* trust and sense of partnership to develop between and within communities, regions and the centre, there must be a loosening of the bonds forged through contemporary modes of governance and fiscal control, accompanied by a *genuine* commitment to local participation and empowerment (as we will see in 2.2 below).

What is also clear from Chapters 4 and 6 is that trust cannot be recaptured without less 'spin' and greater *honesty* (for example, about what works and what doesn't in criminal justice and social policies). Equally, trust may be partly restored through a clearer vision of *'the good society'* which political parties aspire to, as opposed to an unseemly pre-election auction of 'goodies' to tempt middle Englanders. In any event, few believe the bidders' promises, and trust in politicians has been eroded to such an extent that cynicism and disbelief is frequently the default response of the public. In this respect, as we will see in section 3 below, the issue of re-engaging with the politics of belief and conviction is crucial to addressing the trust deficit.

2.2. The democratic deficit – issues of participation and engagement

New Labour has been committed to addressing (what it perceived as) a democratic deficit, most notably through reforms of local government, devolution and electoral change. All of these changes were predicated on the engagement of individuals and communities in the democratisation project – as citizens, voters, service users, carers, young people, neighbourhood and community groups, voluntary and community sector actors and so on. But, at national level, the general election turnout of 70% in

1997 had (despite eight years of the democratisation, modernisation and reform agendas) dropped by 10% in 2005. At local level, the outcomes of initiatives geared to reform local democracy have been disappointing too: recent research confirms that New Labour reforms have, so far, largely failed because 'successful institutional design... depends on diversity' and not on central proscription (Leach et al., 2005). Put simply, you cannot 'legislate' centrally for local leadership and vision because these are the products of context, culture and individual capabilities, and such a positive coalescence is more likely to occur where there are *flexible institutional structures* generating creativity rather than frustration (ibid). 'Experimentation and learning' were and are key factors in effective local political leadership.

While Chapter 5 demonstrated some of the limits of the mechanisms for, and practices of, consultation and participation at local levels, it also pointed to positive examples which were similarly predicated on 'lesson learning'. *Participatory approaches* are being learned and successfully adapted from 'South to North' and are having benefits in deprived UK communities (for example, see http://www.oxfamgb.org/ukpp/work.htm). However, these approaches do involve a long-term investment of time and resources in training, capacity building and the development of new structures for engagement, policy-making and feedback. But, as we saw in Chapter 5, the demands of governance include a requirement to consult across a tapestry of initiatives locally and so 'overload', under-resourcing and short termism remain challenges to participation.

However, there is now, at the very least, a powerful momentum for *participation and empowerment in social policy research, policy and practice* which is itself democratising and offers opportunities for positive change. It is recognised that the participation of users and communities *and* the engagement of the social policy community are *both* essential to counter the negative effects of the reactionary populism of middle England (Beresford, 2001). Building on the foundations of the communities studies tradition, Marilyn Taylor (2002:102) argues that academics need to engage locally in order to 'address the community language', and offer more realistic approaches, and she argues that 'we need to develop this knowledge base not in ivory towers, but through participatory research'. Thus any inclusive and anti-discriminatory welfare future will depend upon the discipline of social policy *embedding* the principles and practices of engagement and participation in its own research and theorising (Beresford, 2001; Taylor, 2002; Bennett and Roberts, 2004; Lister, 2004; Sinfield, 2004).

2.3 Governance

Much has already been said (in 2.1 and 2.2 above) about the negative consequences of governance and governmentality on policies geared to enhancing social justice. Where criminal justice is concerned, the evidence of the preceding chapters has demonstrated what Rutherford (2001) termed the 'misnomer of the "whole systems" approach'. It is true that, in line with the mantra of joined-up-working, a 'strategic plan' for the cjs is produced and issued collectively (by the Home Office, Department for Constitutional Affairs and the Attorney General). But these departments, and the agencies beneath them, all have different goals and agendas (see also 2.5 below). For instance, the goals of the police may conflict with those of the Home Office (as we have seen in Chapter 4, in the case of ICT decisions) and CPS objectives may be at odds with those of their police colleagues. For example, where cases of domestic violence are concerned, the governance of criminal justice gives rise to conflicting goals and policy paradoxes that may adversely affect victims and their families: the CPS's PSI target to 'Narrow the Justice Gap' means speeding up cases, and this could have adverse consequences for some victims who need extra time for support. Their target to 'Bring Perpetrators to Justice' may not be what domestic violence victims themselves want, and may place them at greater risk of repeat victimisation (Cook et al., 2004).

Target setting and managerialism also undermines *independent justice ends* of agencies (notably the CPS) and effectively 'fetters' them to policy goals such as Narrowing the Justice Gap, Bringing Perpetrators to Justice, targeting Persistent Young Offenders, Street Crime and so on – all of which are essentially politically determined priorities. This is particularly problematic for the CPS who, therefore, must work to *political* targets but are in fact constituted as an *independent* prosecuting authority. In this sense, the separation of powers – the judicial from executive – is potentially threatened by the current governance of criminal justice.

Taking a step back and looking at the issues raised in broader terms, it is clear from the examples cited already that frameworks for governance in the criminal justice arena lead to a stress on issues of technical/systems and *means* to deliver policy targets, rather than addressing basic questions about the *ends* to which these policies are directed – that is, *'What [and who] is the criminal justice system for?'* At the same time, the decision to focus on means (and not on ends) is, again, a political one. Rutherford (2001) contends that the 'whole systems' approach therefore obscures the need to articulate the tensions and choices inherent in debates over the *purposes of criminal justice*. Instead, the 'reforms' of criminal justice under New Labour have been 'mesmerised' by the idea of efficiency and assume that legitimacy is merely a function of the 'accuracy' of the system itself (Sanders, 2002; Morgan, 2002).

However, it is important not to entirely deny the possible benefits of new forms of management and governance in enabling organisations to develop more creative approaches as, for instance, in the case of youth justice (Newburn, 2002). Here Newburn argues that the 'corporatist' model of youth justice does offer these positive opportunities, mainly because of values and commitment of staff (who are not, as critics suggest, part of a conspiracy of punitive exclusion). Similarly, Burnett and Appleton argue, in relation to the work of YOTs, that staff engage creatively with new initiatives and modes of governance, and pick out 'their favourites from the "smorgasbord"... of aims, principles and interventions and then concentrate on making those selections work' (Burnett and Appleton, 2004:51).

In terms of ways forward to more progressive criminal justice futures, the *creative role of practitioners* (in the public, private and not-for-profit sectors) is vital. For instance, Hilary Somerland sees value in the 'political lawyer's project in developing a partnership with the client which 'builds and daily operationalizes a discourse which is empowering rather than commodifying' (ibid:359). She goes on to argue that 'creative lawyering' is vital to ensuring the citizenship rights of their clients, as one such lawyer (in the sphere of housing law) confirms:

> I see justice as strongly linked to the issue of power and the extent to which people can achieve their legal rights and the outcomes which flow from those... You can have all the rights in the world but without the means/wherewithal to enforce them there is no justice. The law is the mechanism to achieve the aims, to realize clients' needs... Its about the homeless maximizing their rights to housing. (2001:348)

This creative, empowering and rights-based approach can equally apply to professionals in the spheres of social work, health and social care and community justice, many of whom are more interested in collective problem-solving than the reductionism which accompanies the politics of behavioural control and 'blame'.

2.4 Rights and justice

In Chapters 2 and 6, tendencies towards *the criminalisation of the social* were traced, with particular reference to constructions of 'problem' people and areas and to anti-social behaviour. But the inexorable rise in activities defined as 'anti-social' signals only one example of this tendency: government legislation created over 600 new criminal offences between 1997 and 2003 (Faulkner, 2003:296) and, at the same time, generated a more punitive climate, which was bound to shape judicial practices in relation to a range of offences (Millie et al., 2003). As a consequence, Morgan (2003) rightly observed that 'More offenders are getting mired deeper and deeper within the criminal justice system for doing less and less' and so the prison population has now risen to unprecedented levels. These observations seem to indicate that while we have more laws, we have less justice.

This punitive climate involves a lowering of thresholds of tolerance for certain behaviours which frequently runs counter to the spirit of human rights. These human rights, according to Lord Goodhart, include the right to be 'bloody-minded' and 'make a bit of a nuisance' of yourself because, after all, we are not in an authoritarian state (quoted in Hopkins-Burke and Morrill, 2004:235). As we saw in Chapter 6 in relation to ASB, there is evidence that a significant proportion of the public agree that 'kids will be kids' and so would not wish to invoke the enforcement of the criminal law in a 'zero tolerance' fashion (Millie et al., 2005).

Where 'rights' are concerned, the 'sales pitch' for the 1998 HRA was impressive, but recent research by Luke Clements examining the impact of the Act, on the ground, for socially excluded groups, was less so. He suggests that the HRA is having little impact on the most excluded groups, for many reasons. In the first place, the legislation is used selectively: local authorities are only likely to undertake human rights reviews of policies which are seen to benefit the majority, or 'an influential minority'. As a result, many are left *'stranded victims'* of social exclusion, an important element of exclusion being access to the law. What he terms *'fear of the consequences'* of human rights reviews acts as a barrier to proactive use of the legislation and thus leaves stranded victims outwith the benefits of the human rights agenda (Clements, 2005:43). Clements argues these are the same (broadly three) groups who have also failed to benefit from social inclusion policies, namely: people with physical or mental disabilities or chronic health problems (together with their carers); people with poor skills and no qualifications; and people from some minority ethnic groups (notably travelling people).

How can the compounding effects of social exclusion and differential access to human rights and the law be tackled? One answer would be through the 'creative lawyering' enterprise suggested by Sommerland earlier. A more sustainable solution, however, lies in *cultural change*:

> the promised rights revolution cannot take hold without a cultural shift in the way public service organisations operate... [and] no such cultural shift in attitudes has yet occurred. (Clements, 2005:49)

Public services have over the past eight years endured rafts of changes associated with the New Labour modernisation agenda – some have had positive effects; others not – and now, in its third term, more 'reform' is promised. Whilst in 1997 Blair famously proclaimed that the choice was 'modernise or decline', the choice now is less about modernisation for its own sake, and more about finding ways to encourage deeper, *positive, cultural change*.

But the context – in terms of human rights discourse – for driving forward such cultural change is a challenging one. Here it is useful to draw on the framework outlined by Francesca Klug (2005) who identifies three 'waves' of rights: the first is associated with the Enlightenment and what came to be termed 'the rights of man' [*sic*]; the second wave (as we saw in Chapter 1) developed following the Second World War with the birth of the international human rights movement; and the third wave, follows on from the fall of the Berlin Wall in 1989 and subsequent trends towards globalisation (outlined in Chapter 3). Klug argues that this third wave of 'evolution' in the human rights discourse is proving difficult to sustain after 9/11:

> Since the President of the US has declared war on terror (not on a state but on a noun), human rights standards are once again at the mercy of the whim – not so much of the great powers – but of the one great power and its cohorts. (2005:11)

War on a noun is inevitably an endless war, but it remains essential for its duration to hold on to the principles and the momentum of human rights, and not yield to calls for suspensions of these rights in the face of 'new enemies'.

2.5 Money matters

The values of the Third Way, as Chapter 3 explained, centre on rights, responsibilities, democracy and inclusion. The New Labour project incorporated these values when defining what it was 'about': opportunity, inclusion, radicalism (defined in a non-ideological sense, as 'new' ideas – such as 'what works') and, perhaps above all, responsibility. The principle pathway to opportunity, inclusion and responsibility is paid work, and the welfare-to-work strategy proved the cornerstone of the first New Labour government. What is missing from this list of what New Labour 'is about' is any reference to equality, justice or worth-without-work – and in all of these respects *money matters*.

Chapters 1, 2 and 6 have attempted to demonstrate the ways in which an individual's experiences of citizenship and of criminal justice in contemporary Britain can be patterned along lines of income, wealth, gender, 'race', age and 'otherness'. For many people the currency of this experience (literally) is money[5] – whether they can afford to pay for the rent or mortgage, utilities, council tax, insurance, cars, food, leisure, clothing, birthday presents, toys, holidays... the list is endless. In this respect, money – referring here to *income adequacy* – is an important issue.

Income adequacy is a crucial issue for those who argue that current levels of *welfare benefits* are insufficient to enable those living on them to experience fully social citizenship (see Chapter 1). It is also important for those who *work* for their poverty: the problem of low pay is a chronic one. While the national minimum wage has been an important step forward, it fails to address deeper-seated structural issues:

> If the reduction of extreme poverty is our goal, what most needs reforming is the labour market itself and particularly the spread of low-wage unstable work. We will not sever the links between poverty and crime by increasing the number of poorly paid stressful jobs and forcing low-incomer parents to take them... A far more rational approach is to boost the rewards and the stability of work, in order to strengthen families and stabilize local communities. (Currie, 1998, quoted in Young and Matthews, 2003:15)

The compulsion of the welfare-to-work strategy and stresses of living on inadequate incomes is seen here to (potentially) affect levels of family breakdown and/or crime. While many people would argue with the poverty-crime linkage implied by Currie, the picture painted here does, however, indicate that *rational* policy approaches to poverty, crime and social exclusion would stress the need for *sustainable, meaningful,*

---

[5]This is not to deny the priority of valuing the 'ethic of care' (which is largely absent from discourses centring on the ethic of work) but to argue that income adequacy (for workers, carers and those dependent on welfare benefits) should meet standards of adequacy which reflect wider social norms and aspirations.

well paid work rather than leaving individuals compelled to succumb to the vagaries of the 'flexible' low-pay labour market.[6]

Research on young adults' experiences of social exclusion within derived neighbourhoods supports this view, concluding that the current policy emphasis on training, advice, work incentives and childcare is having only marginal impact on social exclusion. Instead, the authors argued that 'good quality training and rewarding and secure employment' was crucial and that this involved a 'more comprehensive and generous' redistribution – of both resources and opportunities (Webster et al., 2004). However, while much is said of 'opportunities', the issue of 'resource redistribution' remains off limits for New Labour policy discourse.

Although the *adequacy* of incomes – whether in welfare benefits or wages – is vitally important, we should not lose sight of those at the 'top' end of the scale whose incomes are far *beyond* 'adequate'. Chapter 1 indicated the dramatic rise in incomes at the top, where the top 10% of British earners received 28% of total income in 2003/4 compared with a 2.8% share of earnings for the bottom 10%. While government policy has focused on floor targets and a minimum wage, it has failed to broach *ceiling targets* or the idea of a maximum wage. The result is a society in which any decision to raise the highest rate of income tax above its current rate of 40 pence in the pound is regarded as politically unthinkable, and where the Duke of Westminster, Richard Branson and David Beckham (when he is at home) all pay the same rate of tax as I do. Personally, I am more than happy to pay (and to pay more). The problem is that the current top rate of tax applies to all income above £32,400, whether you are a bricklayer, sales representative or a school teacher earning £40,000 a year, or a Premier League footballer earning £100,000 a week. For me, this gross inequality in income coupled with a Conservative[7] tax policy towards the top earners raises issues of both equity and responsibility (to be discussed further in section 3 below).

It is widely accepted (outside the sphere of New Labour politics) that poverty cannot be adequately tackled without addressing inequality at national and international levels and that rising inequality is 'not inevitable' (Lister, 2004:53). The government's commitment to end child poverty and pensioner poverty (discussed in Chapters 1 and 6) would therefore imply a need for redistribution, although what redistribution has occurred since 1997 has done so by stealth, not declared policy. For

---

[6]Where 'the flexible labour market' is concerned, recent research by COMPAS (Centre on Migration, Policy and Society, Oxford University) suggested that migrants made up to 50% of those working in the areas of the economy most liable to forced labour and exploitation. These areas include: agriculture, fisheries, contract cleaning, hotel work, construction, work in care homes and the sex trade. The squalor and violence that often characterise their lives constitute an important (though invisible) feature of a British economy which is able to be competitive and 'flexible' by driving wages down, partly through dependence on exploiting migrant labour. Ironically, these workers are then cast as 'others' and often subjected to harassment and the vitriol of the tabloid press and middle England (see Chapter 6).

[7]Recall, in Chapter 1, that the top rate of tax was reduced to 40% by the (Conservative) Thatcher government in 1988.

New Labour, increases in tax remain 'the great unmentionable'. The received wisdom for this decision derives from the general election defeat of 1992 when the then Shadow Chancellor, John Smith, proposed an increase in the top rate of tax to 50%. However, as John Hills and Kitty Stewart noted, there was no evidence (from opinion polls or otherwise) that a potential higher rate tax increase figured prominently in Labour's defeat (Hills and Stewart, 2005:7) but the party has since held on (defensively) to its predecessors conservative tax policies.

Ironically, the British Social Attitudes surveys conducted since the 1990s have all indicated that the majority feel the gap between rich and poor is too large (Jackson and Segal, 2004). Moreover, when recently asked 'Should the government spend more or less on health, education and social benefits by raising or reducing taxes accordingly?', 62.4% favoured increasing taxes[8] and spending more (British Social Attitudes Survey, 2002). But the moratorium on higher tax rates stubbornly persists, even in the face of more progressive public attitudes and evidence that, with the prospect of declining revenues, we can ill afford such a policy (Emmerson et al., 2005).

At this point it is perhaps worth stepping back to look at a bigger picture and ask the 'utopian' questions posed by Ruth Levitas:

> What is the alternative? Increase the top rate of tax? Certainly. Increase inheritance tax and the baby bond? Perhaps. Renationalise the railways? Definitely. But these are still piecemeal ameliorative policies. The point of the utopian method is that we stop and think about where we are trying to go. (2001:449)

In order to understand why and how social policies ostensibly geared to social justice have side-stepped the *core issue of taxation*, it is necessary to ask bigger (and some may say, utopian) questions. If, as New Labour, 'Where they are trying to go' is *only* back into office (at all costs), then their policy stance is explicable, although not excusable: social justice and criminal justice, as interdependent goals, both rest upon notions of fairness and, in my view, current fiscal polices are simply not 'fair'.

3. Some Principles for Reconciling Criminal and Social Justice

This section will attempt to work towards a sense of 'Where we are trying to go' by sketching some of the key principles that would underpin any attempts to reconcile criminal and social justice in contemporary Britain. In this task we can build a great deal on existing theorising from the spheres of both social policy and criminology. What follows will be based upon this theorising together with the wide-ranging (though, admittedly sometimes terse) arguments that have been presented in this book. As a result this final section is inevitably highly distilled. What follows, then, are ten (good enough – for a start, at least) principles which may usefully inform

---

[8]While extra funding for the NHS has been used to justify recent increases in National Insurance contributions, income *tax* increases for this purpose remain off limits.

attempts to address the challenges described here, and to more effectively reconcile criminal and social justice – in theory, practice and research.

3.1 Recognition&respect

This principle reflects the work of Ruth Lister which marks a fusion of not just two but three essential preconditions for social (and criminal) justice, as she states:

> The struggle for social justice has to involve both redistribution and recognition& respect. (2004:188)

Where the politics of recognition seeks respect for difference, the politics of redistribution seeks to remove unjust differences, but the two are interconnected (and discussion of the material principle of redistribution follows later). This first principle – *recognition& respect* – connotes symbolic and relational struggles against injustice. This conjoined principle encompass the seven components identified by Fiona Williams (1999) as 'good enough' principles for welfare, namely: interdependence, care, intimacy, bodily integrity, identity, transnational welfare and voice (see Chapter 3, page 73). At the same time, the component of 'respect' also recalls criminal justice principles of dignity and human rights (Sanders, 2002). But, the reading of recognition&respect proposed here should not be confused with New Labour's third term 'respect' agenda: this latter version of 'respect' is located within the lexis of order and control.

3.2 Redistribution

This principle builds, in theory, on the work of Nancy Fraser who usefully distinguishes *socio-economic* injustice (rooted in the political-economic structure of society, including economic and social marginalisation) and *cultural or symbolic injustice* (patterns of representation, communication implying disrespect, and/or cultural domination). As discussed in Chapter 1, she goes on to contend that these two manifestations of injustice have in the past been polarised, as had academic debate. But, for Fraser, the idea of a purely 'cultural society', devoid of economic relations did not reflect contemporary social life (Fraser, 2000:111). Following on from this perspective, redistribution (for me) offers one key means of addressing material injustices which lead to poverty and marginalisation. *Redistribution combined with recognition&respect* would also help to remedy a range of very 'real' material injustices suffered along lines of age, gender, sexuality, (dis)ability, religion, ethnicity and 'race'. As Chapters 1 and 2 have shown, such injustices may include those of: income, wealth, employment, health and health care, access to a range of public and private services, pension rights, and access to (and quality of) criminal and civil justice.

Redistribution could additionally serve the symbolic function of 'reprimanding greed', in addition to encouraging (and funding) a shift in social policies away from the primacy of the ethic of work and material accumulation, towards a rewarding of the ethic of care and considerations of what is necessary for a decent life for all. This principle could also be applied through '*inequality-proofing*' policies, to ensure that not only do they not *disadvantage* poorer and vulnerable groups, but that they do not *advantage* richer people (Sinfield, 2004). In all these respects, redistribution is envisaged here not as an end in itself, but as a tool, used together with the other principles described, to address the material basis of many (though, of course, not all) forms of criminal and social injustice.

3.3 Responsibility

The sense in which 'responsibility' is used here is very different from its usual use in New Labour political discourse and focuses, instead, on the responsibilities of the relatively rich to fully meet their obligations as citizens. As argued in Chapters 1 and 3, relatively well-off individuals pay less (relatively, in taxation and for everyday goods and services), have less demanded of them (in terms of behaviour, as they are good citizens, 'givers' to the state) and are less liable to formal and informal censure than poorer groups. But, as Giddens (2000) acknowledged, 'mutual obligations must stretch... from bottom to top'. Put bluntly, if we expect the poor to behave themselves, we should expect the rich to do so too. While new discourse has stressed the responsibilities of the poor and excluded (to work, pay taxes, obey the law and support their families), it has failed to emphasise and to enforce the same responsibilities of the rich. The example of the differential treatment of tax and benefit fraud (discussed in Chapter 2) is a reminder of a double standard applied to rich and poor when they defraud the state. Differential patterns of criminalisation and sentencing similarly demonstrate a double standard whereby being relatively well-off is often an *exculpatory factor* where a crime has been committed (s/he is of good character, hard working, has suffered enough and so on) rather than an *inculpatory* one (s/he is well-off and has no 'excuse', should know better and has betrayed our trust). The principle of responsibility could therefore be used to critique and radicalise the politics of blame which currently pervades contemporary social and criminal justice discourse.

This principle also applies to the *responsibilities of the state* itself: for example, where ex-prisoners are concerned (discussed in Chapter 5), it could be argued that the state has an obligation to try to address the multiple exclusions they suffer (for example, by providing drug and alcohol rehabilitation, skills, education and work programmes, housing and welfare provision, and better services – in every respect – for looked after children and young people). In this sense the response to those who break the law should be one resembling 'state obligated rehabilitation' (Carlen and Cook, 1989).

At the same time, responsibility would work alongside redistribution, both materially and symbolically: in the case of the former, if the rich pay their dues, there will be more resources available for public services and welfare provision (and for state obligated rehabilitation too). In relation to the latter, the principle of responsibility could be beneficial in enhancing a more genuine sense of 'fairness' – and ultimately *legitimacy and trust* – because responsibilities and duties fall (and are seen to do so) on the rich and poor alike.

3.4 Rights

In the challenging times which define the 'third wave' of rights, it is commonplace to hear complaints that rights have 'gone too far': pub talk and tabloid stories of 'asylum seekers', a victim of crime imprisoned for shooting dead a burglar, adults prosecuted for hitting their children, and court cases involving accusations of racial or sexual harassment can all invoke *negative* responses, critical of the 'rights' of 'others'. One essential principle for reconciling criminal and social justice would be the reassertion of a ***positive rights discourse***.

Recalling from Chapter 1, citizenship can be seen in terms of: civil and political; social and economic; environmental; and human rights. But these rights of citizenship in contemporary Britain may be undermined by the wide range of inequalities described in this book. It follows that to address these inequalities it would be essential to redress the rights imbalance. In practice this would entail countering the factors described in Chapter 1 (and visualised in Figure 1.1) which currently undermine rights, by positively stressing the value of:

1. **Civil and political rights:** civil liberties, freedom from harassment, legal rights, participation, trust and empowerment
2. **Social and economic rights:** good quality, accessible, fair and appropriate services for: health, education, welfare, housing, leisure, culture, transport and care; adequacy of income (for those in paid work and those who are not)
3. **Environmental rights:** water, housing, environmental amenity and minimisation of pollution (through harm reduction and precautionary policies)
4. **Human rights:** dignity, recognition&respect, elimination of poverty, 'voice', access to justice, civil and political rights (above).

Stating the need for a positive reassertion of these rights may be seen by some as unnecessary and by others as utopian. But, as Ruth Levitas argued, we have to take time to think (and to make clear) 'Where we are trying to go' before setting out on the journey.

3.5 Sustainability

Two of the main factors which undermined the effectiveness of many New Labour policies (described in Chapters 4 and 5) were failures in consultation and in implementation. Key reasons for both were lack of resources and lack of community engagement. Financial and human resources have, under New Labour, often been allocated to a multiplicity of initiatives and programmes which are time and/or area limited. This proliferation of initiatives needs to be reversed in favour of integration into mainstream budgets (Perri 6 et al., 1999). But the principle of 'sustainability' here refers to more than persistence over time, and more than mainstreaming budgets – it refers also to the sustainability of community networks and social relations.

But, here too, money does matter: as Fiona Williams, for example, has noted 'local, rooted community and self-help groups struggle to survive year after year with little stable funding' and yet these groups offer indispensable services and support (Williams, 2004:419). Chapters 4 and 5 also demonstrated the vital role of voluntary and community, not-for-profit, sector agencies in a range of policy areas, but the problems they face in, for instance, sustaining their role within partnerships, given their constraints of time and resources.

Beyond issues of time and money, the principle of sustainability must also apply to relationships of trust and empowerment in local contexts and, as we saw in Chapter 5, a sense of trust and empowerment can emanate from more participatory methods of engaging those communities. And so, the principle of sustainability offers a more 'nuanced understanding' of the ways in which social and criminal justice exists within the context of complex community-based relations (Kelly et al., 2005). This principle, in turn, offers the prospect for a more holistic approach to policy-making and delivery in complex, community-based contexts.

3.6 Holism

Holistic ways of working attempt to address people and issues in the round, as a whole. In terms of criminal and social justice, the principle of holism attempts to challenge the dangers of pervasive 'silo' mentalities of lead government departments. Returning to Chapter 1, the 'way ahead' in tackling crime and its causes (Figure 1.7) indicated a seperating out of measures designed to tackle crime per se from broader 'social' measures. The dangers for criminal and social justice evident here (and in subsequent policies) are that the *criminal* will be privileged over the *social*; and that crime reduction will be seen as disconnected in organisation and delivery from strategies addressing 'causes' (Stenson and Edwards, 2004). Thus far (as Chapters 3 and 6 have shown) there has been a tendency to criminalise the social, but the principle of holism would attempt to *re-socialise* issues of crime and justice.

One example of a holistic approach which encompasses criminal justice and social welfare interventions is the Specialist Domestic Violence Court. These are largely based upon principles grounded in what has been termed 'therapeutic jurisprudence', which signals a move away from traditional adversarial principles and instead adopts a *co-ordinated and problem-solving approach* in an effort to meet the needs of victims, their families and the community (Ostrom, 2003). But for this holistic approach to work, there must be commitment from all parties – from police and judiciary to health care and voluntary and community sector support workers. It also requires that we envisage and treat victims, survivors and 'clients' as people – not 'cases' – and take account of the complex realities of their daily lives. This may mean acknowledging the potential of the legal system to address crimes (such as domestic violence), while equally acknowledging (from the victim's perspective) that it has many limitations in practice. The holism and flexibility of this approach can be empowering and very beneficial, and illustrates the ways in which more holistic interventions may cross and blur the false boundaries between many 'criminal' and 'social' issues, but potentially offer a truly 'joined-up' response to individuals' needs.

3.7 From managerial to transformative governance

The critique of governance in section 2 concluded that an important component of more progressive welfare and criminal justice futures depended upon the creative role of practitioners. Creative professionalism, an emphasis on rights and accompanying organisational culture change offered ways forward to addressing some of the challenges posed by NPSM modes of governance. But there were also seen to be some advantages arising from some of the new ways of working implied in the term 'governance' (Newburn, 2002; Burnett and Appleton, 2004). Many critics may feel that there is little worth salvaging here, although I doubt that it is either feasible or desirable to attempt to disinvent some of the management techniques that governance currently deploys, and so salvaging what may be positively re-directed to other *ends* (other than the maintenance of governance itself) may be a preferable option. This leads us to the principle of ***transformative governance***.

This term derives from Young and Matthews (2003) who contended that while New Labour delineated the structural causes of crime, it merely stopped at that. The way in which the discourses of crime and its causes were subsumed within the overarching framework of 'social exclusion' could be seen as negating any structural cause – the policy response it invoked was managerial not ***transformative*** (ibid:15 emphasis added). The policy task was thus reduced down to the management of socially excluded and 'problem' individuals, communities and neighbourhoods.

Building on this analysis, I would argue that in order to move towards reconciling criminal and social justice, there is a need to develop new forms of governance which are *transformative* – that help towards achieving just *ends* and not constitute *means* (of governing) alone. This will be essential if transparency, accountability and effectiveness in local (and national) services is to be ensured. At the same time, a better balance needs to be struck between designing systems to assure these positive aims are met whilst, at the same time, allowing for ***local agency, flexibility and innovation***. These tensions currently lie at the heart of New Labour's democratisation and modernisation projects, and have yet to be resolved. In order to provide the basis for such a resolution it is necessary to re-think not only structures of governance, but also styles of leadership (see 3.10 below).

3.8 Embedding

One of the crucial themes emerging from Chapters 4, 5 and 6 was the ***short termism*** of many criminal justice and social policies. This issue is partly addressed by reference to the principle of sustainability – over time and resourcing. But there is also a political and ideological dimension to short-termism: that is, the perceived need to appeal to middle England has led to a desire to tap into their concerns, devise policies geared to achieving 'quick wins' and, thereby, to get (re)elected. But to begin to reconcile issues of criminal and social justice, there is a pressing need to challenge short-termism and to advocate for greater ***societal embedding*** of policy. In this vein,

Daniel Clegg persuasively argues that a progressive future, rather than just seeking short-term effectiveness *in* social policy, would focus on longer-term consensus and legitimacy *over* social policy (Clegg, 2005:235). But the mechanisms for building such a consensus remain unclear and have not emerged under New Labour, despite the rhetoric of democratisation, partnership and participation.

Similar arguments on societal embedding have been put forward in relation to anti-poverty strategies, where greater public support needs to be mobilised: here awareness raising, information and campaigning is seen to be needed to engage an ill-informed public and win popular support for policy (Bamfield, 2005). One important element in this context is **coalition building**, which largely runs counter to the New Labour emphasis on wooing the centre – middle England (Gary Younge, *Red Pepper*, February 2000). If efforts to more effectively reconcile criminal and social justice are to succeed, then coalitions will need to be built between policy-makers and: academics, researchers, campaigners, practitioners, community groups, not-for-profit groups, service users and many (as yet) voiceless 'others'. This last point links with the next principle – what Adrian Sinfield termed 'moving upstream' (Sinfield, 2004).

3.9 Moving 'upstream'

This principle refers to a story rediscovered and quoted by Adrian Sinfield (2004) to illustrate the need for social policy researchers and theorists to address structural causes of poverty and disadvantage. It tells of a doctor who feels his professional dilemma is summed up as follows: standing at the shore of a swiftly flowing river he [*sic*] hears the cry of a drowning man. He jumps in, rescues him, applies artificial respiration and the man begins to breathe, at which point another cry for help is heard. Again he jumps into the river, rescues and resuscitates. Another cry, and again, and again. By this time the doctor is so busy rescuing that he has no time to run upstream to see who is pushing these people into the water in the first place.

Upstream policies seek to address root causes and to prevent inequalities, rather than downstream policies which seek to understand and ameliorate them. The shift to 'upstream' thus entails addressing the structural causes and contexts of inequalities – and that would include studying the benefits and subsidies to the rich as well as those paid out to the poor (Sinfield, 2004). There are lessons here too for academics. As policy researchers and theorists, this principle suggests we need to move upstream and to: move from deconstructive to (re)constructive arguments; from regressive to progressive critiques; and to develop *positive* policy options to enhance criminal and social justice. The need for a positive vision underlies the last principle for reconciling criminal and social justice.

3.10 Idealism

In the principle of idealism, I am referring here to the **politics of conviction and belief**. In the past the term 'conviction politics' was used disparagingly to refer to

Margaret Thatcher's strident new right political stance. But here it is seen to refer to a positive element which is currently lacking in New Labour policy and leadership. As we saw in Chapter 3, New Labour's Third Way politics explicitly rejected the conviction politics of the left and the right in favour of an essentially pragmatic stance. In doing so it seemed to concur with this view:

> Idealism without pragmatism is impotent. Pragmatism without idealism is meaningless. The key to effective leadership is pragmatic idealism.

Interestingly, this view was not expressed in recent years by a New Labour politician, but almost 40 years ago by former US President Richard Nixon (Richard Nixon, quoted in Strober and Strober, 1994:109). However, Nixon's advocacy of 'pragmatic idealism' emanated from his 'brokerable convictions', which was hardly a positive attribute for leadership (ibid).

In the UK context, many have accused Tony Blair of a similar variety of pragmatism which gives rise to 'wooing not leading' the nation, and this failure of leadership, alluded to by Ruth Lister in 2001, was also evident in the 2005 general election (although perhaps less successfully). Indeed, after the victory Blair likened his relationship with the electorate as a 'relationship', but despite all the wooing, concerns around the Prime Minister's sinuousness, pragmatism and leadership style are not going away. Such concerns around leadership are not restricted to the UK: in the context of Canada there have been recent calls for more ideological leadership from politicians; greater recognition between rights and responsibilities across the class divide; a more progressive system of taxation; more analysis of social costs and benefits; and more informed debate on the core issues in globalisation (Faulkner, 2003:293). In the immediate post-2005 election weeks there were similar murmurings in the UK when MPs (some of them even allowing themselves to be named) called for 'different leadership', a 'progressive consensus' and 'conviction politics' (*TimesOnline*, 26 May 2005).

The principle of idealism used here addresses these aspirations, but acknowledges that political conditions – at home and abroad – currently make this difficult. The war on terror being waged in the UK and globally creates conditions under which 'if you believe in nothing, fear becomes the only agenda' (*The Power of Nightmares*, BBC 2 television programme, 27 October, 2004). The challenge now is to engender a sense of belief in *something* in a time of fear. But, beyond just believing in something, (anything), the goal in reconciling criminal and social justice must be to take a ***principled and progressive turn***, which is underpinned by conviction not pragmatism. The 'turn' envisaged here is one of both inflection and direction. It will be a difficult one to make in the current political climate and change may come only by inching our way forward. But we have got to start somewhere...

⊙⊙ **References**

9/11 Commission (2004) *The 9–11 Commission Report: Final Report of the National Commission on Terrorist Attacks Upon the United States, Official Government Edition*. Washington DC, US Government Printing Office.

Accountancy Age (2005) http://www.accountancyage.com/accountancyage/news/2037126/ rich-hide-billion-for-havens (accessed 26 July 2005).

Adam, S. Brewer, M. and Wakefield, M. (2005) *Tax and Benefit Changes: who wins and who loses?* Election Briefing, Institute for Fiscal Studies (IFS).

Ambrose, P. (2004) 'Force, Fraud or Goodwill?' *Poverty* Vol. 18.

Amin, A. (2003) 'Unruly Strangers? The Urban Riots in Britain'. *International Journal of Urban and Regional Research* Vol. 27 No. 2 pp 460–3.

Amin, A. Massey, D. and Thrift, N. (2003) *Decentering the Nation: A Radical approach to regional inequality*. Catalyst. http://www.catalystforum.org.uk/pubs/paper19a.html Accessed 24 February 2004.

Amnesty International (2005) *United Kingdom – Seeking Asylum is not a crime: detention of people seeking asylum*. 20 June 2005. http://www.amnesty.org

Anderson, B. and Rogaly, B. (2005) *Forced Labour and Migration to the UK*. Centre on Migration, Policy and Society (COMPAS) Oxford University/TUC. http://www.compass.ox.ac.uk/ publications/ papers/Forced%20Labour%20Report.pdf

Aslam, D. (2005) 'We rock the boat: today's Muslims aren't prepared to ignore injustice'. *Guardian*, Wednesday 13 July 2005.

Association of Police Authorities (2005) *Competency Frameworks for Members of Police Authorities in England and Wales*. London, APA.

Audit Commission (1998) *A Fruitful Partnership: effective partnership working*. Audit Commission Management Paper.

Audit Commission (2002) Briefing: *Community Safety Partnerships*. London, Audit Commission.

Baldock, J. and Hadlow, J. (2004) 'Managing the Family: Productivity, Scheduling and the Male Veto'. *Social Policy and Administration*, Vol. 38 No. 6 pp 706–20.

Bamfield, L. (2005) 'Making the Case for Tackling Poverty and Inequality'. *Poverty* Issue 121, Summer 2005. London, CPAG.

Barbalet (1988) *Citizenship*. Milton Keynes, Open University Press.

Barnes, M., Newman, J., Knops, A. and Sullivan, H. (2003) 'Constituting "The Public" in Public Participation'. *Public Administration* Vol. 81 No. 2 pp 379–99.

Barrow Cadbury Trust, (2003) *Inside Out: rethinking inclusive communities*. London, DEMOS.

BDO Stoy Hayward (2005) 'Business Failures Set to Rise after Two Year Lull'. Press Release 21 March, 2005.

Beck, U. (1992) *Risk Society: towards a new modernity*. London, Sage.

Bennett, F. and Roberts, M. (2004) *From Input to Influence: participatory approaches to research and enquiry into poverty*. York, JRF.

Beresford, P. (2001) 'Service Users, Social Policy and the Future of Welfare'. *Critical Social Policy* Vol. 12 No. 4 pp 494–512.

Berghman (1995) 'Social Exclusion in Europe: policy context and analytical framework'. In G. Room (ed.) *Beyond the Threshold*. Bristol, Policy Press.

Blair, T. (1998) *The Third Way: new politics for the new century*. London, Fabian Society.

Blanden, J. Gregg, P. and Machin, S. (2005) *Intergenerational Mobility in Europe and North America: a report supported by the Sutton Trust*. Centre for Economic Performance, London School of Economics.

Blunkett, D. (1999) 'The Welfare Society'. Speech to DEMOS. 19 May 1999. London, DEMOS.

Blunkett, D. (2003) *Civil Renewal: a new agenda*. The CVS Edith Kahn Memorial Lecture, 11 June 2003. London, Home Office/CVS.

Blunkett, D. (2005) *A New England: An English identity within Britain*. Speech to the IPPR 14 March 2005.

Boone, M. (2004) 'The Legal Boundaries of What Works'. Paper presented to the *4th Annual Conference of the European Society for Criminology*, Amsterdam, Netherlands.

Bottoms, A. (2005) 'Methodology Matters'. *Safer Society*, Summer 2005. NACRO.

Boyne, G.A. (2003) 'What is Public Service Improvement?' *Public Administration* Vol. 81 No. 2 pp 211–27.

Braithwaite, J. (2002) 'Rewards and Regulation'. *Journal of Law and Society* Vol. 29 No. 1 pp 12–26.

Brewer, M., Goodman, A., Myck, M., Shaw, J. and Shephard, A. (2004) *Poverty and Inequality in Britain: 2004*. London, Institute for Fiscal Studies (IFS).

Brewer, M., Goodman, A., Shaw, J. and Shephard, A. (2005) *Poverty and Inequality in Britain 2005*. London, IFS.

British Social Attitudes Survey (2004) *British Social Attitudes: the 21st Report*. London: Sage.

Brookman and Pierpoint (2003) 'Access to Legal Advice for Young Suspects and Remand Prisoners', *Howard Journal of Criminal Justice*, Vol. 42 No. 5 pp 452–70.

Brown, G. (2000) Chancellor of the Exchequer's Budget Statement 21 March 2000. http://www.hm-treasury.gov.uk/budget/budget_2000/bud_bud00_speech.cfm

Burchardt, T. (2005) 'Selective Inclusion: asylum seekers and other marginalised groups'. In J. Hills and K. Stewart (eds) *A More Equal Society? New Labour, poverty, inequality and exclusion*. Bristol, The Policy Press.

Burnett, R. and Appleton, C. (2004) 'Joined-Up Services to Tackle Youth Crime'. *British Journal of Criminology* Vol. 44 No. 1 pp 34–54.

Burney, E. (2002) 'Talking Tough, Acting Coy: What Happened to the Anti-Social Behaviour Order? *Howard Journal* Vol. 41 No. 5 pp 469–84.

Butt, J. and O'Neill, A. (2004) *'Lets Move on' Black and Minority Ethnic Older People's Views on Research Findings*. York, JRF.

Byrne, D. (2001) *Social Exclusion*. Buckingham, Open University Press.

Cabinet Office (1999) *Modernising Government*. London, Cabinet Office.

Cabinet Office (2000) *e-Government: a strategic framework for public services in the information age*. London, Cabinet Office.

Cabinet Office (2004) *Code of Practice on Consultation*. London, Regulatory Impact Unit, Cabinet Office.

Campbell, B. (1993) *Goliath*. London, Methuen.

Campbell, C., Wood, R. and Kelly, M. (1999) *Social Capital and Health*. London, Health Education Authority.

Cantle, T. (2001) *Community Cohesion: a report of the Independent Review Team*. Home Office. http://www.homeoffice.gov.uk/docs2/pocc.html

Carlen, P. (1989) 'Crime Inequality and Sentencing'. In C.P. Carlen and D. Cook (eds) *Paying for Crime*. Milton Keynes, Open University Press.

Carlen, P. (2002) 'Critical Criminology? In praise of an oxymoron and its enemies'. In K. Carrington and R. Hogg (eds) *Critical Criminology: issues debates and challenges*. Devon, Willan Publishing.

Carlen, P. and Cook, D. (eds) (1989) *Paying for Crime*. Milton Keynes, Open University Press.

Cavadino, P. (2002) *Safer Society* No. 13, Summer 2002.

Charman, S. and Savage, S.P. (1999) 'The New Politics of Law and Order: Labour, crime and justice'. In M. Powell (ed.) *New Labour, New Welfare: the 'third way' in British social policy*. Bristol, Policy Press.

Child Poverty Action Group (2003) *Campaign Newsletter* Issue 30, December 2003. London, CPAG.

Churches Commission for Racial Justice (2005) *Election Briefing*. March 2005.

Citizens Advice (2005a) *Tackling Rural Disadvantage, Our First Thematic Study*. http://www.citizensadvice.org.uk

Citizens Advice (2005b) *Money with Your Name on it?*

Clarke, J. (2004a) 'Dissolving the Public realm? The logics and limits of neo-liberalism'. *Journal of Social Policy* Vol. 33 No. 1 pp 27–48.

Clarke, J. (2004b) *Changing Welfare, Changing States: new directions in social policy*. London, Sage.

Clarke, M. and Stewart, J. (1997) *Handling Wicked Issues: a challenge for government*. Birmingham, Birmingham University School of Public Policy.

Clegg, D. (2005) 'A Rootless Third Way: continental European perspectives New Labour's Third Way revisited'. In M. Powell, L. Bauld and K. Clarke (eds) *Social Policy Review 17*. Bristol, Policy Press.

Clegg, M. Finney, A. and Thorpe, K. (2005) *Crime in England and Wales, Quarterly Update to December 2004*. Home Office Bulletin 07/05, 21 April 2005.

Clements, L. (2005) 'Winners and Losers'. *Journal of Law and Society*. Vol. 32 No. 1 pp 34–50.

Cohen, S. (1988) *Against Criminology*. Oxford, Transaction Books.

Cole, D.H. (2001) '"An Unqualified Human Good": E.P. Thompson and the Rule of Law'. *Journal of Law and Society* Vol. 28 No. 2 pp 177–203.

Coleman, J.C. (1988) 'Social Capital in the Creation of Human Capital'. *American Journal of Sociology* Vol. 94 pp S95–S120.

Coleman, J.S. (1990) *Foundations of Social Theory*. Cambridge M, Belknap.

Colley, H. and Hodgkinson, P. (2001) 'Problems with "Bridging the Gap": the reversal of structure and agency in addressing social exclusion'. *Critical Social Policy* Vol. 21 No. 3 pp 335–59.

Collins, C. (2002) *Separate Silos: Race and the reform agenda in Whitehall*. London, IPPR.

Collins, T. (2005) 'What national police IT fiasco has to teach us for the NHS modernisation programme'. *Computer Weekly* 5 July 2005.

Commission on Poverty, Participation and Power (2000) *Listen Hear: the Right to be Heard. Report of the Commission on Poverty, Participation and Power*. Policy Press/JRF/UKAP.

Commission on Social Justice (1993) *The Justice Gap*. London, IPPR.

Cook, D. (1989). *Rich Law, Poor Law*. Milton Keynes, Open University Press.

Cook, D. (1993) 'Racism, Citizenship and Exclusion'. In D. Cook and B. Hudson (eds) *Racism and Criminology*. London, Sage.

Cook, D. (1997a) 'Social Divisions of Welfare: Tax and social security fraud'. *New Waverley Paper Series*, Edinburgh University.

Cook, D. (1997b) *Poverty, Crime and Punishment*. London, CPAG.

Cook, D. (1997c) 'Criminal Justice and Social Policy: a New Settlement or the Emperor's New Clothes?' Unpublished paper to the Social Policy Association Annual Conference, University of Lincolnshire and Humberside, 15–17 July 1997.

Cook, D. (1999) 'Putting Crime in its Place: the causes of crime and New Labour's local solutions'. In H. Dean and R. Woods (eds) *Social Policy Review 11*. Luton, SPA/University of Luton.

Cook, D. and Roberts, M. (2001) *Looked After Children and Youth Offending in Shropshire and Telford & Wrekin*. Research report. http://www.wlv.ac.uk/pri

Cook, D. (2002) 'Consultation for a Change? Engaging users and communities in the policy process'. *Social Policy and Administration* Vol. 3 No. 5 pp 516–531.

Cook, D. (2003) *Evaluation of Wolverhampton Specialist Domestic Violence Court*. Regional Research Institute, University of Wolverhampton http://www.wlv.ac.uk/pri

Cook, D. and Lyle, C. (2004) *Audit and Feasibility Study for a West Midlands Domestic Violence Voluntary Perpetrator Programme*. Research report. http://www.wlv.ac.uk/pri

Cook, D. and Vallely, C. (2003) *A Study of Witness Non-Attendance at Wolverhampton Magistrates Court: a comparative West Midlands Case Study*. Research Report. http://www.wlv.ac. uk/pri

Cook, D., Roberts, M., Cameron, E. and Watkin, G. (1998) 'Wren's Nest: Crime Audit.' Unpublished report for the Wren's Nest Safety Partnership.

Cook, D., Burton, M., Robinson, A. and Vallely, C. (2004) *Evaluation of Specialist Domestic Violence Courts/Fast Track Systems*. London, CPS/DCA/CJS Race Unit. http://www.cps.gov.uk/publications/docs/specialistdvcourts.pdf

Corner, J. (2004) 'Inaction Plan'. *Safer Society* Issue 22, Winter 2004. London, NACRO.

Cottingham, P., Maynard, R. and Stagner, M. (2004) 'Synthesising Evidence on the Impacts of Programmes and Policies in Education, Crime and Jusitcie, and Social Welfare: practical recommendatioms based on 14 Test-bed Reviews'. *Evaluation and Education* Vol. 18 Nos 1 & 2, pp 28–53.

Cowie, J. (2002) 'Nixon's Class Struggle: Romancing the New Right Worker, 1969–1973'. *Labor History* Vol. 43 No. 3 pp 257–83.

Craig, G., Taylor, M. and Parkes, T. (2004) 'Partnership or Protest? The voluntary and community sectors in the policy process'. *Social Policy and Administration* Vol. 38 No. 3 pp 221–39.

Crawford, A. (1998) *Crime Prevention and Community Safety*. London, Longman.

Crawford, A. (2001) *Public Matters: reviving public participation in criminal justice*. London, IPPR.

Crawford, A. (2003) '"Contractual Governance" of Deviant Behaviour'. *Journal of Law and Society*. Vol. 30 No. 4 pp 479–505.

Credit Action (2005) *Debt Fact and Figures: compiled 8 April 2005*. http://www.creditaction .org.uk

Crime and Society (2005) '"Don't do it our way", Major Giuliani's prisons chief tells Britain'. Press Release, 13 June 2005.

Daguerre, A. (2004) 'Importing Workfare: Policy transfer of social and labour market policies from the USA to Britain under New Labour'. *Social Policy and Administration* Vol. 38 No. 1 pp 41–56.

Daly, M. (2003) 'Governance and Social Policy'. *Journal of Social Policy* Vol. 32 Vol. 1 pp 113–28.

Davies, P. (2004) 'Is Evidence-Based Government Possible?'. Jerry Lee Lecture to the Annual Campbell Collaboration Colloquium, Washington DC, 19 February 2004.

Deacon (1997) in L.M. Mead (ed.) *From Welfare to Work: lessons from America*. Choice in Welfare Series No. 39, London, Institute of Economic Affairs.

Deacon, A. (2002) *Perspectives on Welfare: ideas, ideologies and policy debates*. Buckingham, Open University Press.

Delorenzi, S., Reed, J. and Robinson, P. (2005) *Maintaining Momentum: extending social mobility and life chances from early years to adulthood*. London, IPPR.

Denham, J. (2001) *Building Cohesive Communities: a report of the Ministerial Group on Public Order and Community Cohesion*. London, Home Office.

Dennis, N. and Erdos, G. (1993) *Families without Fatherhood*. London, Institute for Economic Affairs.

Doherty, P., Stott, A. and Kinder, K. (2004) *Delivering Services to Hard to Reach Families in On Track Areas: definition, consultation and needs assessment*. Home Office Development and Practice Report 15. London, Home Office.

Donzelot, J. (1980) *The Policing of Families*. London, Hutchinson.

Dorning, D. and Thomas, B. (2004) *People and Places: A 2001 Census Atlas of the UK*. Bristol, Policy Press.

DTI (Department of Trade and Industry) (2001) *Opportunity for All in a World of Change: white paper on skills, innovation and enterprise*. London, DTI.

Duncan, P. and Thomas, S. (2000) *Neighbourhood Regeneration: resourcing community involvement*. Bristol, Policy Press.

Duncan, S., Edwards, S. Reynolds, T. and Alldred, P. (2003) *Mothers and Childcare: Policies, Values and Theories*. Chichester, John Willey and Sons.

DWP (Department for Work and Pensions) (2003) *Opportunity for All: Fifth Annual Report 2003*. CM 5956. London, DWP.

DWP (2004a) *Fraud and Error in Income Support and Jobseekers Allowance from April 2002 – March 2003*. London, National Statistics.

DWP (2004b) *Income Related Benefits: Estimates of Take-up in 2001/2*. London, National Statistics.

DWP (2005a) *Income Related benefits Estimates of Take-Up in 2002/3*. London, National Statistics.

DWP (2005b) *Jobcentre Plus Evaluation: summary of evidence*. Research report No. 252, Leeds, DWP/Corporate Document Services.

Dwyer, P. (2004) *Understanding Social Citizenship*. Bristol, Policy Press.

ECRI (European Commission Against Racism and Intolerance) (2005) *Third Report on the United Kingdom*. Strasbourg, Council of Europe.

Ekblom, P. (1998) *The Crime and Disorder Act: community safety and the reduction and prevention of crime*. London, Home Office Research and Statistics Directorate.

Emmerson, C., Frayne, C. and Tetlow, G. (2005) *Taxation: election briefing 2005*. London, Institute for Fiscal Studies.

EOC (Equal Opportunities Commission) (2005) *Sex and Power: who runs Britain? 2005*. London, EOC.

Fairfax, P., Green E., Hawran, H., South, J. and Cairns, L. (ND) *Well Connected! A Self-Assessment Tool on Community Involvement for Organisations*. Bradford Action Zone/Building Communities Partnership Initiative.

Farrall, and Gadd, D. (2004) 'Research Note: The Frequency of the Fear of Crime'. *British Journal of Criminology* Vol. 44 No. 1 pp 127–32.

Faulkner, D. (2001) *Crime the State and Citizen: a field full of folk*. Winchester, Waterside Press.

Faulkner, D. (2003) 'Taking Citizenship Seriously: social capital and criminal justice in a changing world'. *Criminal Justice* Vol. 3 No. 3 pp 287–315.

Fawcett Society Briefing (2004) *Equal Pay*. http://www.fawcettsociety.org.uk/

Fenge, L. (2001) 'Empowerment and Community Care – projecting the voice of older people'. *Journal of Social Welfare and Family Law* Vol. 23 No. 4 pp 427–39.

Finn, D. (2003) 'The Employment First Welfare State: lessons from the New Deal for Young People'. *Social Policy and Administration* Vol. 37 No. 7 pp 709–24.

Fitzgerald, M., Stockdale, J. and Hale, C. (2003) *Young People and Street Crime*. London, Youth Justice Board.

Flaherty, J., Veit-Wilson, J. and Dornan, P. (2004) *Poverty: the facts 5th Edition*. London, Child Poverty Action Group (CPAG).

Foley, J. (ed.) (2004) *Sustainability and Social Justice*. London, IPPR.

Follett, M. (2004) 'Who Governs? The changing roles of councillors and officers in local community safety partnerships'. Unpublished paper to the British Society of Criminology Conference, Portsmouth, 6–9 July 2004.

Forest, R. and Kearns, A. (1999) *Joined-up Places? Social Cohesion and neighbourhood regeneration*. JRF Foundations, April 1999 Ref 4109. http://www.jrf.org.uk/knowledge/findings/foundations/4109.asp. Accessed June 2004.

Foster, J. (2002) 'People Pieces: the neglected but essential elements of community crime prevention'. In G. Hughes and A. Crawford (eds) *Crime Control and Community*. Devon, Willan Publishing.

Fraser, D. (1973) *The Evolution of the British Welfare State*. London, Macmillan.

Fraser, N. (2000) 'Rethinking Recognition'. *New Left Review* 3 May 2000.

Fraser, P. (1998) 'Reducing Offending'. *Safer Society* No. 1. October 1998.

Gadd, D. (2004) 'Evidence-led Policy or Policy-led Evidence? Cognitive behaviour programmes for men who are violent to women'. *Criminal Justice* Vol. 4 No. 2 pp 173–97.

Garland, D. (1985) *Punishment and Welfare*. Aldershot, Gower.

Garland, D. (2001) *The Culture of Control: crime and social order in contemporary societies*. Oxford, Oxford University Press.

Garland, J. (2004) The Same Old Story? Englishness, the Tabloid Press and the 2002 Football World Cup'. *Leisure Studies* Vol. 23 No. 1 pp 79–92.

Giddens, A. (1998) *The Third Way: the Renewal of Social Democracy*. Oxford, Polity Press.

Giddens, A. (2000) *The Third Way and its Critics*. Oxford, Polity Press.

Gill, M., Spriggs, A., Allen, J., Argomaniz, J. Bryan, J., Jessiman, P., Kara, D. Kilworth, J., Little R., Swain, D. and Waples, S. (2005) *The Impact of CCTV: fourteen case studies*. Home Office Online Report 15/05.

Gilling, D. and Hughes, G. (2002) 'The Community Safety "Profession"'. *Community Safety Journal*, Vol. 1 No. 1.

Gilroy, P. and Sim, J. (1985) 'Law and Order and the State of the Left'. *Capital and Class*, No. 25.

Girling, E., Loader, I. and Sparks, R. (2000) *Crime and Social Change in Middle England: questions of order in an English town*. London, Routledge.

Goeghegen, L. (2004) 'ICT: Loves New Labour Lost'. Unpublished paper to the Social Policy Association Annual Conference, University of Nottingham 13–15 July 2004.

Goldblatt, P. and Lewis, C. (1998) *Reducing Offending: an assessment of research evidence on ways of dealing with offending behaviour*. Home Office Research Study 187. London, Home Office.

Golding, P. and Middleton, S. (1982) *Images of Welfare*. Oxford, Martin Robertson.

Goldthorpe, J. (2003) 'Higher Education has Benefited the Wealthy and Been Subsidised by the Poor'. IPPR Press Release 8 December 2003.

Gomersall, A. (2005) 'Social Policy and Practice: a UK focused database for social researchers and practitioners'. *Evidence and Policy* Vol. 1 No. 1 pp 127–44.

Goodhart, D. (2004) 'Discomfort of Strangers'. *Guardian* 24 February 2004.

Goodman, A. and Oldfield, Z. (2004) *Permanent Differences? Income and expenditure inequality in the 1990s and 2000s*. London, Institute for Fiscal Studies.

Gould, P. (1998) *The Unfinished Revolution: How Modernisers Saved the Labour Party*. London: Little Brown and Co.

Grabiner Report (2000) '*The Informal Economy*'. London HM Treasury.

Graham, S. and Wood, D. (2003) 'Digitizing Surveillance: catergorization, space, inequality'. *Critical Social Policy* Vol. 23 No. 2 pp 227–48.

Green, A.E., Maguire, M. and Canny, A. (2001) *Mapping and Tracking Vulnerable Young People*. http://www.jrf.org.uk/knowledge/findings/socialpolicy/411.asp

Grover, C. and Stewart, J. (2000) 'Modernizing Social Security? Labour and its welfare to work strategy'. *Social Policy and Administration* September Vol. 54 No. 3 pp 235–52.

Gwinnett, B. (1997) 'From Zones of Toleration to Zero Tolerance: regulating prostitution in the 1990s'. Unpublished paper to the Socio-Legal Studies Association, Annual Conference, April 1997, Cardiff University.

Hagan, J. (1994) *Crime and Disrepute* California, CA, Pine Forge Press.

Hale, C. (1989) 'Economy, Punishment and Imprisonment'. *Contemporary Crises* Vol. 13 pp 327–49.

Hall, S. (1988) 'Even Worms Turn'. *New Statesman* 25 March 1988.

Hall, S., Critcher, C. Jefferson, T., Clark, J. and Roberts, B. (1978) *Policing the Crisis*. London, Macmillan.

Hallsworth, S. (2002) 'Representations and Realities in Local Crime Prevention: some lessons from London and lessons for criminology. In G. Hughes and A. Edwards (eds) *Crime Control and Community: the new politics of public safety*. Devon, Willan.

Halsey, A.H. (1992) *The Decline of Donnish Dominion*. Oxford, Clarendon Press.

Hanley, B. (2005) *Research as Empowerment? Report of a series of seminars organised by the Toronto group*. York: Joseph Rowntree Foundation.

Hasluck, C. (1999) *Employers and the Employment Option of the New Deal for Young Unemployed People: employment additionality and its measurement*. Cacenty, University of Warwick, Institute for Employment Research.

Haylett, C. (2001) 'Modernization, Welfare and "Third Way" Politics; limits to theorising in thirds?'. *Transitions: the Institute of British Geographers* 26 pp 43–56.

Heeks, R. (1999) *Reinventing Government in the Information Age*. London, Routledge.

Henman, P. and Adler, M. (2003) 'Information Technology and the Governance of Social Security'. *Critical Social Policy* Vol. 23 No. 2 pp 139–64.

Her Majesty's Inspectorate of Probation (2002) *Annual Report 2001–2*. London, Home Office.

Herd, D., Mitchell, A. and Lightman, E. (2005) 'Rituals of Degradation: administration as policy in the Ontario Works Programme'. *Social Policy and Administration* Vol. 39 No. 1 pp 65–79.

Hester, M. and Westmorland, N. (2004) 'Tackling Street Prostitution: towards a holistic approach'. Home Office Research Study 279. Home Office RSD.

Hill, J. and Wright, G. (2003) 'Youth, Community Safety and the Paradox of Inclusion'. *The Howard Journal* Vol. 42 No. 3 pp 282–97.

Hills, M. and Stewart, K. (2005) *A More Equal Society? New Labour, poverty, inequality and exclusion.* Bristol, Policy Press.

Hilton, D. (2001) 'New Labour, New Cliché'. *Open Democracy* 16 May 2001.

Hirsch, D. (2002) 'How Much Work for Those Who Can?'. Unpublished presentation to IFS Conference Social Security Policy Under New Labour, 22 May 2002.

Hirsch, D. (2003) 'How Much Work for Those Who Can?' Presentation to the Institute for Fiscal Studies Conference – *Social Security Policy Under New Labour* 22nd May 2002.

HM Treasury (2000) *Budget 2000.* http://www.hm-treasury.gov.uk/budget/budget_2000/bud_bud00_index.cfm

HM Treasury (2004) Speech by the Cancellor of the Exchequeur, Gordon Brown at the British Council Annual Lecture, 7 July 2004.

HM Treasury (2005) Speech by the Chancellor of the Exchequer Gordon Brown to the London Business School, 27th April 2005. London, HM Treasury.

Hodgson, L. (2004) 'Manufactured Civil Society: counting the cost'. *Critical Social Policy* Vol. 24 No. 2 pp 139–64.

Holloway, K., Bennett, T., Farrington, D. (2005) *The Effectiveness of Criminal Justice Interventions in Reducing Drug-related Crime.* Home Office Online Report 26/05.

Holmes, E. (2003) *Anti-Social Behaviour and Young People in the West Midlands: Questionnaire Findings February 2003.* Birmingham, Home Office Regional Research Team.

Home Office (1999) *Reducing Crime and Tackling its Causes: a briefing note on the crime reduction programme.* London, Home Office Communication Directorate.

Home Office (2003a) *Statistics on Race and the Criminal Justice System – 2002.* London, Home Office.

Home Office (2003b) *The Role of Police Authorities in Public Engagement.* Home Office Online Report 37/03.

Home Office (2003d) *Public Perceptions of Police Accountability and decision-making.* Home Office Online Report 38/03.

Home Office (2003e) *Respect and Responsibility – Taking a Stand Against Anti-Social Behaviour.* Cm 5778. London Home Office.

Home Office (2003f) *Home Office Departmental Report.* Cm 5906. London, Home Office.

Home Office (2003g) *Streets Ahead: the Street Crime Initiative Joint Inspection Report.* London, Home Office.

Home Office (2004a) *Statistics on Race and the Criminal Justice System – 2003.* London, Home Office.

Home Office (2004b) *Defining and measuring anti-social behaviour.* Home Office Development and Practice Report 26.

Home Office (2004c) *Cutting Crime, Delivering Justice: a Strategic Plan for Criminal Justice.* Cm 6288. London, Home Office.

Home Office (2005a) *Statistics on Race and the Criminal Justice System – 2004.* London, Home Office.

Home Office (2005b) *Terrorism Act 2000 – arrest and charge.* http/www.homeoffice.gov.uk/docs3/tact_arrest_stats.html Accessed 12th April 2005.

Home Office (2005c) *Updated and Revised Prison Population Projections 2005–2011.* Home Office Statistical Bulletin 10/05, July 2005.

Home Office (2005d) *Improving Opportunity, Strengthening Society: the Government's strategy to increase race equality and community cohesion.* London, Home Office.

Home Office (2005e) *Anti Social Behaviour Orders Issued by the Courts 2004* http://www.crimereduction.gov.uk/asbo2/htm Accessed July 2005.

Home Office (2005f) *Penalty Notices for Disorder Statistics 2004.* Home Office Online Report 35/05.

Home Office (2005g) *Controlling Our Borders: making migration work for Britain.* Cm 6472. London Home Office.

Hope, T. (2002) 'The Road Taken: Evaluation, Replication and Crime Reduction'. In G. Hughes and J. Muncie (eds) *Crime Prevention and Community Safety.* London, Sage.

Hope, T. (2004) 'Pretend it Works'. *Criminal Justice* Vol. 4 No. 3 pp 287–308.

Hopkins-Burke, R. and Morrill, R. (2004) 'Human Rights vs Community Rights: the case for Anti-Social Behaviour Orders'. In R. Hopkins-Burke (ed.) *Hard Cop, Soft Cop: dilemmas and debates about contemporary policing.* Devon, Willan Publishing.

Horgan, G. (2005) 'Child Poverty in Northern Ireland: the limits of welfare to work policies'. *Social Policy and Administration* Vol. 39 No. 1 pp 49–64.

Hough, M. (2004) 'Modernization, Scientific Rationalism and the Crime Reduction Programme'. *Criminal Justice* Vol. 4 No. 2 pp 239–53.

Households Below Average Income (2005) www.dwp.gov.uk/asd/hbai2004/contents.asp

House of Lords (2004) *The International Covenant on Economic, Social and Cultural Rights. Twenty-first Report of Session 2003–4.* HL Paper 183 HC 1188. Joint Committee on Human Rights.

Hudson, B. (1987) *Justice Through Punishment.* London, Macmillan.

Hudson, B. (2001) 'Punishment, Rights and Difference: Defending justice in the risk society'. In K. Stenson and R.P. Sullivan (eds) *Crime Risk and Justice: the politics of crime control in liberal democracies.* Devon, Willan Publishing.

Hudson, B. (2003) *Justice in the Risk Society: challenging and re-affirming justice in late modernity.* London, Sage.

Hudson, J. (2003) '*e*-galitarianism? The information society and New Labour's repositioning of welfare'. *Critical Social Policy* Vol. 23 No. 2 pp 268–90.

Hughes, G. (2004a) 'The Community Governance of Crime, Justice and Safety: challenges and lesson drawing'. *British Journal of Community Justice* Vol. 2 No. 3.

Hughes, G. (2004b) 'Crime and Disorder Reduction Partnerships in England and Wales: grounding Garland's culture of control thesis'. Unpublished paper to the British Society of Criminology Conference, Portsmouth 6–9 July 2004.

Hughes, G. and Gilling, D. (2004) 'Mission Impossible? The habitus of the community safety manager and the new expertise in local partnership and governance of crime and safety'. *Criminal Justice* Vol. 4 No. 2 pp 129–49.

Humphrey, J.C. (2003) New Labour and the Regulatory Reform of Social Care'. *Critical Social Policy* Vol. 23 No. 1 pp 5–24.

Hunter, C. and Nixon, J. (2001) 'Taking the Blame and Losing the Home: women and antisocial behaviour'. *Journal of Social Welfare and Family Law* Vol. 23 No. 4 pp 395–410.

Hutton, W. (1997) 'Lack of a Welfare State Causes Poverty'. *Observer*, 21 December, p 22.

IPPR (2004) *Housing Equality and Choice.* London, IPPR.

Inland Revenue (2002) *Inland Revenue Annual report for the Year Ending 31st March 2002.* Cm 5706. London, Inland Revenue.

Inland Revenue (2003) *Report of the Commissioners of Her Majesty's Inland Revenue for the Year ending 31st March 2003.* Cm 6050 London, Inland Revenue.

Jackson, S. and Thomas, N. (1999) *On the Move Again? What works in creating stability for looked after children.* London, Barnardos.

Joint Council for the Welfare of Immigrants (2005) *Recognise Rights, Realise Benefits: a JCWI analysis of the Government's five-year plan on immigration.* JCWI, June 2005.

Joint Review Team (2001) *Delivering Results: Joint Review Team Fifth Annual Report 2000/1.* London, National Assembly for Wales/SSI/Audit Commission.

Jones, T. and Newburn, T. (2001) *Widening Access: improving police relations with hard to reach groups.* Police Research Series Paper 138. London, Home Office Policing and Reducing Crime Unit.

Joseph Rowntree Foundation (JRF) (1994) *Community participation and empowerment: putting theory into practice Housing Summary 4, August 1994.* http://www.jrf.org.uk/ knowledge/findings/housing/H4.asp

JRF (2000) 'Resourcing Community Involvement in Neighbourhood Regeneration'. http://www.jrf.org.uk/knowledge/findings/housing/320.asp.

JRF (2003) '*Developing People – regenerating place: achieving greater integration for local area regeneration*'. Findings Ref 753. http:/www.jrf.org.uk/knowledge/findings/hounsing/753.asp accessed 6 August 2003.

JRF (2004) *Monitoring Poverty and Social Exclusion 2004. Findings*, December 2004. York, JRF.

Juby, H. and Farrington, D. (2001) 'Disentangling the Link Between Disrupted Families and Delinquency'. *British Journal of Criminology* No. 41 pp 22–40.

Jupp, B. (2000) *Working Together: creating a better environment for cross-sector partnerships*. London, DEMOS.

Kantola, J. and Squires, J. (2004) 'Discourses Surrounding Prostitution Policies in the UK'. *European Journal of Women's Studies* Vol. 11 No. 1 pp 77–101.

Keith, Lord (1983) *Keith Committee Report on the Enforcement Powers of the Revenue Departments*. Cmnd 8822, London, HMSO.

Keith, M. and Cross, M. (1993) 'Racism and the post modern city'. In M. Keith and M. Cross (eds) *Racism, the City and the State*. London, Routledge.

Kelly, K.D., Caputo, T. and Jamieson, W. (2005) 'Reconsidering Sustainability: some implications for community-based crime prevention'. *Critical Social Policy* Vol. 25 No. 3 pp 306–24.

Kennedy, H. (2004) *Just Law*. London, Chatto and Windus.

Klug, F. (2005) 'Human Rights: above politics or a creature of politics?'. *Policy and Politics* Vol. 33 No. 1 pp 3–14.

King, D. (1995) *Actively Seeking Work? The politics of unemployment and welfare policy in the United States and Great Britain*. Chicago, IL, University of Chicago Press.

Kirschler, E., Maciejovsky and Schneider, F. (2002) 'Everyday representations of tax avoidance, tax evasion and tax flight: do legal differences matter?'. *Journal of Economic Psychology* Vol. 24 pp 535–53.

Kundnani, A. (2001) 'From Oldham to Bradford: the violence of the violated'. *Race and Class* Vol. 43 No. 2 pp 105–31.

Leach, S., Hartley, J., Lowndeds, V., Wilson, D., Downe, J. (2005) *Local Political Leadership in England and Wales*. York, Joseph Rowntree Foudation.

Leadbeater, C. (1997) *The Rise of the Social Entrepreneur*. London, DEMOS.

Lederman, D., Loayza, N. and Menendez, A.M. (2002) 'Crime: does social capital matter?' *Economic Development and Cultural Change* Vol. 50 No. 3 pp 509–39.

Lemos, G. (2005) *The Search for Tolerance: challenging racist attitudes and behaviour amongst young people*. York, JRF.

Levitas, R. (2001) 'Against work: a utopian incursion into social policy'. *Critical Social Policy* Vol. 21 No. 4 pp 449–65.

Liberty (2005) *Court Judgement Savages Government's 'Anti-Yob'/Anti Child Policy*. Liberty, Press Release, 20 July 2005.

Ling, T. (2002) 'Delivering Joined-Up Government in the UK: Dimensions, Issues and Problems'. In *Public Administration* Vol. 80 No. 4 pp 615–42.

Lister, R. (1990) *The Exclusive Society: Citizenship and the Poor*. London, CPAG.

Lister, R. (2000) 'Towards a Citizens' Welfare State: the 3 R's and 2 R's of welfare reform'. Paper to the Social Policy Association Annual Conference, Roehampton, July 2000.

Lister, R. (2001) 'New Labour: a study in ambiguity from a position of ambivalence'. In *Critical Social Policy* Vol. 29 No. 4 pp 425–47.

Lister, R. (2004) *Poverty*. Cambridge, Polity Press.

Loader, B. (2004) *Challenging the Digital Divide? A review of online community support*. York, JRF.

London School of Economics (2005) *The Identity Project. An assessment of the UK identity cards bill and its implications*. Department of Information Systems, London School of Economics.

LPC (Low Pay Commission) (2005) *National Minimum Wage: Low Pay Commission Report 2005*. Cm 6475. London: Low Pay Commission.

Lynn, N. and Lea, S. (2003) 'A Phantom Menace and the new Apartheid: the social construction of asylum seekers in the United Kingdom'. *Discourse and Society* Vol. 14 No. 4 pp 425–52.

MacDonald, K. (2003) *Sustaining Networks: how regeneration partnerships learn and develop*. York, JRF.

McBarnett (2001) 'After Enron: corporate governance, creative compliance and the uses of corporate social responsibility'. In J. O'Brien (ed.) *Governing the Corporation*, Chichester, John Wiley.

McGregor, A., Glass, A., Higgins, K., Macdougall, L. and Sutherland, V. (2003) *Developing People – Regenerating Place: achieving greater integration for local area regeneration*. Bristol, Policy Press.

McLaughlin, E. (2002) '"Same Bed, Different Dreams": postmodern reflections on crime prevention and community safety'. In G. Hughes and A. Crawford (eds) *Crime Control and Community*. Devon, Willan Publishing.

McManus, J. (2004) 'Crime and Disorder Reduction Partnerships: leadership, governance and effectiveness in a sample of English CDRPs: an organisational perspective'. Unpublished paper to the British Society of Criminology Conference, Portsmouth 6th–9th July 2004.

McPherson, Sir W. (1999) *The Stephen Lawrence Enquiry*. Cm 4262-1. London, TSO.

McRobbie, A. (2000) 'Feminism and the Third Way'. *Feminist Review* Vol. 64 No. 1 pp 97–112.

Maguire, M. (2004) 'The Crime Reduction Programme in England and Wales. Reflections on the vision and the reality'. *Criminal Justice* Vol. 4 No. 3 pp 213–37.

Marshall, T.H. (1950) *Citizenship and Social Class*. Cambridge, Cambridge University Press.

Marshall, T.H. (1981) *The Right to Welfare and Other Essays*. London, Heinemann.

Mayer, M. (2004) 'The Onward Sweep of Social Capital: causes and consequences for understanding cities, communities and urban movements. In *International Journal of Urban and Regional Research* Vol. 27 No. 1 pp 110–132.

Milburn, A. (2004) *Localism: the need for a new settlement*. Speech at DEMOS Seminar, 21 January 2004. London, DEMOS.

Millie, A., Jacobson, J. and Hough, M. (2003) 'Understanding the Growth in the Prison Population in England and Wales'. *Criminal Justice* Vol. 3 No. 4 pp 369–87.

Millie, A., Jacobson, J., McDonald, E. and Hough, M. (2005) *Anti-Social Behaviour Strategies: Finding a balance*. Bristol, Policy Press.

Ministerial Group on Public Order and Community Cohesion (2002) *Building Cohesive Communities: a report of the Ministerial Group on Public Order and Community Cohesion*. London, Home Office.

Monaghan, G. Hibbert, P. and Moore, S. (2003) *Children in Trouble: time for a change*. London, Barnardos.

Morgan, R. (2002) 'Magistrates: the Future According to Auld'. *Journal of Law and Society* Vol. 29 No. 2 pp 308–23.

MORI (2005) http//www.mori.com/polls/2005/es050411.shtml#96

Murray, C. (1990) *The Emerging British Underclass*. London, IEA.

Murray, C. (1994) *Underclass: the crisis depends*. London, IEA.

Murray, C. (1996) *Charles Murray and the Underclass: the developing debate*. London, IEA Health and Welfare Unit.

Myhill, A. and Allen, J. (2002). *Rape and Sexual Assault of Women: the extent and nature of the problem*. Home Office Research Study 237. London.

NACRO (1986) *Enforcement of the Law relating to Social Security*. London, NACRO.

National Statistics (2005) *Focus on Social Inequalities: 2004 edition*. London, TSO.

Newburn, T. (2002) 'Young People, Crime and Youth justice'. In M. Maguire, R. Morgan and R. Reiner (eds) *The Oxford Handbook of Criminology* 3rd edn. Oxford, Oxford University Press.

Newman, J., Barnes, M., Sullivan, H. and Knops, A. (2004) 'Public Participation and Collaborative Governance'. *Journal of Social Policy* Vol. 33 Part 2 pp 203–23.

NOMS (2005) *Prison Population and Accommodation Briefing for 8th July 2005*. Estate Planning and Development Unit, National Offender Management Service.

Office of the Deputy Prime Minister (ODPM) (2004a) *Empowering Communities, Improving Housing: involving black and minority ethnic tenants and communities*. London, ODPM.

ODPM (2004b) *Mainstreaming Community Cohesion*. Speech by Housing Minister Keith Hill, 14 October 2004.

ODPM (2004c) *Tackling Social Exclusion: taking stock and looking to the future*. London, ODPM.

ODPM (2005a) *New Localism: Citizen Engagement, Neighbourhoods and Public Services: Evidence from Local Government*. London, ODPM.

ODPM (2005b) *Citizen Engagement and Public Services: Why Neighbourhoods Matter*. London, ODPM.

Oldham Independent Review (2001) *Panel Report* [Ritchie Report]. http://www.oldhamir.org.uk

ONS (2002) *Census 2001: first results on population in England and Wales*. London, TSO.

Ortivska, M. and Hudson, J. (2002) 'Tax Evasion, Civic Duty and the Law Abiding Citizen'. *European Journal of Political Economy* Vol. 19 pp 83–102.

Ostrom, B.J. (2003) 'Domestic Violence Courts'. *Criminology and Public Policy*, Vol. 3 No. 1 pp 105–8.

Palmer, G., North, J., Carr, J. and Kenway, P. (2003) *Monitoring Poverty and Social Exclusion 2003*. York, Joseph Rowntree Foundation.

Parmar, A., Sampson, A. and Diamond, A. (2005) *Tackling Domestic Violence: providing advocacy support to survivors of domestic violence*. London, Home Office Development and Practice Report 34.

Paton, C. (1999) 'New Labour's Health Policy: the new healthcare state'. In M. Powell (ed.) *New Labour, New Welfare: the 'third way' in British social policy*. Bristol, Policy Press.

Pawson, R. (2001) 'Evidence Based Policy II the Synthesis'. ESRC, CEBPP Working Paper 4.

Pawson, R. and Tilley, N. (1997) *Realistic Evaluation*. London, Sage.

Paxton and Dixon (2004) *The State of the Nation: An Audit of Injustice in the UK*. London: IPPR.

Peck, J. (1998) 'Workfare: a geopolitical etymology'. *Environment and Planning: Society and Space* Vol. 16 pp 133–61.

Perri 6 (1995) 'Governing by Cultures'. *Demos Quarterly* Issue 7/1995. London, DEMOS.

Perri 6, Leat, D., Seltzer and Stoker, G. (1999) *Governing in the Round: strategies for holistic government*. London, DEMOS.

Perrons, D. and Sykers, S. (2003) 'Empowerment through Participation? Conceptual exploration and a case study'. *International Journal of Urban and Regional Research* Vol. 27 No. 2 pp 265–85.

Pilger, J. (2003) 'The Awakening of Liberal England'. *New Statesman* 13 October 2003.

Platt, L. (2002) *Parallel Lives? Poverty among ethnic minority groups in Britain*. London, CPAG.

Pleace, N. and Fitzpatrick, S. (2004) *Centrepoint Youth Homelessness Index: an estimate of youth homelessness for England*. Centre for Housing Policy, University of York.

Powell, M. (ed.) (1999) *New Labour, New Welfare: the 'third way' in British Social Policy*. Bristol, Policy Press.

Powell, M. and Boyne, G. (2001) 'The Spatial Strategy of Equality and the Spatial Division of Welfare'. *Social Policy and Administration* Vol. 35 No. 2 pp 181–94.

Prideaux, S. (2001) 'New Labour, Old Functionalism: the underlying contradictions of welfare reform in the US and the UK'. *Social Policy and Administration* Vol. 35 No. 1 pp 85–115.

Prison Reform Trust (1991) *The Indentikit Prisoner*. London, Prison Reform Trust.

Prison Reform Trust (2005) *Prison Factfile: Bromley Briefings, May 2005*. London PRT. www.prisonreformtrust.org.uk

Public Accounts Committee (2003) *Tackling Fraud against the Inland Revenue*. First Report of Session 2003/4. HC 62. London, The Stationery Office.

Putnam, R.D. (1993) 'The Prosperous Community: social capital and public life'. *American Prospect* Vol. 4 No. 13.

Rawls, J. (1971) *A Theory of Justice*. Oxford, Oxford University Press.

Raynor, P. (2003) 'Research in Probation: from nothing works to what works'. In W.H. Chui and M. Nellis (eds) *Moving Probation Forward*. Oxford, University of Oxford Centre for Criminological Research.

Raynor, P. (2004) 'The Probation Service "Pathfinders". Finding the path and losing the way?'. *Criminal Justice* Vol. 4 No. 3 pp 309–25.

Read, T. and Tilley, N. (2000) *Not Rocket Science? Problem solving and crime reduction*. Crime Reduction Research Series paper 6. Home Office, Policing and Crime Reduction Unit, RSD.

Refugee Council (2004) *Asylum and Immigration Act 2004: main changes and issues of concern*. Refugee Council Briefing September 2004. London, Refugee Council.

Refugee Council, (2005a) *Asylum and Immigration Act 2004: an update*. March 2005. London, Refugee Council.

Refugee Council (2005b) *Tell It Like It Is: the truth about asylum*. London. Refugee Council, Scottish Refugee Council, Welsh Refugee Council, Refugee Action, Student Action for Refugees (STAR).

Reiman, J. (1990) *The Rich Get Richer and the Poor Get Prison*. London, Macmillan.

Roberts, R. and Garside, R. (2005) *Briefing Paper: Punishment before justice? Understanding Penalty Notices for Disorder*. Crime and Society Foundation, March 2005. http://www. crimeand society.org.uk/pjustice.html

Roberts, M. and Roche, M. (2001) *Community Life and Social Well-being in the Black Country: towards indicators of social capital*. Report for The Black Country Consortium/West Midlands NHS Executive. http://www.ac.uk/pri.

Robinson, A. (2003) *The Cardiff Women's Safety Unit: a multi-agency approach to domestic violence*. Cardiff, Cardiff University.

Roche, M. (2004a) 'Social Policy and Social Capital: a clear case of putting merit before method?'. *Social Policy and Society* Vol. 3 No. 2 pp 97–111.

Roche, M. (2004b) 'Complicated Problems, Complicated Solutions? Homelessness and joined-up policy responses'. *Social Policy and Administration* Vol. 38 No. 7 pp 758–74.

Rose, D. (1996) *In the Name of the Law*. London, Jonathan Cape.

Rouse, J. and Smith, G. (1999) 'Accountability'. In M. Powell (ed.) (1999) *New Labour, New Welfare: the 'third way' in British Social Policy*. Bristol, Policy Press.

Rowe, M. and Devanney, C. (2003) 'Partnership and the Governance of Regulation'. *Critical Social Policy* Vol. 23 No. 3 pp 375–97.

RRI/CIDT (2003) *Report of Conference: 'Consultation for a Change: involving communities in making policy'*. http://www.wlv.ac.uk/pri

Rutherford, A. (2001) *Criminal Justice Choices: what is criminal justice for?* London, IPPR.

Sainsbury (2001) 'Getting the Measure of Fraud'. *Poverty*, Winter No. 108 pp 10–14.

Sanders, A. (2002) 'Core values, the Magistracy and the Auld Report'. *Journal of Law and Society* Vol. 29 No. 2 pp 324–41.

Scampion Report (2000) *Organised Benefit Fraud*. http://www.dwp.gov.uk/publications/dss/2000/scampion/main.pdf

Sebba, L. (2001) 'On the Relationship between Criminological Research and Policy: the case of crime victims'. *Criminal Justice* Vol. 1 No. 1 pp 27–58.

SEU (Social Exclusion Unit) (1998) *Bringing Britain Together: a National Strategy for Neighbourhood Renewal*. Cm 4045. London, TSO.

SEU (1999) *Annual Report*. Cm 4342. London: The Stationery Office.

SEU (2000) *National Strategy for Neighbourhood Renewal – Report of Policy Action Team 8: Anti-Social Behaviour*. http://www.cabinet-office.gov.uk/seu/2000/pat8/ default.htm

SEU (2002) *Reducing Reoffending by Ex-prisoners*. London, Office of the Deputy Prime Minister.

Shaxson, L. (2005) 'Is Your Evidence Robust Enough? Questions for policymakers and practitioners'. *Evidence and Policy* Vol. 1 No. 1 pp 101–11.

Shearing, C. and Wood, J. (2003) 'Nodal Governance, Democracy and the New "Denizen"'. *Journal of Law and Society* Vol. 30 No. 4 pp 400–19.

Sherman, L.W., Gottfriedson, D.C., MacKenzie, D.L., Eck, J., Reuter, P. and Bushwau, S.D. (1998) *Preventing Crime: what works, what doesn't, what's promising*. Washington DC, National Institute of Justice, US Department of Justice Report. http://www. preventingcrime.org

Sinfield, A. (2004) 'Preventing Poverty in Market Societies'. Paper to ESPAnet Annual Conference, Oxford, 9–11 September 2004.

Sipilä, J. and Kröger, T. (2004) 'Editorial Introduction: European families stretched between the demands of work and care'. *Social Policy and Administration* Vol. 38 No. 6 pp 557–64.

Skidmore, P. and Harkin, J. (2003) *Grown Up Trust*. London, DEMOS/Nationwide seminar series.

Social Trends (2005) *Social Trends No. 35*. London, ONS.

Solesbury, W. (2001) 'Evidence Based Policy: whence it came and where its going'. ESRC CEBPP Working Paper 1.

Solomos, P. (1993) 'Constructions of Black Criminality: racialisation and criminalisation in perspective'. In D. Cook and B. Hudson (eds) *Racism and Criminology*, London, Sage.

Somerland, H. (2001) 'I've Lost the Plot': an everyday story of legal and lawyers'. In *Journal of Law & Society* Vol. 28 No. 3 pp 335–360.

SPARK (2004) A Review of the DWP Benefit Fraud Scheme. DWP In-House Report 149. London, HMSO.

Sparks, C. and Spencer, S. (2002) *Them and Us? The public, offenders and the criminal justice system*. London, IPPR.

Spicker, P. (1998) '"Our Budget Under Attack": estimating social security fraud"'. In *Radical Statistics*. http://www.radstats.org.uk/no070/article2.htm

Squires and Measor (2001) 'Rounding up the Usual Suspects: police approaches to multi-agency policing'. In S. Balloch and M. Taylor (eds) *Partnership Working: Policy and Practice* Bristol: Policy Press.

Stanley, R. (2005) 'Truth Commissions and the Recognition of State Crime'. *British Journal of Criminology* Vol. 45 pp 582–97.

Stedman-Jones, G. (1981) 'The Threat of the Outcast in London'. In M. Fitzgerald, G. McLennan and J. Pawson (eds) *Crime and Society.* London, RKP.

Stenson, K. (2000) 'Some Day Our Prince Will Come: zero tolerance policing and liberal government'. In T. Hope and R. Sparks (eds) *Crime Risk and Insecurity.* London, Routledge.

Stenson, K. and Crawford, A. (2001) 'Rethinking Crime Control in Advanced Liberal Government: the 'third way' and the return to the local'. In K. Stenson and R. Sullivan (eds) *Crime Risk and Justice.* Devon, Willan Publishing.

Stenson, K. and Edwards, A. (2004) 'Policy Transfer in Local Crime Control: beyond naive emulation'. In T. Newburn and R. Sparks (eds) *Criminal Justice and Political Cultures: national and international dimensions of crime control.* Devon, Willan Publishing.

Streets Ahead (2002) *A Joint Inspection of the Street Crime Initiative.* HMIC, Ofsted, SSI, HMCPSI, MCSI, Court Service, HMIP.

Strober, G. and Strober, D. (1994) *Nixon: an oral history of his presidency.* New York, Harper Collins.

Swain, S. (1999) '"I Am Directed to Remind You of Your Duty to Your Family": public surveillance of mothering in Victoria, Australia, 1920–40. *Women's History Review* Vol. 8 No. 2 pp 247–59.

Tawney, R.H. (1931) *Equality (1964 edition)* London, Unwin Books.

Taylor, M. (2002) 'Community and Social Exclusion'. In V. Nash (ed.) *Reclaiming Community.* London, IPPR.

Taylor-Gooby, P. (2001) 'Risk, Contingency and the Third Way: evidence from the BHPS and qualitative studies'. *Social Policy and Administration* Vol. 35 No. 2 pp 195–211.

Tax Justice Network (2003) Declaration of the Tax Justice Network. http://www.taxjustice.net.

Tax Justice Network (2005) *Briefing Paper: The Price of Offshore.* March 2005. http://www.taxjustice.net. Accessed July 2005.

Taylor, M. (2003) *Public Policy in the Community.* Basingstoke, Palgrave MacMillan.

Thompson, E.P. (1975) *The Making of the English Working Class.* Harmondsworth, Penguin Books.

Tilley, N. (2001) 'Evaluation and Evidence-led Crime Reduction Policy and Practice'. In R. Matthews and J. Pitts (eds), *Crime, Disorder and Community Safety.* London, Routledge.

Tilley, N. (2002) 'The Rediscovery of Learning: crime prevention and scientific realism'. In G. Hughes and A. Crawford (eds) *Crime Control and Community.* Devon, Willan Publishing.

Tilley, N. and Laycock, G. (2002) *Working Out What to Do: evidence based crime reduction.* Crime Reduction Research Series Paper 11. Home Office.

Tomlinson, S. (2001) 'Education Policy, 1997–2000: the effects on top, bottom and middle England'. *International Journal in the Sociology of Education,* Vol. 11 No. 3 pp 261–77.

Tonry, M. (2004) *Punishment and Politics: evidence and emulation in the making of English crime control policy.* Devon, Willan Publishing.

Toynbee, P. and Walker, D. (2005) *Better or Worse? Has Labour delivered?* London, Bloomsbury Publishing.

Tseloni, A., Osborn, D.R., Trickett, A. and Pease K, (2002) 'Modelling Property Crime Using the British Crime Survey'. *British Journal of Criminology* Vol. 42 pp 109–28.

Uglow, S. (1984) 'Defrauding the Public Purse'. *Criminal Law Review,* March 1984.

Vallely, C., Robinson, A., Burton, M. and Tredidga, J. (2005) *Evaluation of Domestic Violence Pilots sites at Caerphilly (Gwent) and Croydon 2005/2005 – Independent Report.* http://www.cps.gov.uk/publications/equality/index.html

Vennard, J. and Hedderman, C (1998) *Effective Interventions with Offenders. Part 111.* Home Office Research Study. No. 187. London. Home office.

Vennard, J., Sugg, D. and Hedderman, C. (1997) *Changing Offenders' Behaviour: what works?* Home Office Research Study 171. London, Home Office RSD.

Walker, R (2003) 'Employment, support and security'. *New Economy.* IPPR.

Walklate, S. (2000) 'Trust and the problem of community in the inner city'. In T. Hope and R. Sparks (eds) *Crime Risk and Insecurity*. London, Routledge.

Webster, C., Simpson, D., MacDonald, R., Abbas, A., Cieslik, M., Shildrick, T. and Simpson, M. (2004) *Poor Transitions: social exclusion and young adults*. Bristol, Policy Press.

Welsh, B.C. and Farrington, D.P. (2002) *Crime Prevention Effects of Closed Circuit Television: a systematic review*. Home Office Research Study 252. Home Office, RSD.

Welsh, B.C. and Farrington, D.P. (2003) *Effects of Closed Circuit Television Surveillance on Crime: Protocol for a Systematic Review*. Submitted to Campbell Collaboration Crime and Justice Group. 4 November 2003.

West Midlands Police (2004) *Best Value Review of Public Consultations and Expectations*. West Midlands Police Performance Review Department.

Wheelock, J. and Jones, K. (2002) '"Grandparents are the Next Best Thing": informal childcare for working parents in urban Britain'. *Journal of Social Policy* Vol. 31 No. 3 pp 441–63.

White, M. (2005) 'Big reform agenda to seal Blair legacy'. *Guardian*, 18 May 2005.

Whyte, B. (2004) 'Responding to Youth Crime in Scotland'. *British Journal of Social Work* Vol. 34 pp 395–411.

Wiles, P. and Pease, K. (2001) 'Distributive Justice and Crime'. In R. Matthews and J. Pitts (eds) *Crime Disorder and Community Safety*. London, Routledge.

Wilkinson, D. (2003) *New Deal for Young People: evaluation of unemployment flows*. PSI Discussion Paper 15. London, Policy Studies Institute.

Williams, K. (1981) *From Pauperism to Poverty*. London, RKP.

Williams, F. (2000) 'Good-enough Principles for Welfare'. *Journal of Social Policy* Vol. 28 No. 4 pp 667–87.

Williams, F. (2004) 'What Matters Is What Works: why every child matters to New Labour. Commentary on the DfES Green Paper *Every Child Matters*'. *Critical Social Policy* Vol. 24 No. 3 pp 406–27.

Williamson, A.P., Beattie, R.S., Osborne, P. (2004) 'Addressing Fragmentation and Social Exclusion through Community Involvement in Rural Regeneration Partnerships: evidence from the Northern Ireland Experience'. *Policy and Politics* Vol. 32 No. 3 pp 351–69.

Wilson, M. and Wilde, P. (2003) *Benchmarking Community Participation: developing and implementing the Active Partners benchmarks'*. York, Joseph Rowntree Foundation.

Wood, M. (2004) *Perceptions and Experience of Anti-social Behaviour: findings from the 2003/4 British Crime Survey*. Home Office Online Report 49/04.

Worrall, A. (1990) *Offending Women*. London, RKP.

Worrall, A. (1997) *Punishment in the Community*. London, Addison Wesley Longman.

Yaqoob, S. (2005) 'Our Leaders Must Speak Up: failure to oppose the official line creates extremists'. *Guardian* Friday 15 July 2005.

Young, J. (2002) 'Critical Criminology in the Twenty-first Century: critique, irony and the always unfinished'. In K. Harrington and R. Hog (eds) *Critical Criminology: issues, debates, challenges*. Devon, Willan Publishing.

Young, J. and Matthews, R. (2003) 'New Labour, Crime Control and Social Exclusion'. In R. Matthews and J. Young (eds) *The New Politics of Crime and Punishment*. Devon, Willan Publishing.

Zephaniah, B. (2003) 'Me? I thought, OBE me? Up yours, I thought'. *Guardian*, 27 November 2003.

⊙⊙ **Index**

Entries in *italics* denote publications and specific initiatives.

16 hour rule, benefits 36

access to law 13, 179
active citizenship 82, 83
administrative penalties, benefit fraud 56–7
African poverty 173
age factors
  tax evasion 48
  see also older people; young people
Amnesty International 162–3
anti-social behaviour (ASB) 164–8
  definition 79–80
  human rights 178
  policy paradoxes 165–6
  'problem' places 45
anti-social behaviour orders (ASBOs) 164–5
area
  otherness 153–8
  see also place
area-based partnership initiatives 139–40
ASB *see* anti-social behaviour
ASBOs *see* anti-social behaviour orders
asylum 158–64
  five year plan 163–4
  identity 159–61
  immigration policy 161–3
  politics 159
Asylum and Immigration Acts 162
Auld, Robin 118–19

Balsall Heath, Birmingham 168
Beck, Ulrich 61, 62–3
behaviour *see* anti-social behaviour
benefit fraud
  agenda 58–60
  guesstimating and prosecuting 54–8
  identity cards 112

benefit fraud *cont.*
  politics 53–4
  public perceptions 49
  responses 46–60
  versus benefit take-up 59–60
benefit system, 16 hour rule 36
benefit take-up 27–8, 59–60
Best Value consultation 132
black communities
  consultation 126, 129–30
  policing 18–19
  prison numbers 17–18
  see also ethnic groups; race...; racial...
Blair, Tony
  criminal justice 75–6
  general election 2005 172–4
  pragmatic idealism 189
  'problem' families 43
  social justice 23–4
  Third Way 64–6
  see also New Labour
blame culture 43
bodily integrity concept 73
bottom-up approach, consultation 125
'Britishness' 159–61
Brown, Gordon 69, 70–1
Burney, Elizabeth 164

Campbell, B. 44–5
Canadian welfare policy 113–14
Cantle Report 156–7
capital *see* social capital
capitalism 13
care concept 73
cautions, benefit fraud 56–7
CCT *see* compulsory competitive tendering
CCTV 116–17

CEBSS *see* Centre for Evidence Based
     Social Services
ceiling targets, income 181
centralisation 153–4
Centre for Evidence Based Social
     Services (CEBSS) 97, 99
child abuse 87–8
     see also domestic violence
child protection policies 165–6
Child Tax Credit 36
childcare 37
children
     immigration policy 162
     policies post-1997 147, 148
     poverty 25, 147
     see also young people
Children's Trust Fund 70
Christianity 160
Citizens Charters 96
citizenship
     benefits 11–12
     inequalities 9–12
     rich law, poor law 46–60
     social justice 20–2, 82
     two-way street concept 4–9, 11–12
     undermining 7, 9–10
     see also social citizenship
civic duties 49
civil rights 5, 7, 185
CJS *see* criminal justice system
claimant classification 36
Clements, Luke 178–9
client control/prescription 100–1
Climbié child abuse case 87–8
clothing, anti-social behaviour 166
coalition building 188
Coleman, James 82–3
Commission on Social Justice (CSJ) 21
communism 63
community 71–2, 77–8, 185–6
community cohesion policy 157–8
community consultation 121–2, 123–31
     see also consultation
community informatics initiatives 138
community safety strategies 77–8, 104–5
compliance
     Penalty Notices for Disorder 110
     tax fraud 48, 49–53
compulsory competitive
     tendering (CCT) 132
Connexions 88
Conservative party
     asylum attitudes 163
     criminal justice 75–6
     general election 2005 172

Conservative party *cont.*
     'what works' origins 95, 96
     see also New Right; Thatcher...
constants and dissonants 33–60
consultation 121–3
     aims 128–9
     empowerment 132–5
     hard to reach groups 126–8
     overload 129–30
     participatory approaches 135–7
     theory and practice 123–31
consumer choice 96
contexts, evidence-based policy 104
contractual governance 118
conviction politics 188–9
co-production 82
Corner, Julian 145
costs
     consultation 135
     housing 26
     tax fraud 49–51
'court' structure (area) 153–4
CPS *see* Crown Prosecution Service
'creative practice' 177–8
crime
     cause and effect 31–2
     as indicator and cause 15
     middle England 152
     patterns of criminalisation 16
     positivistic approaches 95–6
     'problem' families 38–40
     psychological approach 100
     spatialisation 44–5
     young people 141–2
crime prevention
     CCTV 116–17
     Thatcherism 75
     'what works' 99–100
Crime Reduction Programme
     (CRP) 78, 105–6
Criminal Justice: The Way Ahead
     (Home Office, 2001) 30–1
criminal justice
     definition 14–16
     social justice reconciliation 171–89
     Third Way 74–8, 80
criminal justice system (CJS) 15–17
     exclusion 30
     information and communications
          technology 89–92, 115–16
     legitimacy 21
     race 18
'criminalising the social' 78–80, 166–7
Crown Prosecution Service (CPS) 89–90, 177
CRP *see* Crime Reduction Programme

CSJ *see* Commission on Social Justice
cultural change 175, 179
cultural injustice 183
cultural issues
    information sharing 89
    realistic evaluation 102
curfew orders 164–5, 167

decision-making, 'what works' 97–9
'delivery' agenda 66–7, 94
democracy 21
democratic deficit 175–6
Department for Work and
        Pensions (DWP) 53, 55–7, 59
dependency culture 34–7, 47
'deserving' poor 33–8, 72
detention of immigrants 162–3
devolution 159
digital divide 87, 138
disabled people, New Deals 36–7
'disconnections' ('what works') 103–5
disorder 79
    see also anti-social behaviour
dissolution of public services 67
dissonants and constants 33–60
distribution of wealth 26
domestic violence 11
    governance 177
    holistic interventions 186
    'problem' families 42
    'what works' interventions 98, 99, 107–8
double standards 184
'down-up' empowering research 106
duties of citizenship 11–12, 49
DWP *see* Department for Work and Pensions

EBP *see* evidence-based policy
ECHR *see* European Convention
        on Human Rights
economic context
    criminal/social justice reconciliation 174
    social capital 83–4
    socio-economic injustice 183
    see also money matters
economic rights 7, 185
education
    middle England 154–5
    'opportunities for all' 29
    policy impact 147
    tax evasion factors 48–9
e-galitarianism 91–2
e-government strategy 86–7, 138
electronic dossiers 88
electronic monitoring 162
embedding 176, 187–8

employment policies post-1997 147
employment system, 16 hour rule 36
empowerment
    consultation 132–5
    research 176
    'what works' 106–7
engagement 120–50
    democratic deficit 175–6
    participatory approaches 135–7
    Third Way 70
'Englishness' 159–61
enterprise culture 47
environmental rights 7, 185
environmental risks 6
equality
    Blair 23–4
    as inclusion 69–71
    law 16–20, 21
    Third Way 91–2
    see also inequalities
'equality of opportunity' 69
    see also 'opportunities for all'
equity divide 28
errors, benefit fraud figures 58
ethnic groups 17, 148
    see also minority ethnic groups
European Convention on Human
        Rights (ECHR) 6
evaluation research 102–3, 106–7
evidence-based policy (EBP) 95–7, 99–100
ex-prisoners 143–6
exclusion
    Third Way 69–70
    see also social exclusion
exculpatory factors, responsibility 184

fairness concept 20–2
families *see* lone parents;
        'problem' families
Faulkner, David 8
feedback loop (community
        consultation) 125
financial lexicon 70
five year plan, asylum 163–4
flexible labour market 181
football, racism 161
'fortress Britain' 45
Fraser, Nancy 183
fraud and error 58
    see also benefit fraud; tax fraud
Fukuyama, Francis 82–3
function creep (identity cards) 111

G8 summit 2005 173
Garland, David 41–2, 61–2

gender 11, 13–14
  see also women
general election 2005 163–4, 172–6
generative approach, 'what works' 99, 108
geographical barriers, information
    sharing 89
Giddens, Anthony 64–6
Gingrich, Newt 92
globalisation 63, 68, 86
'the good society' 175
governance 176–8
  consultation 122, 126–8
  New Labour 67–8
  transformative 187
  trust deficit 175
  'what works' 100–2, 105–6, 117–19
Grabiner Report 48, 52–3
grand narratives of modernism 62
'guesstimations', benefit fraud 54–8

Handsworth riots 75
hard to reach groups 126–8
Hattersley, Roy 66
health 9–10, 148
Heeks, Richard 87
hidden economy 48, 52
high net worth individuals (HNWIs) 173
historical themes 33–60
HNWIs *see* high net worth individuals
holism 186
honesty 175
housing 9–10
  costs 26
HRA *see* Human Rights Acts
human rights 6–9, 178, 185
Human Rights Acts (HRA) 8, 178–9
Hutton, Will 77

ICESCR *see* International Covenant on
    Economic Social and Cultural Rights
ICT *see* information and communications
    technology
ID cards *see* identity cards
idealism 188–9
identity
  area 153
  asylum 159–61
  welfare policy 73
identity (ID) cards 111–12
identity theft 112
illegal immigration 112
  see also immigration
imagined identities 159–61
immigration 112, 158–64
implementation failures, 'what works' 117

inclusion
  responsibilisation 122–3
  Third Way 69–71, 92
  young people 140–2
  see also social inclusion
income adequacy 180–2
income inequality 24–6, 70, 147, 180–2
inculpatory factors, responsibility 184
independent justice 177
industrial society 62
inequalities
  centralisation 153–4
  citizenship 9–12
  contemporary 24–9
  criminal justice system 15
  as exclusion 69–70
  law 16–20
  money matters 180–2
  New Labour 68–74
  policies post-1997 146–9
  social justice 21
  see also equality
'inequality-proofing' policies 184
information and communications
    technology (ICT)
  criminal justice system 89–92
  public sector reform 88
  social inclusion 138
  technological fix 112–17
  Third Way 85–92
information sharing 87–9
Inland Revenue compliance work 49–53
institutional racism 10–11
integrated approach
  barriers 139–40
  information sharing 89
interdependence concept 73
International Covenant on Economic
    Social and Cultural Rights (ICESCR) 6, 8
intimacy concept 73
Iraq War 81

Jobcentre Plus 113–14
joined-up government (JUG) 67, 119, 129
Joint Review Team (JRT) 132
Joseph, Keith 39
Joseph Rowntree Foundation
    (JRF) 123–4, 126
JRT *see* Joint Review Team
JUG *see* joined-up government
July 7th 2005 158, 171
justice
  criminal/social justice
    reconciliation 178–9
  law 12–14

justice *cont.*
  tax compliance 52–3
  Third Way 74–8
  two-way street concept 4–32
  young people 140–2

Kinnock, Neil 24
Klug, Francesca 179
knee-jerk politics 109, 111, 143

Labour party *see* New Labour; Old Left
Laming Enquiry 87–8
LAs *see* Local Authorities
law
  criminal justice 14
  equality 16–20, 21
  information sharing barriers 89
  justice 12–14
  rich law, poor law 46–60
law and order discourse 74–5
Lea, S. 160–1
leadership styles 189
learning initiatives, ICT 138
legitimacy 21
less eligibility principle 35
lexicon of finance 70
Liberal Democrats 172
Lister, Ruth 8, 73, 183
Local Authorities (LAs) 55–7, 59
local autonomy/spatial equality 154
local governance 117, 119
localism
  crime control 78
  'local solutions to local problems' 130–1
  participatory research 137
  partnerships 139
  trust deficit 82, 175
location factors 44, 154–5
  see also place
London
  centralisation 153–4
  July 7th 2005 158, 171
lone parents
  New Deals 37, 38
  'problem' families 39–40, 42
Lynn, N. 160–1

McLaughlin, E. 101–2
McPherson Report (1999) 10
Magistrates' Courts 89, 91
Make Poverty History campaign 173
managerialism 117–18, 134, 187
Marshall, T.H. 5–6
means-tested minimum income
  guarantee (MIG) 27–8

measurement, social capital 84–5
meta-analyses 97–9, 109
middle England 151–70
MIG *see* means-tested minimum
  income guarantee
minimum wage policy 25
minority ethnic groups
  consultation 126–8, 129–30
  gender 11
  law 17–20
  poverty 28
  social citizenship 11
  see also race...; racial...
modernisation, Third Way 63, 68
modernism 62
'Mondeo Man' 151–2
money matters 180–2, 185–6
  see also economic context
moralisation of families 41
mugging 74
multi-agency framework, governance 119
multipliers (benefit fraud) 55
Murray, Charles 34, 39

national governance 117
national identity 159–61
National Institute for Clinical
  Excellence (NICE) 97
NDLP *see* New Deal for Lone Parents
NDYP *see* New Deal for Young People
negative othering 169–70
  see also otherness
neighbourhood renewal 32, 45
net-widening effects, Penalty Notices
  for Disorder 110
networks
  deciding 'what works' 97
  governance 106
  social capital 83, 84, 86
New Deal for Lone Parents (NDLP) 37
New Deal for Young People (NDYP) 38
New Deals 36–8
New Labour
  asylum five year plan 163–4
  benefit fraud policies 54, 55
  criminal justice 30–2, 75–8
  democratic deficit 175–6
  general election 2005 172–4
  governance 187
  idealism 189
  inequalities 25, 68–74
  information and communications
    technology 86–7
  middle England 151–2
  participation and engagement 120–50

New Labour *cont.*
   social justice 68–74
   socialisation of crime 79–80
   Third Way 64–8, 92–3
   trust deficit 81–2
   'what works' 94–119
   see also Blair, Tony
New Poor Law (1834) 35
New Public Sector Management
      (NPSM) 117–19
New Right 63, 66
New York policing 168
Newman, Kenneth 44
NICE *see* National Institute for
   Clinical Excellence
normalisation of families 41
'nothing works' approach 96
NPSM *see* New Public Sector Management

obligations
   citizenship 5–9
   rule of law 12–14
offshore assets 173
Old Left 66
older people
   consultation 134–5
   means-tested minimum income
      guarantee 27–8
   policies post-1997 147, 148
   see also age factors
Oldham disorders 156–8
on the spot punishments 109–11
On Track programme 127
'opportunities for all' 22–4, 29
   see also equality of opportunity;
      'pathways' of opportunity
otherness 151–70
   anti-social behaviour 164–8
   area 153–8
   asylum and immigration 158–64
   middle England 168–70
   prostitution 167–8

participation 120–50, 175–6
participatory research 135–7
partnerships 139–40
   domestic violence interventions 107
   'local solutions to local problems' 130–1
   New Public Sector Management 119
   participation and engagement 121
   Third Way 67, 71–2
'pathways' of opportunity 71
patterns of criminalisation 16
pauperism 34–5
Peck, Jamie 104–5

Penalty Notices for Disorder (PND) 109–11
'people' perspective, participatory
      research 137
personal debt 28–9
PFI *see* private finance initiatives
Pito *see* Police Information
      Technology Organisation
place
   mythologies 155–6
   otherness 153–8
   'problem' places 43–5
PND *see* Penalty Notices for Disorder
Police Information Technology
      Organisation (Pito) 115–16
policing
   anti-social behaviour 167
   black communities 18–19
   consultation aims 128–9
   criminal justice system 15–16
   governance 177
   hard to reach groups 126–7
   information and communications
      technology 89–90, 115–16
   problem-solving approach 102–3
   on the spot punishments 109–11
   zero tolerance 168
policy-based evidence-making 109, 112
policy engagement 120–50
policy impact 120, 122
   partnerships 139–40
   social inclusion agenda 137–46
   summary 146–50
policy implementation, 'what works' 117–19
policy research 109
political rights 5, 7, 185
politics
   asylum 159
   benefit fraud 53–4
   concept-shaping 31–2
   idealism 188–9
   middle England 151–2
   social capital 85
   Third Way 92
Poor Laws 34–5
positive rights discourse 185
positive welfare 72
positivism 95–6
postcode lottery 154–5
postmodernism 61–4
poverty
   Africa 173
   asylum function 161
   citizenship 11–12
   contemporary 24–5, 26–7
   definitions 20

poverty *cont.*
'deserving and undeserving' poor 33–8, 72
housing and health 9–10
human rights 8–9
law 46–60
minority ethnic groups 28
personal debt 28–9
policies post-1997 146–9
'problem' families 39–42
'problem' places 45
Third Way 70, 72
PPPs *see* public private partnerships
practitioner creativity 177–8
pragmatism
idealism 189
Third Way 65–6
'what works' 94
prison populations
ethnicity 17
ex-prisoner social inclusion 143–6
social characteristics 144–5
private finance initiatives (PFI) 67, 91
private sphere (law) 13–14
'problem' families 38–43
'problem' places 43–5
see also place
problem-solving approach, policing 102–3
professional autonomy displacement 118
programme fetishism 108
projects, definition 68
property rights 13
prosecutions, benefit fraud 54–8
prostitution 167–8
psychological approach to crime 100
public perceptions
mugging 74
tax and benefit fraud 49
public private partnerships (PPPs) 67
public services
dissolution 67
information and communications
technology 88
social justice 20
public sphere (law) 13–14
Putnam, Robert 82–3

qualifications (education) 29
quality of life indicators 155
'quick wins' 133–4

Race Relations (Amendment) Act (2000) 10
race/racialisation
criminal justice system 18
law and order discourse 74–5
place intersection 156–8

race/racialisation *cont.*
'problem' places 44, 45
see also black communities;
minority ethnic groups
racial incidents/racism
asylum attitudes 163
citizenship 9–10
football 161
institutional racism 10–11
law 16–17
Rawls, J. 20–1
Raynor, Peter 101
realistic evaluation 102–3, 106–7
reciprocity 71
recognition 22, 183
redistribution 183–4
reflexive modernisation 63
reform agenda, New Labour 173, 176
regeneration
area-based partnership initiatives 139–40
local partnerships 130–1
middle England 155–6
Oldham disorders 157
Reiman, Jeffrey 4–5
relativity, Third Way 68
reoffending reduction strategies 143–6
replication, evidence-based policy 104
reputation (area) 153, 155
research and evidence
empowerment 176
participatory research 135–7
university involvement 96
'what works' 95–119
resources
consultation 134–5
realistic evaluation 102–3
'respect' agenda 173, 183
responsibilisation strategies 122–3
responsibilities
citizenship 11–12
criminal/social justice reconciliation 184
human rights 8
Third Way 70, 71
reverse engineering 124–5
'the rich'
law 46–60
responsibility 184
rights
citizenship 5–9, 11–12
criminal/social justice
reconciliation 178–9, 185
rule of law 12–14
Third Way 71
riots 43–5, 74–5
risk society 62–3, 80

risks
    citizenship 12
    environmental 6
rookeries 43
'rubbishing the messenger' 109, 112
rule of law 12–14
Rutherford, Andrew 29–30, 176–7

SCCU see Special Claims Control Units
SCI see Street Crime Initiative
scientific realism 98
scientific reductionism 98, 106
Scotland 159–60
scroungermania 53
SDVCs see Specialist Domestic
    Violence Courts
sentencing 8
September 11th 2001 19
SEU see Social Exclusion Unit
'shooting the messenger' 109, 112
short-termism 187–8
'silos', youth crime initiatives 141–2
Sinfield, Adrian 188
situational crime prevention 75, 99–100
skills for realistic evaluation 103
social capital
    consultation 133
    definition 84
    information and communications
        technology 86
    measurement 84–5
    Third Way 82–5
social citizenship 5, 9–10, 11
social exclusion 20
    criminal justice system 30
    human rights 179
    New Labour 79
    'us' and 'them' 156
    see also exclusion
Social Exclusion Unit (SEU)
    78–9, 137–8, 143–6
social inclusion
    agenda 137–46
    anti-social behaviour 165
    criminal justice 30
    ex-prisoners 143–6
    information and communications
        technology 138
    policies post-1997 146–9
    'problem' places 45
    responsibilisation 122–3
    see also inclusion
social justice
    active citizenship 82
    criminal justice reconciliation 171–89

social justice cont.
    definition 20–2
    New Labour 68–74
    'opportunities for all' 22–4
    principles 21
social problems, families 38–9
social rights 5, 7, 185
Social Security Fraud Act (2001) 57
social segregation 156
    see also social exclusion
socialisation of crime 78–80, 166–7
societal embedding 187–8
socio-economic injustice 183
Somerland, Hilary 178
south of England 153–4
spatial equality/local autonomy 154
spatialisation of crime 44–5
Special Claims Control Units (SCCU) 53–4
Specialist Domestic Violence Courts
    (SDVCs) 107–8, 186
state responsibilities 184
stigma of place 155–6
street crime 141–3
Street Crime Initiative (SCI) 142–3
surveillance systems 116–17
suspension of benefits 57–8
sustainability 185–6
symbolic injustice 183
symbolic locations 44
systematic reviews 97–9

Tawney, Richard 24
tax avoidance 47
Tax Credits 36, 51, 114–15
tax evasion 47–9, 52, 54, 173
tax flight 47
tax fraud
    compliance 49–53
    costs 49–51
    responses 46–60
taxation
    inequalities 181–2
    rich law, poor law 46–7
    social justice 23–4
technical challenges, information
    sharing 88–9
technicist view 103–4
technology
    social inclusion 138
    Third Way 85–92
    'what works' 112–17
terrorism
    identity cards 111
    risk society 63
    war on terror 19, 174, 179

Thatcher, Margaret/Thatcherism 66
  enterprise culture 47
  law and order 74–5
  taxation 23–4
  'what works' origins 94–5
thematic partnership initiatives 139
Third Way 61–93
  criminal justice 74–8, 80
  idealism 189
  information and communications
      technology 85–92
  middle England 151
  narrowness 64–8
  social capital 82–5
  social justice definition 69–70
  trust deficit 80–2
Thompson, E.P. 12–13
tokenism 126
'tough' talking 31–2, 75–7, 80
training opportunities 29
transformative governance 187
transnational welfare 73
trust deficit 80–2, 174–5
tutelage, families 41
two-way street concept
  justice 4–32
  trust deficit 175

underclass concept 33–4, 39, 44
underpaid benefits 59
'undeserving' poor 33–8, 72
United States (US)
  workfare solutions 104–5
  zero tolerance policing 168
Universal Declaration of Human Rights 6
university research 96–7
'unjust consequences' 154
  see also inequalities
'upside down duck' analogy 120–1, 150
upstream policies 188
US see United States
'us' and 'them' categorisation 152, 156
  see also otherness
the 'usual suspects' 126–7

victim information 90–1
violence 42, 156–8
  see also domestic violence; riots
voice (welfare principles) 73
voluntary sector groups 135
vulnerable young people 87–9, 149

Wales 159–60
war on terror 19, 174, 179
wealth distribution inequalities 26
welfare policy
  asylum 162
  postmodernism 63
  Third Way 72–3
  'what works' 113–15
  see also policy...
welfare-to-work strategy
      36–8, 113–14, 140, 180–1
'what works' 94–119
  dynamics and 'disconnections' 103–5
  empowerment 106–7
  governance 100–2, 105–6, 117–19
  policy research pitfalls 109
  rise of 95–7
  theoretical and practical issues 97–107
  use and misuse 107–17
'whole systems' approach 176–7
'wicked issues' 67
Williams, Fiona 73
women 11, 42
  see also gender; lone parents
'Worcester Woman' 151–2
work
  income adequacy 180–2
  'worth' 22–3, 35–6
worker classification 36
workfare solutions 104–5
workhouse test 35
Working Tax Credit 36
'worth', work condition 22–3, 35–6

YOTs see Youth Offending Teams
young people
  anti-social behaviour 164–5, 166–7
  inclusion and justice 140–2
  information sharing 87–9
  New Deals 38
  policy impact 149
  see also children
youth justice governance 177
Youth Offending Teams (YOTs) 119, 177

zero tolerance policing (ZTP) 168
Zimbabwean asylum seekers 163–4
ZTP see zero tolerance policing